DogPerfect

S E C O N D   E D I T I O N

The User-Friendly Guide to a Well-Behaved Dog

- A Quick, Fun and Easy Approach
- Simple Steps You Can Apply to Everyday Life
- User-Friendly Terminology
- An Entire Encyclopedia of Canine Etiquette

BY SARAH HODGSON

HOWELL
BOOK
HOUSE

To Job Michael Evans,
My mentor and friend
As long as we remember, you'll never die.

Howell Book House
Published by Wiley Publishing, Inc., Hoboken, New Jersey
Published simultaneously in Canada

For general information on our other products and services or to obtain technical support please contact our Customer Care Department within the U.S. at 800-762-2974, outside the U.S. at 317-572-3993 or fax 317-572-4002.

Wiley also publishes its books in a variety of electronic formats. Some content that appears in print may not be available in electronic books. For more information about Wiley products, visit our web site at www.wiley.com.

Library of Congress Cataloging-in-Publication Data:
Hodgson, Sarah.
    DogPerfect : the user-friendly guide to a well-behaved dog / by Sarah Hodgson.— 2nd ed.
        p. cm.
    Includes bibliographical references.
    ISBN 0-7645-2499-2 (alk. paper)
    1. Dogs — Training. 2. Dogs — Behavior. — I. Title: Dog perfect. II. Title.
    SF431.H728   2003
    636.7'887 — dc21
                        2002156455

Manufactured in United States of America

10 9 8 7 6 5 4 3

Second Edition

Book design by Marie Kristine Parial-Leonardo
Cover design by José Almaguer
Book production by Wiley Publishing, Inc. Composition Services

Table of Contents

Acknowledgments

Thanks to my publisher and editor, Dale Cunningham, who got all rolled into one for this rewrite.

A quick note of deep appreciation for the many great theorists and teachers who have influenced me, and have in turn touched the lives of the dogs and people I teach: Karen Pryor for her clicker work, Sue Sternberg for her ongoing shelter dog work and theories on aggression, Jack and Wendy Volhard and others — Carol Benjamin, Job Evans and my first teacher, Mickey Niego.

My clients, both dogs and people, are too many to name personally. My apologies! You have been my learning source as much as I've been your teacher. I'm lucky to have found you.

Thanks to the many people, from past clients to good-hearted veterinarians, pet supply stores, groomers and other trainers, who have kept my name in circulation. I would not be where I am, professionally, without you.

My friends and family. Four-legged and two. Thanks for keeping me sane.

A Welcoming Wag

When my publisher approached me to update *DogPerfect,* I jumped at the chance! Having written the first edition in 1995, I knew my teaching style and theories had evolved, but I had no idea how much! The biggest change? I have adopted a more cheerful, positive flair. I've evolved into a YES teacher rather than a NO trainer, using anything and everything to encourage good behavior. And everyone seems to be enjoying the process even more!

One gigantic epiphany? That everybody, human and dog alike, likes attention for doing something right. ("Gee, Mom, that was a great dinner." "What a great job you did mowing the lawn." "Thank you for helping out. You're the best kid in the world!") Rather than addressing a dog when he misbehaves, the time has come to focus first on the good stuff and on teaching a mutual language: "Good dog for chewing your bone." "Good sit! Good stay!" "Three cheers for chasing your ball." As the accolades for good behaviors continue, a dog builds a strong sense of what he can do right and a good feeling about being with people. When situations arise that need refocusing (inappropriate chewing, jumping, accidents and so forth), this approach allows for discouragement with positive redirection! The training ends on a high note, not with isolation or frustration.

Are some of you crossed-eyed now, thinking, "My dog never does anything right!"? Start to look for the little stuff. When your dog is asleep or stretching, chewing a bone or eating a meal, praise that. Be creative!

Before we jump in, however, I want to clear the air about something. There is no such thing as "DogPerfect," no single animal who embodies it all. In fact, there are as many ideals of perfection in dogs as there are in people. Perfection, when it comes right down to it, is a very personal thing.

Whether your goals are short-term problem-solving or long-term off-lead control, with a dog or a puppy, this book will show you how to get where you want to go with your dog. As you read along, I'll sometimes take a little break to share my and others' personal experiences. I promise, these stories will also relate to your own situation. You'll recognize them by this picture:

You will also notice a question and answer section after each new concept or command is described. In addition to this book, you can purchase its companion video to visualize the training methods and techniques I'll explain here. Like the book, the video is upbeat yet educational. Check out my website (www.dog perfect.com) for more information.

One more thing: I know it might be hard for some of you to imagine, but you and your dog really do want the same things. You both want to get along with one another and be happy. While your jump-all-over-you, run-when-you-say-come, nip-at-your-trousers Fido may appear to be having a blast, he's having no more fun than you are. He's confused. He interprets your frustrated behavior, your body language, your bark (the human yell) as interactive, not corrective. You're out of control. So instead of correcting his activities, you're encouraging them. He gets more wild. You get more frustrated. Wild. Frustrated. Wild. Frustrated. Help!!!!!

Whether this sounds too familiar, or you're simply striving to preserve your dog's wonderful disposition, you'll find empathy within these pages. This book not only answers and instructs, it provides insight into the causes and effects of your relationship with your best friend.

Enjoy this book. Think of me as your coach and translator. Dogs are more fascinating when you understand them.

Why Bother Training?

Exley, named after the writer Frederick Exley, is a three-year-old German Short-haired Pointer who lives in Brooklyn, New York. His owner rescued him from a shelter when he was one year old. Although Exley pulled on the leash, only listened to commands when the mood struck him, was destructive when his owner left for work and was a headache around company, the relationship worked. Or so his owner thought. Until a friend pointed out that Exley wasn't so happy. His habitual pacing and whining were not signs of a mentally balanced dog. Neither was the destructive chewing that went on when he was left alone. Or the pulling on the leash, which left Exley choking on the way to the park. That was when I entered the picture.

My first impression? Exley was a blur of excitement. Too happy. He didn't know what to do with himself. Quickly I reached for a ball and one of my Teaching Leads. Ball for Exley. Teaching Lead for me. After just a few minutes, I discovered a highly intelligent dog who eagerly soaked up every direction I gave him. He was a dog willing to cooperate. He just didn't know what his owner wanted from him. He was like a spoiled brat crying out for some guidance. Unfortunately, it's an all-too-common problem. From Exley's point of view, he was the leader: first to greet company at the door, got attention whenever he wanted it and led his owner to the park.

So who could solve Exley's problems? Only his owner. He had to take responsibility for creating the problem as well as for solving it. He could do all this by training. By making a commitment to give Exley direction. By becoming his leader.

And you, my readers — with your Exleys or Fluffys or Baileys or Sams — I hope you can see the importance of training, too. Whether or not your problems are similar to Exley's, training is still the solution. It defines the hierarchy. It puts you in charge and gives your dog the freedom to be a dog. You'll both be happier, more content with one another and less stressed out. And, as this book will show, training never breaks a dog's spirit. On the contrary, it can set him free.

Chapter 1

Who Is My Dog and How Does He Learn?

This question seems pretty simple. Who is your dog? Take a look. Big or small? Pup or grown-up? A special breed from a specific country? How about your dog's ancestors — did they do anything fancy for their keep, like hunting, herding or pulling a sled? And what about that personality? Is your dog a sweetie pie, all soft eyes, belly rubs and sweet kisses, or an athlete bent on continuous activities, or the bossy type?

Jodi Buren

Who is your dog and what does he think about?

Your answers to these questions will shape how you map your way through this book. Dogs are as individual as snowflakes. In addition, you are another component in your dog's behavior and training. Each of you has different lifestyles, schedules and social commitments. To help you, I'll need to cover all the angles. You and your dog are a unique pair!

DOG PSYCHOLOGY 101

I can imagine some of you rolling your eyes saying, "Great, I've got this nutty dog running my life who, in addition, is unique and special. Very poetic. But how can that help me train him?" Well, nutty or not, the first step in teaching your dog how to behave is learning to understand him. He's not human. He doesn't think, look or feel like you. He isn't born knowing a house from a hole in the ground, a rug from the grass or a stick from a table leg. He's a dog. A preciously simple dog. Since he can't fully grasp what it means to be a human, make the effort to imagine what life feels like in his paws. Take psychology to a canine level.

The most fascinating thing? Your dog, or puppy, thinks you're a dog too. Family, friends, kids in the neighborhood — to your dog we're all the same species. Unable to imagine what we're thinking, dogs translate all our actions into Doglish, their native language. Yes, dogs are the quintessential product of our domestication efforts. We did such a good job they think we're all the same species. One big, happy dog family. Quite a compliment.

Jodi Buren

Your dog is no less a member of your household team than you are. The question is, in your dog's mind are you the captain or is he?

Stand Up, Sit Down

some of you wondering if it's
to get down and play on your
's level? The answer is yes!
t's half the fun of sharing your
together. The rule is: Stand up
ight and calm when instructing
r dog. Get down for interaction
play.

Lesson #1: Once the dog is fitted with a humane training collar or harness, I teach the people how to hold the leash and control their dog without choking him. I calmly let them know that the chaos is normal and their dog is wonderful, albeit a bit confused. With a handful of treats or a bone, the person is instructed to reward their dog for quieting down. And you know what? The dogs, all of them, calm down pretty quickly. Why?

se I got the people to calm down! Most dogs would rather follow directions
ive them. And it all starts with a relaxed, upright posture — one that says,
worry, I know what's going on."
e are some rules about body language:

x

e posture communicates confusion or excitement. Let's say you meet some-
the street and you're expecting your dog to pull on the leash. You tense up,
ur tension travels down the leash to your dog. He gets tense, too, and starts
. Instead, remind yourself to relax.

Ahead

r dog is in front of you, guess who's not in charge? To communicate direc-
d leadership, you must position yourself in front of your dog. The leader
leads.

Centered

se your dog barks wildly at the door and you, disturbed from a quiet nap
couch, jump up and start yelling. Since a yell is as good as a bark in Dog-
our dog will naturally feel reinforced for his alerting instincts. Bark-yell-
ell!!!! When your dog gets nervous, stay centered and calm.

ch

people take their dog's behavior personally. When a dog behaves poorly in
l situation, the owner can become giddy listing every excuse for the dog's
n. This only makes the problem worse, because rambling and bent body
es communicate chaos and confusion. When your dog acts up, calm down.
yourself from the situation. Keep your cool and take a deep breath. Your
eds a level-headed leader — and it's up to you to be one!

The first step in our journey will be to train you how to think, act and perceive the world from your dog's perspective. It's a fascinating process. When all is said and done, you'll find that the solutions to everything you wondered were inside you all along. It's common sense, canine style.

The Leadership Principle

Dogs aren't terribly democratic. Instead, they live in a hierarchy, in which group members are classified according to their leadership potential. There's a lot of terminology out there (alpha dog, master, top dog or pack leader), but I like to explain it as being part of a team.

Whether you and your dog are a team of two, or whether there are seven people in your home, teams have certain rules and regulations that are universal. First off, every successful team needs a captain or a set of co-captains. That way, there's order within the group. The hierarchy that follows is based on many factors, including age and authority. And to keep the team balanced and healthy, constant communication between all members is a must.

Communicating team structure to your dog comes down to helping your dog with two very simple principles: organizing his space and activities. A dog needs to know where to go and what to do in every situation from play to settling on a mat when you're having your meals to handling company at

Do Dogs Really Like Being in Charge?

Being a team captain is not all it's cracked up to be. There's a lot of responsibility and worry that goes along with a 24-7 job. For dogs it's totally unnerving: keeping track of our comings and goings, directing our space and activities, monitoring the home territory. They usually end up in the top job by default, because no one else stood up for the role. When you step up to the plate, your dog will be so relieved!

the door. If you don't give your dog direction he won't know what to do, and that can feel pretty scary. When a dog feels out of control and undirected he becomes nervous, and often acts hyper or frightened.

It's better to learn your dog's language and take charge. Organize his space and activity with words you both recognize and you'll all feel better. You've made a big decision in sharing your life with a dog. Now it's time to take on the responsibility and give your dog the greatest gift of all: the gift of direction.

The Attention Factor

Dogs love attention! They're motivated by it. And they don't care whether it's negative or positive. If an action gets a reaction, they'll repeat it. Period.

Imagine your dog's energy level on a scale from 1 to 10. One is asleep; 10 is wild and manic or extremely fearful.

1   ☺   8   ☹   10
●——●————————●

Now let's split the scale. The 1 to 8 dog is cooperative, connected and contained. A team player. The 8 to 10 dog, however, is just too excited or afraid. He's over the top, disconnected from the team, and nothing you do influences the way he reacts to his world.

Now here's the tough part: Can you guess what is motivating your dog's behavior? It begins with an "A" . . . That's right — attention! And, once again, your dog doesn't care whether the attention is negative or positive. Negative attention, in fact, is often perceived as confrontational play! If your dog steals a sock, for example, and you chase him, you're playing his game. He'll steal the sock not because he's naughty, but because he wants to play with you. Yell at your dog for grabbing your breakfast off the counter and he'll do it again, not because he's bad but because you're suddenly competing for the same prize and competition conveys importance. Chase your runaway dog shouting COME! and your dog will run whenever he hears COME because you keep following him. Push a jumping dog, yell at a barker, clean up accidents in front of a housesoiler and you're guaranteed a repeat performance.

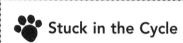

Stuck in the Cycle

Negative attention is most often perceived as confrontational play. "You want to play rough; I can play rougher." "You want to chase me; look at me run!" Dogs caught in the vicious cycle of misbehaving, in the 8 to 10 zone, are not happy. They simply do not know what to do and are more stressed because no one is giving them any direction.

Fortunately, the opposite is also true. Pay attention to your dog when he's behaving and he'll repeat good behavior with the same gusto. If the Four Paw Rule (keeping his four paws on the floor except when he's invited to do otherwise) gets rewarded, it will become a habit. Focus on your dog when he's chewing his bone or greeting company with a ball in his mouth rather than with his fur flying, and your dog will catch on that this is the preferred behavior. In this book you'll learn to focus on what your dog is doing right before harping on him for being naughty.

Doglish

Although many people are convinced their dog is a furry person, the opposite is true — your dog thinks you're a dog. English is the foreign language! Put yourself in your dog's paws. Imagine you're in a country where you don't speak the language and you're stuck alone in a room with a boisterous bunch of foreigners.

Abducted by Aliens

Imagine you've been abducted by alie[ns] twice your size and odd looking. Th[ey] two-hour adventure in their giganti[c] put you in a room where everything [is] unfamiliar. You're confused and are feeling your way aroun[d] ited by one of the aliens. This creature is super excited, gra[bbing] of your hand and putting them up high where you can't [reach] he lifts you up, making goofy noises that are totally unfam[iliar] races out of the room. A few minutes later another alien [enters] one moves slowly and calmly. He places a human-size ch[air] gives you reading material and a lamp. He stands tall and [in] front of him, says "ugg." Not your language exactly, but th[e mean]ing and clear: You should sit down and relax. Which ali[en are you] more comfortable seeing again? The second one, right? Th[e one who] helped you organize your space and activities, where you sh[ould sit,] you should do. *Now* you can relate to your dog.

They're not unfriendly, just super chatty and you can't [understand.] Suddenly someone steps out of the crowd and says in broke[n] English, "Please have a seat." Instantly your heart relaxes. Y[ou wait] for another message from the person who spoke your langu[age.]

Now that you've got the mental image, let me teach you [the] native tongue. You'll be the one stepping out of the crowd [making] connected and at ease.

Doglish consists of three elements: body language, eye co[ntact] is not born into the world knowing the meaning of words [.] Sure, sure we can help him learn, but he'll learn from the wa[y] the sound of your voice and the direction of your eyes. Let'[s]

BODY LANGUAGE

The best example of body language out of control is the fir[st] The dogs arrive straining at the end of their leashes. Dragg[ing] are their people. The dogs are either hyper with excitemen[t or] on the defensive. The people run the gamut: some are be[gging] and soothe. Others are shouting in run-on commands: "sit-[stay]-heel" as they hold on for dear life. It's really quite entertain[ing]

Whether you're asking your dog to sit or controlling him around a new person or situation, a relaxed, upright body posture communicates purpose and understanding. Tensing up, jerking about or shoving tells your dog you're out of control too. And if you're out of control, who's going to set the example?

When teaching your dog, remember the calmer you are, the cooler you are. Assume what I call the Peacock Position: Stand tall, throw your shoulders back and you'll emanate authority from your head to your toes.

EYE CONTACT

Eye contact is central to your whole relationship. The less you look to your dog, the more he'll look to you. Unfortunately, most people get it backwards. They spend every shared moment gazing lovingly at their dog, only to leave the dog wondering what to do.

Constant eye contact conveys a sense of confusion. If I invited you into my house and gazed at you the whole time, wouldn't you feel like I needed some help? If you stare too much at your dog, he might think you're unsure; that you're the one in need of a captain, a leader, a director of affairs. Nothing personal — it's just hierarchy. In the next chapters, I'll be coaching you through lessons that make you look cool in your dog's eyes and encourage him to watch you for direction.

Eye contact lessons straight from mother.

For now, reconsider the 1 to 10 energy level scale. Whatever you look at, you reinforce. Focus on good behavior. Look at your dog when he's in the 1 to 8 zone, not the 8 to 10. A loving glance when your dog is chewing on the right bone goes a long way. Stare at a dog with your favorite pillow in his mouth, and I guarantee he'll find that pillow tomorrow when you're on the phone and he wants your attention.

TONE

Think "team captain" again, this time in terms of the sound of your voice. For an everyday example, think about asking a family member to pass the ketchup. Would you yell, "PASS THE KETCHUP!"? Or say it in a sing-song voice? Or would you repeat the request: "Sarah, pass the ketchup, the ketchup, ketchup, ketchup, ketchup"? If you used any of those tones, I'd be puzzled. When teaching your dog new words and giving direction, speak calmly and clearly. Remember you're the captain.

Dogs recognize four tones: happy, directional, corrective and high-pitched squeals.

- Use *happy tones* to praise good behavior. Some dogs need more enthusiasm than others do. Test your dog to see what level works.

- The *directional tone* is your pass-the-ketchup tone. It should always come as a non-optional direction given in your dog's (and your team's) best interest. If you have children, make a habit of over-enunciating your commands (for example, say SITTT, emphasizing the *t* sound); your kids will follow your lead and the dog will respond better to the whole family. Good team captains choose their words wisely and speak in a confident, directive tone. In the next chapters I'll introduce you to the words you'll use to give your dog direction. Think of these words as establishing a mutual language to help your dog understand the team's plan.

- Let's look at *corrective tones*. Are you a yeller? Well, guess what? Yellers make matters worse. It's the human equivalent of a loud bark. Sure, some dogs cringe and crawl away on their belly, but that's not a sign of understanding, it's a sign of terror. And who'd want to terrorize their helpless doggie? Not you. So what's a good alternative when your dog has done something wrong? I act ashamed, disappointed or totally surprised, using words like "shame" and "that's unacceptable," in a reasonably disappointed voice.

- A *high-pitched squeal* is the only sound that can work against you. It communicates fear, confusion or submission. Kids often squeal, as do many women. If you can help yourself, stop.

THE SAME, ONLY DIFFERENT

Now that I've listed our differences, let's look at what we have in common with our four-footed friends — after all, we're animals, too! There are actually lots of similarities. Let's look at four of them: personality profiles, breed differences, drives and the age issue.

Personality Profiles

Some people think only humans have a real personality. Anyone who has ever had a dog knows better, though. Dogs, like us, have their own personalities. Some are extremely funny. I call this rowdy bunch *the comedians.* They can be frustrating as heck, constantly dancing on the edge of good behavior, but in your most serious or sad moments, they'll make you laugh. Then we have *the eager beavers,* the dogs many of us dream of. They'll do anything that earns your approval. Sounds fantastic, but they'll be bad, too, if that gets attention. There are also *the sweet peas* of the planet — quiet souls who prefer the sidelines over the spotlight. Taking the sweet thing a step too far are those dogs who are *truly timid.* Almost anything will freak them out. Poor creatures, they require a lot of understanding. Then there is *the boss.* This fellow thinks a little too highly of himself. He needs lots of training to tame his egotism. And finally, there's *Joe cool.* Male or female, this dog takes it all in stride. Although training often puts *Joe cool* to sleep, it can't be overlooked for his own safety. Take a look at where your dog fits in because, like us, all dogs learn differently!

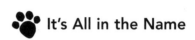 **It's All in the Name**

Or at least in the way you say the name. When you call your dog's name, think about how you'd like someone to call your name. How would you feel if they called out your name in a high, squeaky, fairy voice, or if they sounded really frustrated or angry? Not cool. Remember that as you teach your dog to respond to his name. Use a happy voice that's powerful and inviting.

Breed Differences

Breeds are the equivalent of cultures. Same species, different styles. The American Kennel Club recognizes more than 150 breeds, and other registries recognize even more. Besides looking different, each breed has instincts and drives that make them unique — instincts and drives humans helped create. The Doberman Pinscher was bred by the Germans for protection; the Alaskan Malamute was developed by the Eskimos to help them pull their sleds; the Collie bred for herding and the Shih Tzu for companionship.

So what about your warm bundle? What were his ancestors doing? With few exceptions, a dog's skills are no longer necessary to our survival, but don't tell that to your dog. His instincts and breeding still make him think his skills are very much in demand. Finding out what they were will help you understand how he views his role in the world today.

So what if every dog is different? Can't they all adapt?

With training, all behaviors can be modified to some degree. But adaptation is relative. Most breeds can adapt only so much. For example, suppose you're having a house party. A Golden Retriever in that situation would consider it a marvelous opportunity to make new friends and show off his latest tennis ball collection. Maybe a bit too cheery, but he'll do just fine. A German Shepherd, however, bent on keeping track of his territory, might suffer career stress watching the comings and goings. With training, he may become more accepting, but don't expect him to lie belly-up at just anyone's feet. Only yours will do. Lessons help get a handle on your dog's instincts, but you can never eliminate them.

If you have a mixed-breed dog, don't worry! Your job is a little more adventurous. Try to identify the mix, and then read over the description that follows for each group. Study your dog's behavior and decide where he fits in.

THE GROUPS

In the American Kennel Club, breeds are categorized into seven groups: Sporting, Hound, Working, Terrier, Toy, Non-Sporting and Herding. These groups are organized according to shared characteristics. After determining which group your dog is a member of, read the following corresponding description to determine some predictable character traits. Breeders, trainers and veterinarians can help determine what breed your dog is if you're not sure.

The Sporting Group

Originally bred to spend the entire day in the fields seeking out and collecting game on land and in the water for their masters, this bunch is an energetic, loyal, happy lot who thrive on group interaction. Trusting, friendly and bright, they take well to training and generally view all strangers as potential friends. These easy-going dogs make excellent family pets, but prolonged isolation does upset them. Left alone, they'll develop diversionary habits like destructive chewing, barking, digging and jumping. They are annoyingly enthusiastic when left untrained. Examples are Labrador Retrievers, Golden Retrievers, Irish Setters, German Shorthaired Pointers and Cocker Spaniels.

The Hound Group

These guys were bred to pursue game, using their eyes (sighthounds) or their noses (scenthounds). They are dogs with a mission! Active, lively and rugged, they make fun-loving, gentle pets — but with an independent streak. Not bred to look to humans for direction, they usually don't. Consequently, training them can be slow and challenging; they'd rather trail a rabbit than do sit-stays. Generally sweet, lively and tolerant, hounds thrive on family involvement, and accept children and strangers with ease. Examples are Basset Hounds, Greyhounds, Beagles and Rhodesian Ridgebacks.

The Working Group

This is the most diversified group in terms of their breed functions. Some pull sleds, others guard flocks and still others protect the homestead. They do, however, have one common bond: They were all bred to serve humans, helping us survive and advance along the evolutionary scale. As pets, the working breeds are still very serious about their roles as workers and need a serious commitment to training. Intelligent, fearless and dignified, they can make devoted, loyal pets. Misunderstood, isolated or untrained, they'll be unhappy, nervous and in some cases, overly aggressive. Examples are Rottweilers, Mastiffs, Doberman Pinschers and Siberian Huskies.

The Terrier Group

Originally bred to control the varmint population, these dogs are a self-assured, spirited and lively bunch. Agile, independent and energetic, they're always ready to face a diversion and, outdoors, need to be leashed. They make great pets for all but the control freaks and often leave their owners marveling at their spunk and good humor. When untrained or isolated, however, these little acrobats can become chronic barkers, destructive chewers, urine makers or territorial aggressors over their home, objects, food and other animals. Examples are Bull Terriers, Airedales, West Highland White Terriers, Jack Russell Terriers and Scottish Terriers.

The Toy Group

These little guys were bred for one thing and one thing only: companionship! In keeping with their ancestry, they continue to perfect the art of being adorable. Because they are playful and affectionate, it's easy to neglect training, but owner beware! Without direction they can become quite tyrannical, ruling the house with constant barking and snapping. To get the most from these critters, train them! Examples are Papillons, Chihuahuas, Yorkshire Terriers, Pomeranians and Maltese.

The Non-Sporting Group

Unlike other groups, this bunch has little consistency of personality because these dogs were all bred for different tasks. Some take to training better than others. Many were originally bred for specific work, but when that work was no longer necessary, they became companions. If you've got a dog from this category, you can determine more about him from breed-specific books. Examples are Bulldogs, Dalmatians, Bichon Frises and Standard and Miniature Poodles.

The Herding Group

These dogs were bred to move flocks and herds. Agile and alert, they're always on the lookout and will settle for kids or bikes if sheep aren't available. Easy to train that people are shepherds, not sheep, they are devoted to their families and are not prone to roaming. They can be protective, preferring family members to outsiders. Isolated or ignored, they may become timid, bark or develop chasing and pacing habits. Examples are German Shepherd Dogs, Collies, Pulik and Corgis.

Drives

One of the early influences in my career was the work of dog trainers Jack and Wendy Volhard, who have written *What All Good Dogs Should Know* and *Dog Training For Dummies*. The Volhards talk a lot about "drive"; the idea is that once you discover what motivates your dog's behavior, you can use that knowledge to shape your teaching approach. What follows is a crib sheet. For true insight, get their books or visit their website at www.volhard.com.

Jodi Buren

Every dog, like every human, has a driving force, an instinctive passion that motivates much of their behavior. For my terrier mix, Hope, it's a close tie between the neighbor's cat and my lunch. For my Border Collie mix, Shayna, it was her Frisbee. Every dog is unique, and although breed traits can provide clues, to get the full scoop you'll have to go to your dog. What revs his engine? Is it your neighbor's cat, a knock on the door or does he live and breathe for your attention?

Can you guess what drive is coursing through this Beagle's veins? Serious prey drive.

There are three basic drives that motivate a dog's behavior. One predominates (which one depends on

🐾 Small Dog Syndrome

Jodi Buren

Anyone who has ever shared their life with a small dog will tell you they're adorable, especially when they're puppies. Spoiling them comes naturally. After all, their behavior is so miniaturized that it's rarely a problem. Living the unstructured life, however, and being doted on night and day, is just as harmful for them as it is for big dogs. Intelligent little creatures, they conclude they must be top dog, since there are no rules to follow and everyone is bowing to their every desire. The result is what I call Small Dog Syndrome. Here are four typical personality types:

It's hard not to spoil them, I know! But for their own sake be a good leader.

- The chronic yapper: This one's in charge of all household activities.
- The nipper: This one can't be disturbed when eating, chewing or resting.
- The growler: Basically, this dog is a brat who'd be happy to fight you to have his way.
- The marker: This one has a true Napoleon complex. Concerned that each new noise or human behavior may mean a defection in the ranks, he uses urine (also known as marking) to leave a social reminder that he still exists and he exists to rule.

So treat your little guys like dogs, not play toys. And remember, when well-trained, small dogs can be selectively spoiled!

the dog), but all three exist and interact at different times and at different levels. They are:

- Prey
- Pack
- Defense

A dog with high prey drive is excited by sound and motion, specifically the sound and motion of moving animals and objects. A dog with high pack drive is motivated by what the members of a group are doing — a follow-in-kind reaction. A dog with high defense drive is motivated by the fight or flight response.

What preoccupies your dog's waking hours? Chasing or surveying squirrels, cars, children or the cat? This is prey drive in motion. Is he more concerned about staying with you? This is a pack animal first and foremost. Or does your dog spend his days patrolling and surveying the activities around your home? This dog is in the defensive mode.

How you approach your lessons should be influenced by what is motivating your dog. For example, high prey drive dogs love food and need frequent and sometimes firm tugs to discourage their chasing impulses. The pack drive dog focuses on his group and is more concentrated on pleasing his people than hunting down the neighbor's rabbits. When the defensive drive rules, any noise that reaches the ears will be of interest. If you don't redirect the drives with the right amount of discouragement and praise, problem patterns could emerge and be hard to contain.

The Age Issue

Age is a big thing. If there's a pup nibbling on your shoelace, bless you. By starting to teach him when he is young, you can condition a lot of good habits before the bad ones set in. The more you encourage what your puppy is doing right, the less he'll do what's wrong.

Aside from some obvious differences, young puppies and children are a lot alike. As babies they're sensitive to the impressions of their environment and act according to the acknowledgment and consistency they receive from you. They both need supervision, because as youngsters they have tons of energy and a budding curiosity about the world around them.

In addition, they have a natural tendency to test their superiors. Remember this as your blood pressure is rising. Nothing they do is out of spite. Yelling at a young pup for mouthing, nipping and exploring makes about as much sense as yelling at a one-year-old for grabbing your hair. They can't understand what they're doing yet, so what's the point of losing your temper? It only makes them more afraid and anxious, and anxious puppies are even more oral and nervous. So relax! Tolerance, patience and loving understanding are what you need to raise your puppy. Focus on what your puppy is doing right and he'll feel super and will want to repeat it.

As your puppy grows, he'll go through many of the same stages human children go through — adolescence, puberty, sexual maturity — and with many of the same misbehavior parents endure: the canine equivalent of the teenage eye roll, the "in-a-minute" attitude and assertive and territorial behavior.

But you've got the edge. You're holding this book. Solutions to common problems lie ahead, as do teaching exercises to help your pup understand you and mature. You'll know how to think, speak and teach your puppy throughout all his normal and healthy phases. Just like kids, he'll be grown up before you know it!

Mixed Messages

Here's an example of how easy it is to confuse a pup. Pie, a five-month-old Welsh Corgi-Jack Russell Terrier mix, lives happily with his two adult owners. Well-intending and conscientious, they read every book. They handle most situations with calm and ease, but Pie still has one major problem: He was born with springs in his legs. Although they've tried to resolve his jumping problem, Pie keeps it up. Why? First, the cute factor. Every time he jumps for attention, guess what? He gets it. Next, although the wife ignores jump-man Pie when she comes in, the husband, well, he can't resist. Pie gets a mixed message. Whenever somebody new enters, he must determine whether they'll be more like Mom or more like Dad. Pie also jumps for food scraps, and sometimes he gets lucky. The optimum reinforcer. Now can you see why Pie spends more time on two legs than on four? (If you're experiencing this problem, stay tuned. A step-by-step solution is provided in Chapter 8.)

For those of you with older pups or dogs who have developed naughty behaviors, don't be discouraged. It's never too late. Many older dogs who I train adapt to the educated life as if they'd been waiting for it all their lives. Others may initially roll their eyes, but with persistence they too are grateful for having a team captain, a teacher who is committed to taking care of them.

So where does all this leave you? Let me end this chapter with a thought: Your dog is not as responsible for his habits as you are responsible for having encouraged them. As a pup, his main focus was determining the hierarchy and figuring out what behaviors got the most attention. If you're holding this book, you may have put off lessons and ended up with a dog whose idea of fun may not reflect your idea of good behavior.

Don't worry! Where there are bad habits, I'll help you teach your dog a new way. Where there are misunderstandings, I'll teach you how to communicate direction calmly. If your blood pressure rises when the doorbell rings, you'll have options to control the situation. Rest assured, we'll bring this darling good dog of yours up to snuff.

Chapter 2

Tools of the Trade

In *DogPerfect,* the first edition, I never encouraged the use of treats. Well, in short, I'm a born-again treat giver! Whether it's the sound of a dog eating snacks (how precious), the twinkle in their eye as they swallow or the overall positive attitude that emerges between both the people and dogs I have worked with, I'm forever sold. Using treats during the initial phases of teaching a dog a new behavior is just plain nice. And you know what? Once a dog learns a behavior and it's part of your everyday routine, you won't need a treat to convince her to do it. She'll respond because she's clever and you ask her to. She'll listen because she likes you. Treats to start, phased out gradually, will make learning a lot more fun. I guarantee it!

My dog's favorite snacks are a Cheerio-type breakfast food I get at the health food store (lower in salt). Find a snack your dog likes and break it into small pieces so that she can swallow them quickly and maintain her healthy figure. It's not the size of the treat that counts, it's the act of sharing.

Still don't want to use treats? Is your dog too food oriented to concentrate when you're holding a treat? Or does your dog not care much for treats? The methods in this book will still work for you! Use a favorite toy to motivate or an extra helping of heartfelt praise where you read "treat," and follow the exercises right along.

DRESSING FOR THE OCCASION

Let me tell you the story of the gigantic Pez dispenser . . .

Imagine being in a room with an ill-mannered dog who, in her defense, has never been taught how to behave. Around your waist there's a snack pack (think fanny pack) filled with all sorts of yummy goodies. Playing mute, you walk around the room tidying this and that, basically ignoring the dog. You'll soon learn an age-old secret: You're more interesting when you're busy. If, every time the dog (we'll call her Daisy) walks over to you she gets a snack, what's going to happen? That's right — she'll be your little shadow. Soon, however, Daisy will get demanding. She'll jump. She'll bark. She wants more, more, more! This behavior you ignore. No attention, no treats. Frustrated and confused, Daisy sits down. This gets a treat and a smile. She barks, no treat. She jumps, nothing. When she sits, you share.

Now some people may argue that Daisy is only working for food. But I'd disagree. Daisy, like all dogs, loves to interact. She also likes a puzzle, and this little exercise taught her plenty. It taught her that she can influence your relationship and get attention when she feels the need. But instead of learning that jumping gets attention and rewards, she learned that sitting politely is most effective.

The Snack Pack

A snack pack is a fanny pack done up doggy style. There are companies that make special pouches for pooches, though I've found a generic fanny pack will do just fine. In your snack pack you can put all or some of the following:

- Treats
- A clicker
- Treat cup
- A poop bag
- Chew bones or a special toy
- Grannick's Bitter Apple or Binaca breath spray (to deter problem behaviors, as described in Chapter 8)
- Any other goodies you think will aid you in your learning adventure

When wearing your snack pack, your dog may view you as a life-size Pez dispenser. But as long as she's doing all the right things — following the Four Paw Rule (keeping all four paws on the ground), sitting politely and hanging out with you calmly, treats are a magical way to ensure you get a repeat performance!

Treat Cups

Take an empty deli container — the plastic type used for potato salad or coleslaw. Make sure it's clean and dry. Fill the container half full with some tasty dog treats broken into small pieces. Cut a small hole in the lid of the container, just large enough for one goody to fit through. Now shake the cup and treat your dog until she makes the connection that the shaking sound means "snack." If you're starting with a puppy, pair this early with her name. Keep the treat cups handy; we'll use them throughout the book, from early COME conditioning to game playing and problem solving.

If you've got kids, have them decorate the cups. It's a great way to get them involved in the dog's training and share in the adventure.

A kid-decorated treat cup in action!

Jingle Jar

If your dog's a peanut butter fan or a consort of cream cheese, designate a jar for him and tape a small jingle bell to it. Jingle the jar and let him have a quick lick. Jingle, lick. Jingle, lick. The jingle jar can be used in play, lessons, problem solving and to relieve the stress of new experiences, such as visits to the veterinarian. It's especially useful to help shy dogs overcome fear, rowdy dogs learn the Four Paw Rule, aggressive dogs learn new associations to visitors and to condition the response to words like INSIDE and COME.

COOL COLLARS AND OTHER FRIENDLY RESTRAINTS

Out there in dogland, I'm sure you've discovered endless products and lots of people who claim to be in the know about them. A neighbor or uncle or stranger on the street claims to have just the right tool even without meeting your dear doggie. In this chapter, I'll give you the scoop: an overview of the different equipment I've encouraged, and when and on what dogs I find them most helpful.

The Gentle Leader

I love the Gentle Leader: love the concept, the humaneness, the philosophy. It has saved the lives of many dogs I've worked with and the sanity of their people. In the past I've called it a "chin lead," and it is also known as a head collar because the strap rests over a dog's nose and the leash is clipped under their chin. Often people's first reaction is that it looks like a muzzle, but in fact it doesn't restrict any oral activity, from eating to panting to chewing.

Whenever clients hesitate, I explain that the difference between the Gentle Leader and a neck collar is like the difference between holding their hand and grabbing their shirt collar. It eliminates confrontation. It communicates control passively. It's a kinder approach. Instead of teaching by applying pressure around the neck, it guides dogs gently by their head, like a halter on a horse, and conditions long-term cooperation. Your dog will see you as a friend rather than a combatant.

For those people who can get beyond the odd appearance and endure their dog's initial head scratching, the Gentle Leader gives a huge leg-up in teaching the basics, conditioning good behavior and diminishing the naughty routines, like jumping and barking. Another plus is that leading by the Gentle Leader requires minimal physical strength, so nearly everyone can use it — kids, too!

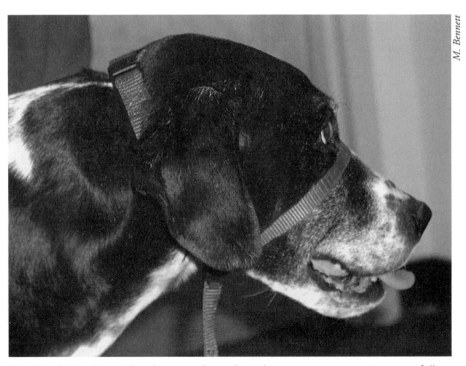

M. Bennett

The Gentle Leader guides dogs gently, and nearly everyone can use it successfully.

The Gentle Leader works well with many dogs of every breed and personality type, although I have found it especially valuable in working with extreme cases: overexcited, aggressive, excessively shy or headstrong dogs and puppies. If this sounds too familiar, the Gentle Leader may be the perfect solution. It communicates to your dog that impulsiveness is not cool. By maintaining a sense of calm and giving direction, your dog will learn to mimic your relaxed attitude.

So how does this wonder collar work?

It's similar to a halter on a horse. The guiding pressure of the Gentle Leader is distributed over your dog's entire head, and, like the cliché says, "Where the head goes the body will follow."

But the Gentle Leader goes deeper than that, working on what I call the Mommy Principle. When your dog was a pup, her mom would curb her wildings by grasping her muzzle or shaking her by the neck. This communicated, "Hey wild one, settle down!" The Gentle Leader has the same effect. It communicates leadership passively — just by putting it on her, you're letting your dog know she's no longer in charge. When the collar is left on during play, the gentle pressure on the nose discourages rowdiness and mouthing with other dogs and people. By using it with a leash, jumping, barking and pulling can be affected as the nose pressure encourages a more submissive outlook. And last but not least, leash walks and teaching times are kinder as you guide your dog gently along.

SIZING YOUR GENTLE LEADER

Gentle Leaders come in petite, small, medium, large and extra large. They also come in a rainbow of colors. Personally, I'm a fan of matching the color to a dog's coat, but you don't have to. If florescent pink floats your boat, your dog will certainly wear pink with style.

With the Gentle Leader in hand, adjust the neck strap. Fit it snugly just behind your dog's ears (about as tight as a watch band), leaving enough room to insert one finger. Don't worry about it being too tight; the underside rests on your dog's jaw bone, not her neck.

Unclip the neck strap and adjust the nose band. Stand behind your dog so

 **High Honors**

The Gentle Leader was designed by a veterinary behaviorist, R. K. Anderson, and a dog trainer and judge, Ruth Foster. In May 2002, I was at a banquet in their honor. The accolades from friends and associates in the dog world brought more than a few tears to my eyes. The most exciting appreciation came from the Smithsonian Institution in Washington D.C., which added it to their Summer 2002 Inventions at Play exhibition (right along with the telephone and Post-it notes)!

that you're reaching over her head, not facing into her (you'll look scary). If your dog is restless, put some peanut butter or cream cheese on the side of a wall for her to lick while you take care of business. The nose band should be loosened to enable your dog to open her mouth comfortably, and the band itself should lie under your dog's eyes and just past the corners of her mouth.

Once the nose band is fitted, reconnect the neck collar behind your dog's ears and hook the leash to the metal loop under your dog's chin. Away you go!

We got the Gentle Leader on, but our Lucy got it off her nose in less than a minute. Now what?

Houdini! Go back to square one and make sure the neck adjustment is snug behind the ears (just one finger's space!) and the nose band is properly adjusted. The most common mistake people make is fitting the neck collar too loosely. Think of a wristwatch or a shoelace — it should be that snug. Then the nose band can be adjusted to allow your dog's mouth to be comfortable, which will make Lucy more accepting of her new attire.

My dog hates this thing! She's scratching at her nose something awful.

Initially, some dogs are less than thrilled with their new headpiece. This reaction passes relatively quickly — some dogs take 20 minutes to acclimate, others may fuss a day or two. When you see your dog flopping about like a flounder, take a deep breath and ignore it (remember the attention equation). Initial responses are the most flamboyant. Once your dog realizes she can't get it off, she'll forget about it. And if she still scratches at it from time to time, in a parental manner tell her THAT'S ENOUGH, (like when you were a kid and you heard "stop scratching that bug bite").

My dog won't budge on the Gentle Leader. He just lies flat and looks at me. What do I do?

Your dog is having leadership withdrawal symptoms. Because the Gentle Leader communicates your authority, she's offering up some passive resistance. Stay the course. If you soothe, talk to, or even look at her, you'll be reinforcing the resistance. Lean forward and apply steady pressure as you cluck and whistle happily. The moment she cooperates, praise her enthusiastically and give her a tasty goodie! (If you're using the clicker, treat cup or jingle jar, these are super tools to encourage a positive association to the Gentle Leader. Use them often when you're starting out.)

How long should my dog wear this during the day?

This question can only be answered by your dog. If yours is relatively well behaved, use it exclusively during teaching time. If she's the mouthing-jumping-barking-maniac type, leave it on whenever you're around. Remove it at night or when you're away from home.

Is this a forever collar, or will we graduate to a regular collar some day?

The coolest thing about the Gentle Leader is that it can be transformed into a neck collar by removing the nose strap and sliding the slack around your dog's head. Clipped on the same ring, you now have a regular collar with the nose strap acting like an extension. And the beauty of it is that if you're out walking and your dog gets too excited or overwhelmed, you can transform the collar back to the Gentle Leader for easy control.

> ### 🐾 When Your Dog Is Not Faking
>
> Sometimes the Gentle Leader can cause a nose irritation. To prevent this, take extra care during fitting. If your dog has sensitive or dry skin, go to the pharmacy and ask for moleskin (they'll know what it is). Place the moleskin or felt on the underside of the nose strap where it rests on your dog's nose. If her skin looks dry when you take it off, lubricate the dry patch with Vaseline. If an irritation forms, remove the Gentle Leader.

I've seen other brands of these collars in stores, haven't I?

Yes, there are other versions that have a similar or identical effect. The most common is the Halti Head Collar. Each brand is effective. I've long recommended the Gentle Leader because I find the fabric soft and their support system for its use most understandable.

If you're interested in buying a Gentle Leader, talk with your veterinarian or an expert you trust at a pet supply store. The company has a video and a booklet about the collar. You can't buy the Gentle Leader through their website (www.gentleleader.com), but you will find more information there.

Neck Collars

The collars listed here all have one thing in common: They go on your dog's neck. The only one that is essential is the buckle collar, which is where you put your dog's identification tags. The other collars are for training — but please, take every measure to learn their proper use, from talking to other dog owners to hiring a professional trainer. If used improperly, your dog will instinctively pull against the restraint and wind up gagging. It's an awful sound and the only lesson she learns is that walking with you is unpleasant. If that sounds like your situation, review how to use the collar properly or reconsider your choice. A Gentle Leader or a no-pull harness may be better options.

BUCKLE COLLAR

This one's a staple. Your pet supply store might also refer to it as a tag collar. This collar fits around your dog's neck and carries her identification and inoculation tags. Whether your dog is two months or two years old, weighs two pounds or

Hi-Tech ID

Microchip your dog! Call your veterinarian and set up an appointment to do it. A quick and virtually painless procedure, inserting an identification chip into your dog's shoulder is another way to increase the chances of your dog's safe return if she gets lost or stolen.

200, find her a nice collar and attach those tags! (Dognappers are a real threat, so keep an eye on your dog whenever she's outside. To safeguard her as well as your home, limit the tag information to a phrase like: "Please help me get home — 555-555-5555.")

Some dogs can be trained with just a buckle collar. If a tug on a regular buckle collar convinces your dog to stay by your side, look no further. You can use your buckle collar for all your teaching endeavors. If your dog falls into this category, count your blessings.

TRAINING COLLARS

This collar fits over a dog's head and, to be most effective, should fit snugly just behind her ears. A training collar is worn with a leash. If your dog is off leash, the training collar must be removed to prevent a choking accident. Avoid using a training collar on small dogs or puppies under four months old, because the pressure on a small or developing neck can damage the trachea. This is in addition to the fact that infant dogs, like infant humans, can't even understand the concept of being bad. Ahh . . . to be young again! Wait until your dog is 16 weeks old before using a training collar.

There are three types of training collars, and choosing one will depend on your dog. Find a collar that works from the following selection (try them all if you have to), and go with it. Good luck!

The Slip Collar

These collars come in nylon, leather and chain versions. A lot of people call them choke collars, which is soooo misleading — it's the sudden tug or sound of the collar, not the restraint, that communicates your expectations. Constant pulling and choking only aggravates problems: You're forcing your dog to stay close out of fear of asphyxiation, rather than choice. I know everyone would rather use it properly than hear their dog hacking during walks, but most people just don't know how to make the darn thing work.

First off, let me help you put the collar on correctly. If you put it on backwards, it will cause your dear doggie lots of discomfort. When the collar is fitted improperly, it will catch in a vise-like hold around your dog's neck and do what the collar is not supposed to do: choke. Getting it on right takes some initial concentration, but it becomes easy and obvious in short order.

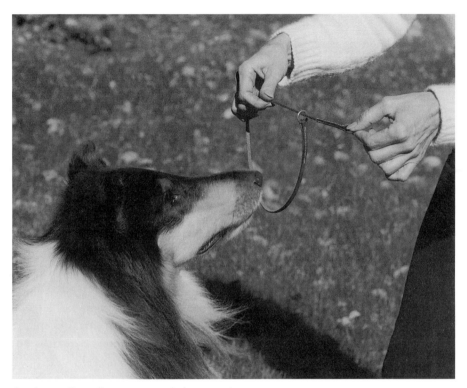

Putting a slip collar on correctly is a must!

First, decide which side you want your dog to walk on, left or right. Be consistent! The left side is traditional, so I'll use it in my example.

1. Take one end loop of the collar and slide the slack through it.
2. Pretending you're on *Sesame Street*, create the letter P with the collar.
3. Holding it out, stand in front of your dog and show her your creation.
4. With the P still facing in your direction, slide the collar over your dog's head as you praise her.

If your dog is not cooperating, use a dab of peanut butter on the roof of her mouth or another tasty snack to give this procedure a more positive spin.

To check the result, slide the rings up behind her ears and stand at her left side. Grasp the moveable ring and pull it toward your leg. Does it slide freely through the stationary loop (that's correct!), or does it bend over the stationary loop (try again)?

Mastering the quicktug is the second step. Quicktug is not a typo, it's a very fast correction. Even faster than quick tug! Once again, it's the suddenness or sound of the collar, not the restraint that teaches. Used properly, the quicktug (with a chain collar it sounds like a zipper) will inhibit your dog's impulse to disobey or lead you.

How do I master the quicktug?

Practice the following exercise:

1. Place the collar on your dog. Check to make sure it's on right and fits properly.
2. Attach a leash and slide the collar between the dog's ears. Stand calmly on her left side.
3. Take the lead in your left hand.
4. Relaxing your arm in a straight position, hold the lead behind your thigh.

Here's the important part: When your dog surges forward, pretend there is a hinge in your elbow. Snap your forearm (from your elbow) back as though you were trying to hit a person behind you. Once you've snapped back, release the pressure *immediately.* This loosens the collar so your dog gets a good feeling when she's back at your side. Remember, the quicktug is done with a relaxed, straight arm. It's a tricep flex, keeping the tug in line with your dog's body. Pulling up, curling your arm — a bicep flex — would be the equivalent of a giant pulling up on your necklace or shirt collar. A choking feeling comes to mind. Totally unpleasant. It should be suddenness or sound, not restraint. Don't forget!

Different Choices

Josie, my friend's Collie mix, and I are walking in the park. Suddenly, we both notice Buster, her Bullmastiff friend, sniffing along with his owner, Tom, trailing behind. Buster immediately recognizes us and digs in to drag poor embarrassed Tom over for a visit. Although he must stop occasionally, hacking to relieve the nagging pressure around his neck, Buster doesn't understand that his coughing could be prevented if only he'd walk behind Tom. Perhaps it's because the pressure never lets up! Once he has caught his breath, he's back on course.

Josie, on the other hand, behaves differently. Although she squirms to be with her friend, she is quickly alerted to a zipping sound by her right ear. No vice hold, just a quicktug. A sound rather than a feeling. That, coupled with the command BACK! urges her to reconsider. She tries once more to pull ahead but is checked again with a tug. She chooses to wait for Buster at my side. Good choice. "Good girl, Josie!"

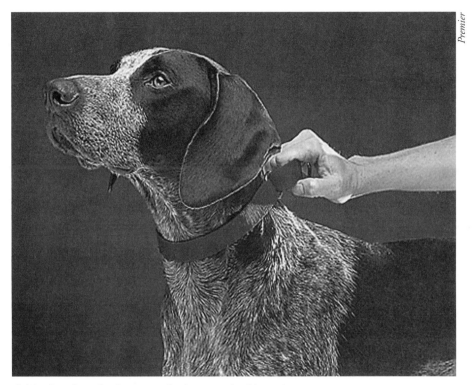

Premier

A Martingale collar is a must for long-necked breeds.

Martingale Collar and Check Chain

The Martingale collar is a hybrid: three-quarters thick, fabric flat collar and one-quarter nylon slip collar that's a must for long-necked sighthounds such as Greyhounds and Whippets. It also works well on other short-coated breeds. It is less cutting than a thin collar and limits the stress to both fur and throat. Other fabric collars of this design work well for a calm dog who just needs an occasional reminder to pay attention.

The check chain is similar in design, but the slip section is chain and the fabric is not as wide. It is the sound of this collar that alerts a dog's attention.

The "Self-Correcting" Collar

Yes, I know it looks like a torture device. However, in the right circumstances it can make the difference between a dog who can stay with you and one who has to go because she's too much to handle. It's not inhumane when used correctly, especially if your dog refuses the Gentle Leader or falls into the I-can't-stop-choking-myself category when using slip collars.

This collar gives a dog the equivalent of a scruff shake — a dominant dog grab-the-neck behavior that ensures containment and respect. Your dog will quickly learn that assertive leash pulling and other dominant behaviors don't fly and that cooperation is met with companionship, rewards and praise. This is far less damaging than a crushed trachea.

If you decide to give this collar a try, be sure to have someone with experience help you fit it on your dog and give you a quick lesson on its use. *Never* leave the collar on your dog unsupervised.

If you decide to try this collar, I need to warn you that occasionally they pop off. To prevent an emergency, buy an oversized nylon slip collar and attach your leash to both collars when you are walking in an unconfined area.

Body Harness

When I think of a harness I think back to Kyia, a sweet-natured Siberian Husky mix I rescued from the pound. That first winter she found her calling hitched to a harness behind a sled. Although it was a professional and properly fitted harness, had it been a generic harness I'm certain her pulling impulse would have been the same. In fact, any breed from a Maltese on up, will instinctively pull against restraint. And that is the biggest negative to using harnesses for walking or teaching purposes.

 **No-Pull Harness**

Yes, such a thing really does exist. The physics of it are baffling, but in essence it hinders forward motion and can be quite effective, especially when handling young, misguided puppies and older dogs during casual walks. In most cases it is not an effective teaching tool, although when used in constant conjunction with a clicker and/or treats, walking cooperatively can become a habit.

There are situations where a body harness is a good idea: small breeds with tracheas too fragile to bear any resistance; dogs with medical conditions that make the use of a collar risky; or if you're training a sled dog. Harnesses are also useful to secure a dog in a car.

LEADS AND LEASHES

There are so many leashes on the market. I've even invented one of my own! No matter which one you choose, the first step is to hold your leash the right way.

Think of holding your dog's lead like holding a friend's hand. Unfortunately, I see a lot of white knuckling out there in dogland. Many people curl their fingers under the leash and muscle up their arm, which is incorrect. If your arm feels like it will fall off or your hands suffer chaffing rope burn, something's not right.

Too much tension on the leash makes it tempting for you to pull forward and lift up. Instead, hold the leash with a relaxed arm, your knuckles over the leash, palm facing back and your thumb wrapped around the underside of the leash.

Confused? Here's a little exercise: Hold your left arm straight out from your body. Pointing your thumb downward, lower your arm. As you do, curl your thumb under the leash and wrap your knuckles over the top! Ta da!

The Teaching Lead Transformer

It sounds like a space age kid's toy, but this leash will affect your life with your dog in many ways. This one leash can be used in three ways: to lead, anchor or station your dog. Use it to teach your dog to be civilized and contained around the house.

Although I've patented my own version of the Teaching Lead (you can learn more about that at www.dogperfect.com), you can easily make your own. You'll need a six-foot leash and a clip with two heads from the hardware store. There are many leashes on the market, so you'll have to make some choices — nylon versus leather (I don't suggest chain), thin versus thick and so on. I'll leave the material choices up to you.

Once you've got your leash, attach the double-headed clip to the handle. Now you have choices! Hold the leash in your hands or secure it around your waist to free up your hands. Secure it to something immovable inside or a tree outside. Why is this important? The story of "What Kyia Taught Me," will answer the question best.

The Teaching Lead uses a leash in the metaphoric role of holding your dog's hand. It is designed to communicate direction and condition household manners without force, discipline or isolation. In the next chapter, you'll learn and understand how to use a Teaching Lead to

- Take the place of a crate when you're at home
- Teach basic obedience skills
- Gain control when walking outside
- Housetrain your dog
- Discourage nipping and jumping
- Encourage good chewing habits
- Calm your dog around company
- Teach more advanced obedience

What Kyia Taught Me

When I was just a pup (a teenager), I found a beautiful, silvery white Husky mix at a pound in Michigan. She was about six or seven months old and had been rescued from the woods, sick with worms and caked with mud. At the shelter, she hung back in her kennel, confused and shy. Everyone passed her by. Everyone, that is, except me.

Although I asked the attendant many questions, all I can remember her saying was, "She has a day to live." That was it. When I took the dog outside, she peed quickly. Good, I thought, she's housebroken. "I'll take her," I said, as a tear trembled down my cheek.

I named her Kyia (which means "white" in Hawaiian), and she wasn't housebroken. She also loved chewing wood — inside and out — was an avid digger, peed every time a voice was raised or anyone bent to greet her, growled at her food dish and, in the height of play, jumped and nipped above the waist. OK, so who's perfect?

Some training was definitely in order. I read some books. Crate, crate, crate, they instructed. It didn't resonate with me. How could confining her teach anything? But I bought a crate anyway. She gave me a desperate look, too similar to her first pitiful stare at the shelter. I folded up the crate and stuck it in the attic. Years later I used it with a puppy, but crates aren't for every dog and it sure wasn't right for Kyia.

So what next? More books. *How to Be Your Dog's Best Friend,* by the Monks of New Skete, mentioned something about keeping a dog with you on a leash. A light bulb went off. That was the answer.

Since holding the leash all the time was cumbersome, I tied it around my waist. I led her when she was in the house and when she was out. Whenever she sniffed the carpets, I chanted OUTSIDE as we raced for the backyard.

The Short Lead

Short leads are wondrous for the quick, easy grab. How short your lead should be depends on the size of your dog. A short lead should not be more than eight inches long; for small dogs, one inch will do.

Use the short lead to encourage good manners and to teach off-leash skills. Many dogs know the Teaching Lead drill: A little halo appears and when it's on they don't do anything naughty. Take the Teaching Lead off, however, and sometimes the old devil emerges. Suddenly, grab-and-go becomes the game of the hour.

Whenever she approached a tissue basket or wooden decoration, I pulled her back and said NOPE! Being good at heart, she learned quickly. Within a few weeks, I let her drag the leash behind her, and eventually I stopped using the leash altogether. She had learned the concepts of GOOD GIRL and NOPE and, as common sense would tell you, she strived for the positive.

So in those novice years I discovered an alternative to the crate. This procedure felt more natural to me and to Kyia, and it worked. She was more secure and learned quickly. We bonded. It felt great.

Years later when I started my own training business, I didn't forget. As I listened to my clients complaining of their own guilty feelings about over-isolation, I empathized and shared my story. I also told them about the Monks' book and two other books by dog trainers and authors Carol Lea Benjamin and Job Michael Evans that describe the process as "umbilical cording." Following my suggestions, my clients gave it a try and it worked in nearly every situation. Year after year, I expanded on this process, creating ideas of my own until my techniques and teachings took on a personality all their own. The Teaching Lead Method was born!

Kyia, my dog and my friend.

Jumping on company becomes quite exciting. Unfortunately, the old patterns of attention-seeking re-emerge and the benefits of on-leash lessons are hard to recover.

Fortunately, a short leash can serve as a nice transition from on leash to full-fledged freedom. Leaving it on your dog reminds her that you're still watching and have something to grasp if things get out of hand.

When you do off-leash work, you can also use the short lead as a reminder. In addition, it's something you can hold if your dog slips up.

Jodi Buren

The short lead serves as a great reminder.

The Flexi-leash

I used to be a big fan of the Flexi-leash, back when it was new. Since then, I've discovered some drawbacks, although I still recommend it for specific off-lead exercises and solitary walks away from crowds or traffic.

First of all, the button holding the line taut can pop open, either due to improper handling or a defective mechanism. This happened to my nine-year-old neighbor when she was out with her Pug. The dog we all loved ran into the street (still on her Flexi-leash) and was instantly killed by an oncoming car.

Some of my clients told me they got horrible rope burns on their legs and hands — some requiring stitches — from grabbing the line when it wouldn't reel in. Others felt too comfortable with their Flexi-leash and their dog, running off, pulled it right out of their hand! So like everything, learn how and when to use the Flexi-leash, and limit it to those times.

Long Lines

Here's one of my favorite tools, both for play time and off-leash lessons. Long lines are great for dogs of any age, and dogs and puppies both benefit from the freedom it gives them to explore and exercise. Used for teaching, the long line simulates off-leash freedom while still giving you a sense of security.

A long line can range from 10 to 50 feet. Attached to your dog's buckle collar, harness or Gentle Leader, you can take your dog to a safe field or yard and let her go. You read right: Let her go. Most people cringe, thinking their dog will head for the hills (if you're honestly concerned, hold the end of the line), but are surprised when their dog just sniffs around. The line is a mental as well as a physical tether.

In Chapter 7 we'll use the long line when we get into more off-leash stuff, so keep it handy. But for now, with your dog on a long line you can begin to encourage the COME command (without even using the word!) and condition the following behaviors. Try these two exercises.

COME ON OVER

Most people call their dog's name when she's running away from them, which only teaches that COME means run. With treats in hand, you're going to call out your dog's name when she's with you. Each time she meanders over, call out her name as you offer a treat. What will start to happen more frequently? She'll keep checking in, of course! And in the beginning, you can't reinforce her enough.

If you're having trouble getting your dog to check in, don't nag. Play with something she'll find interesting — start swinging a stick or tossing a ball. Shake the treat cup and pretend to eat the snack yourself. Lie on the ground and make a funny noise. When she races over to check you out, call her name as you give her a treat.

FOLLOW ME

Teaching your dog to follow you happily requires one very important thing: that your dog wants to follow you! On the long line you can encourage good following skills using a treat cup or a clicker (to learn about how to use a clicker, take a look at Chapter 3). It's better to have a dog who likes to hang out with you than one who's only there

 Ouch!

Long lines are generally made of canvas or rope. If yours is made of rope, be mindful when using it around people. A quick tangle can leave someone with an ugly rope burn.

out of fear or force. Simply walk around patting your leg, acting silly and doing whatever it takes to encourage your dog to follow you — dispensing clicks and/or treats along the way. It will be a great game to play!

CANINE CONTAINMENT

Many behaviors that we consider bad are self-rewarding for a dog. For example, no dog needs to be encouraged to eat garbage, because it's full of free fabulous food scraps. Chewing on the sofa leg, tearing up pillows and running around at breakneck speed are equally rewarding without any input at all from you.

Sometimes the best way to head off these bad habits is to make sure your dog never develops them in the first place. And so canine containment.

Indoor Containment

Whether you need gates, crates and other confinements will depend on your dog. Is she a diplomat, civilized and well mannered as she meanders through the halls of your home? Or are you hiding under the couch as your dog ricochets off your walls? Most of you probably fall between these extremes, so let me explain when these devices come in handy and how to use them humanely.

GATES

These are sometimes called "baby gates," and the benefit of using them to confine both dogs and babies is that the little dears can be kept out of trouble — or at least, all the trouble can be confined to one room. All the hair, the chaos, any destruction or mania, is confined to, say, the kitchen. Once you leave the kitchen, the house will be like it was before you had a dog. That's unless your dog starts to bark to protest your separation or she cruises the counters in order to get your attention. Then gating has some drawbacks.

Although gating long term may create more problems than a sound training regime, there are situations where gates are invaluable: conditioning young puppies to manage freedom; closing off a play area; confining a dog-in-training while you're out; isolating them from off-limit areas; or blocking dangerous stairways, ledges or porches.

 The Right Room

When considering where to confine your dog, keep these things in mind:

- Pick a space with linoleum or tiled floors in case of mishaps or accidents.
- Keep the area clear of loose objects that might be tempting to chew or swallow.
- Keep all electrical cords secure. If they're on ground level, tape them securely to the wall. Left alone, some dogs get mischievous and chew on these cords.

Be sure to buy gates made of high quality wood, metal or nontoxic vinyl mesh, and ones that are designed to fit the width of your doorways. If you have breeds known for their athletic ability, look for extra-tall versions, or else buy two and stack them one atop the other.

We can't leave our dog alone in another room when we're home. She just howls and gets so destructive.

Unfortunately, if you break down and go back to calm her, you'll be reinforcing the problem behavior with — what else — attention. Another vicious cycle is created. Your dog is suffering from isolation anxiety. Being a social creature, she doesn't understand why she can't be with you. Although at this point you'd fear her freedom, consider the Teaching Lead methods of leading and stationing as safe ways to keep your dog with you. If household freedom is not an option at this point, consider using a crate or playpen — smaller spaces are more calming.

CRATES

A crate is basically a big cage made of metal, plastic or wood. Available in a variety of sizes, the crate should be large enough for your dog to stand up and easily turn around. Crates are not mandatory, although for puppies or dogs suffering separation anxiety or those with destructive habits, they can make your life much easier and your dog's life more understandable.

Most dogs think crates are cool: "My own special space!" When used properly, dogs feel secure and safe in them, just like their ancestors did in their dens. Crates also encourage good sleeping habits and discourage mischief and inappropriate elimination. Happy dog, happy owner.

For you, a crate can be tremendous teaching tool and stress reliever. It's great when used in the following situations:

- When you must leave your dog alone for less than six hours
- When you sleep (for a not-yet-housetrained or destructive pup or dog)
- As a feeding area for an easily distracted pup or dog
- As a safe confinement in the car

My dog protests being crated by barking relentlessly.

Whatever you do, don't pay attention to her. The barking will never stop and it will transfer to any situation in which she's not getting her way. Ignore the barking if you can (earplugs are a must!) and wait it out. Also try leaving her with a challenging toy such as a hollow bone filled with peanut butter or cheese, to keep her busy. I've found the Gentle Leader to be calming — left on only while you're there to supervise her reaction, of course! Let her out of the crate when she has calmed down and is not barking.

You can't just stick the crate anywhere and slam the door shut, though. When leaving your dog in her crate, be sure to

- Leave her in a dimly lit area (to encourage sleep).
- Leave the radio tuned to a classical music station (no hard rock).
- Avoid grandiose departures, which your dog interprets as, "Oh no, they're leaving me!"
- Stay cool during arrivals. Good manners start with you!
- Avoid corrections for anxiety behaviors such as shredding or messing. Corrections only convey the message that the isolation results in a frustrated reunion. You'll be increasing her anxiety and the chance of the behavior happening again.

Dogs can go nuts if left in a crate more than six consecutive hours, day after day. Like us, they have active minds that demand companionship and stimulation. If you must leave your dog for long stretches, gate her in a kitchen or bathroom, buy a fold-out dog pen from the pet supply store, and hire a dog walker to break up the monotony of the day. Given more space, she can stretch, play a little and move about as she awaits your return.

What happens if a dog is crated too long?

Frenetic barking. Overly enthusiastic jumping and excited nipping when released. And let's throw in destructive chewing for good measure. Some dogs even chew on themselves. Poor creatures. It's not their fault! I don't mean to insult anyone who uses crates a lot. Many books encourage crating when a dog cannot be watched all the time. It's good advice, because you don't want a destructive dog or untrained pup ravaging your house. For good-hearted people on the go, however, that means a lot of crate time for the dog left behind. This is what can backfire. Alternatives are coming up shortly!

Are there any long-term effects of over-crating?

Yes, in some situations. Many of the dogs I've seen have developed what I call hyper-isolation anxiety. Too much isolation produces anxiety, and the anxiety produces hyper behavior. The dog acts clinically hyper when she's really not. Let me explain. A dog who's confined is not learning how to behave. When she's finally permitted some freedom, she has so much pent-up energy and so little understanding of good behavior that she starts tearing around the house like a lunatic. Yelling and chasing (on your part) make matters worse, and so begins another vicious cycle in which the dog gets confined because no one knows how to handle the situation. Ugh!

Indoor pens can be invaluable, especially if your dog is spending long hours alone.

I want to keep my dog with me when I get home, but she's too hyper. I feel guilty having to put her back into the crate. What's my option?

The alternative is to keep your dog with you on leash, using the Teaching Lead method. It'll work wonders for you and your dog. It's humane and fair, and makes rational sense to both humans and dogs. Learn all about the Teaching Lead method in the next chapter.

PUPPY PLAYPEN

Do you work all day? Or are you in and out frequently, not a big fan of crating yet concerned about leaving your dog gated in a room? Consider purchasing a canine playpen. A big one gives your dog plenty of room to stretch and move about. When you're home for the night, they fold down nicely and can be stored in a closet. If you're paper training your dog, a section of the pen can be designated for that.

Outdoor Containment

The convenience of an outside enclosure can't be argued. We all face the morning rush, family chaos, hard days at work. A free romp for your dog combines walks and play into one. And all that running makes for a peaceful evening around the fire.

As good as it sounds, full freedom outside can have some drawbacks. Your dog will develop SLD: Selective Listening Disorder. Your direction can be considered and reconsidered. COME suddenly has new possibilities — "not come" being among them. Alone outside, dogs learn to fend for themselves, often re-organizing priorities from listening to the instant gratification of running free. Yards get re-landscaped, plants get chewed and little children become the focus of all chasing activities.

Do not despair. There are many benefits of a fenced area, as long as you know that time alone outside can never take the place of your interactions or lessons together.

I get a lot of questions about the difference between pens, physical enclosures and electric fences. Here's my take on them all.

Dog Pens and Tie Outs

An outdoor pen may be an option for an older, well-educated dog. For a young, untrained dog or puppy, being left out in a pen with no one to interact with often results in hyper-isolation anxiety (see page 36). Depending more on social interaction, they get anxious when left alone. This anxiety translates into excessive barking, digging, territorial behavior or frantic activity when reunited with people.

Tie-outs or runner lines create similar issues as an isolated outdoor pen. Used with supervision and interaction, however, the expanded play area can be a good option. These lines offer sturdier confinement than an outdoor pen. For pups who are escape artists, a tie out offers more security than an outdoor pen.

Fenced Yard

This is a great option for many dogs, giving them full freedom to join you in all your outdoor activities. You also have the option of installing a doggy door in one of your entranceways, enabling your dog to come and go as she likes. Nothing so dreamy, however, comes without a few drawbacks.

Left alone outside too long, your dog may pine for companionship and may try to chew her way into the house to find you or dig to relieve separation anxiety or boredom. Then there are the acrobats who may try to jump the fence or dig their way under and set out to find you. If you decide to fence in your property, let your dog out only when you're there to supervise.

Invisible (Electric) Fencing

An option growing in popularity is electric fencing. This seemly magical invention keeps dogs contained through the power of electricity. An underground wire is buried along the perimeter of your property. The location of the wire is then marked with flags stuck in the ground. Your dog wears a battery-operated collar, and if she approaches the perimeter line the battery gives her a shock. Eventually she learns to avoid the flags, and after that, she learns to avoid the edges of your property even when the flags aren't there.

When it works, it's beautiful. And when taught properly (I get dogs to believe I'm getting shocked and am angry at the flags for a solid week before they even wear the collar), it's more humane than letting a dog run the streets. However, it does require some serious training at the outset. And if your dog is headstrong or insensitive to pain, or you're forgetful about changing the collar battery each month, this may not be the way to go.

An electric fence also offers no protection for your dog. Anyone can come in and tease her, hurt her or even steal her. Other dogs and wild animals can also wander into your yard and make trouble. And if your dog does cross the fence line and gets out, she'll have a very good reason not to come home.

Car Control

Driving is a job in itself! Avoid being preoccupied with your dog while doing it, because it's a safety hazard for both of you — not to mention for other motorists. Letting your dog ride in your lap or hang her body halfway out the window may seem cool, but it's really not. Maybe I've witnessed too many accidents, but to me, cars aren't toys and your dog is too precious to lose in a fender bender.

Here's my safety rule: Confine your dog while driving. There are car gates, crates and car leads that, once connected to the seat belt, can be attached to your dog's harness or buckle collar.

Car gates confine dogs to a back cargo area. If you go this way, promise to get the best gate your money can buy. When I was in college at Michigan State University, I bought a bargain brand gate to confine Kyia in my station wagon. We were on our way home to New York when the thing collapsed. Poor Kyia! Such a sweet pea, she was sure she had caused the crash and was remorseful the rest of the trip home. Moral of story? If you're going to buy a gate, buy the best!

Although **crates** are cumbersome to lug in and out of the car, no one can argue about their safety. It may be easier to get two crates and leave one in the car all the time. Another alternative is to secure your dog in the back of a wagon area or on a seat belt with a short lead. Here's the deal.

Jodi Buren

Keep your dog safe and contained. Driving is enough of a job!

A **seat belt safety lead** is a short lead that fastens onto a seat belt. It can be left in the car permanently or removed for handling. When securing your dog, place her in a harness or buckle collar in the backseat to prevent injuries. Now decorate that space! A blanket and some toys will help your dog feel right at home! When you bring your dog to the car, tell her ON YOUR MAT as you point to the area. Offer a treat for cooperation.

In the cargo area of most large vehicles, there is a security clip on the floor. Secure a **cargo lead** to the clip, measuring its length to prevent your dog from jumping into the backseat. Add toys and a mat — give your dog the works back there! Say ON YOUR MAT as you direct her to the area and secure her cargo lead on a harness.

Car containments protect your dog the way your seat belt protects you. Your dog will feel more secure and calm knowing her place, and you're both ensured of a safe arrival.

OTHER ESSENTIALS

Did you think you were finished shopping? If you want a well-trained dog, there's still more on your list of essentials.

Flat Mats and Cozy Beds

Go into each room you'd like your dog to share with you and pick an area for her. Maybe near the couch in the TV room or by the bed in the bedroom, but away

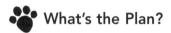

from the table in the dining area. Decorate each area with a flat, washable mat, towel or cushy bed. Place a selection of chewies on the mat. From now on we'll call each location a *play station* (I'll explain stationing in much more detail in the next chapter). Creating cool places for your dog in each room really helps her feel welcomed, connected and calm.

Just telling your dog to sit on her mat may not be enough to persuade her. If she's restless, tie a leash to something immovable near her mat and secure her at appropriate times. When you bring your dog to her station, tell her SETTLE DOWN, show her a chewie toy and secure her until sitting still becomes a habit.

The best application of all this is that no matter where you go, you can take your mat and the whole stationing concept with you. Your dog sees her mat and knows just what to do. At the veterinarian, just think how much better she'll feel having her mat (or in this case, her security blanket) on that cold hard table! Or, if you're going on vacation, leave

🐾 What's the Plan?

Dogs, like humans, prefer a plan. Both species like to know where to go when they walk into a room. Imagine coming into my home and having no idea where to put yourself. Or, what if I gave you too many options? You'd feel confused or nervous or fearful. If, on the other hand, I welcomed you with a smile and said, "Here's a seat, make yourself comfortable," you'd know just what to do and would feel much better. Dogs are the same; they need to know where to go and what to do.

Mary Bloom

A flat mat is easy to wash and transport. Dogs think of it as a security blanket.

it with her at the kennel or take it along to give her a sense of her own space. Her play stations will help her feel safe, calm and connected everywhere! (For this reason I'm a big fan of flat, washable mats. They are easy to clean and transport.)

Chew Toys and Bones

Is your dog having difficulty differentiating her toys from other household objects? Take a look at how many toys are in her basket. More than one? I know, they were all special presents. But it's confusing, trust me. Too big a selection gives the dog the illusion that everything on the ground is fair game.

Try this approach: Pick one or two favorites and buy identical replicas to disperse around the house. If you have a die-hard chewer, be sure to select a chew bone that will satisfy her gumming needs, avoiding soft toys that might feel like a couch cushion or a rope toy that looks like the fringed rug. Each time you give your dog her object, emphasize the word: "Here's your TOY" or "Here's your BONE." When the chewing impulse strikes or she's excited, she'll have your voice ringing in her ears.

Take your discarded toys and bones to a local animal shelter. They'll be appreciated more than you know.

Chapter **3**

The Teaching Lead and Other Training Strategies

The Teaching Lead method can be used to communicate direction and to condition good household manners without force, discipline or isolation. Please remember, however, that how you use leashes and your collar will be shaped by your four-footed participant; no single technique works on every dog.

In addition, I want to introduce you to the latest and greatest in dog training philosophies, and you'll find this information starting on page 57. You may have heard about techniques like clicker training and targeting, but are not sure what they are. Although entire books have been written on these topics, you'll get the crib notes here.

THE TEACHING LEAD METHOD

The Teaching Lead is the only training method I can take partial credit for. Of course, nothing is the sole brain child of any one person. In my case, I was influenced by many of the great dog trainers, including Job Michael Evans and Carol Lea Benjamin.

This method offers three applications: leading, anchoring and stationing. Leading involves holding or securing your dog to your side as you teach specific commands and quickly discourage all inappropriate behavior. Since giving a dog too much freedom too soon can be a big mistake, it's good to know you have an option.

Anchoring teaches your dog that when you're calm, he must be calm too. It is a way to teach your dog to lie calmly at your side while you're eating, watching TV, visiting or talking on the phone.

Stationing provides a special place in each room for your dog and gives you a place to direct him to during meals or when things are hectic. Although initially

Remember!

Before we get started, accept these truths:

1. To your dog, you're a dog. So am I. It's a major compliment, so don't be embarrassed.

2. Being a dog, you need to think about your place in the hierarchy. Think of your group as a team. Do you want to direct the team or be directed? Organize the players, or be organized yourself? Teach or be taught?

3. Rank is determined by who organizes the space and activities of the group. The leader decides where to go and what to do. In all situations 24/7.

4. You can decide to be a follower, essentially being trained by your dog and relinquishing any hope of behavior improvement or obedience, or . . .

5. You can decide to become the team captain. The leader. The program director. The queen or the king!

This is your moment . . . the big decision. If you want to be a follower, read no more. Burn this book. But if you want to be the leader — the team captain — well then, read on! The rest of my book is dedicated to you.

you may need to persuade him to stay at his station by securing him on a leash, eventually he'll go to his specified areas automatically.

Leading

Keeping your dog with you around the house may sound like a drag (literally!), but it's only temporary until he can be trusted off-leash. Leading enables you to passively communicate your leadership and teach good manners as you enjoy time together — with the emphasis on conditioning good behavior. Your success mantra is: Encourage more than you discourage.

Some of you may need to lead your dog only when company's around or maybe not at all. Read over the following three categories to see where you and your dog fit in:

1. Do tornado winds start to blow every time you let your dog loose in the house?

2. Home alone with you, he's a gem, but once the kids come in or company rings the bell, his personality does a turn for the worse.

3. Your dog is Little Ms. Perfect: Mannerly in the home and polite around the guests. No problem.

Did your dog fall into Category 1? You need to use the Teaching Lead whenever you're around, either stationing or leading. Remember, it's not forever. For now, your dog must unlearn old habits and learn better manners from the bottom up.

Did your dog fall into Category 2? I suggest you practice leading periodically when you're home alone to get your dog used to the procedure. Use it full time when you're expecting company.

What about Category 3? We're all jealous! You need not worry about the lead inside, but you'll find it handy for the obedience and off-leash training sections.

If you fall into Category 1 or 2, don't be frustrated. Using the Teaching Lead method is better than losing your sanity or your favorite shoes or confining your dog. It is definitely better than giving up. And it's just until your dog learns the plan.

Remember, to teach your dog anything, he must respect you and want to follow your program. Like a child, you can't force a dog to respect you just because you say so! In Chapter 1, you learned that group structure is of primary importance to dogs. Thinking of your group as a team, you need to be the captain. Leading your dog communicates this idea. Where you go, he goes. If directional decisions are to be made, you make them. No arguing for control. No monkey business. There can be only one decision maker, one captain, and it must be you.

LEADING 101

First things first. Put your dog's teaching collar on and secure it to the Teaching Lead. Either hold the leash at your waist or secure it around you like a belt. Position the leash on one side — either left or right. Pick one side, tell everyone in the family about it and be consistent. Dogs are creatures of habit and are easily confused.

Take your dog into a quiet area. Say his name and LET'S GO, then start walking. Don't look at your dog — you're the team captain so stay focused on your surroundings, not your dog. As you are walking around, remember *you're* the one to watch. If you want to

Leading leaves your hands free and your mind at ease.

The Indoor Drag Lead

Once your dog is catching on to the new plan, it's tempting to just unclip the leash and see what happens. Promise me you won't do that! Instead, if you really want to test things out, attach a lightweight nylon lead onto his buckle collar and supervise those initial ventures! This drag lead will have two benefits: The weight on his collar will serve as a gentle reminder, and the lead itself will give you a way to direct him should he get hyper or confused.

go in the living room but your dog would rather check out the kitchen, it's the living room. If he races ahead, change direction. Don't deliberate, just go! Although he may pull or strain to have his way, just ignore him. Keep your head facing the living room and walk on. Your dog will accept your decision and respect you more for making it.

Once your dog is cooperating on the leash, keep him tied to you in your home as often as possible. Where you go, he goes. If holding/wearing his leash isn't convenient or you need a bathroom break, direct him to one of his play stations (remember, I explained those on page 41), securing him there until he learns to stay put.

THE MULE WANNABES

Initially, some dogs strain to move in one direction or stop moving altogether when you first introduce them to leading. Some are cooperative creatures who are just confused. For these fellows, I suggest kneeling down ahead of them and encouraging them with a treat cup or jingle jar. Use a clicker or YES to cheer on any cooperation. Pretty soon, they'll get the idea and be back on track.

Other dogs, however, are less cooperative. They're the tantrum throwers. When they walk on lead, they imitate mules: Instead of walking, they just stop. Period. Won't move. Passive resistance. And, if you look back, pet them or pick them up, you're sunk. You guarantee even more resistance and determination to do only what they want, when they want. Dogs like that are hard to live with and no fun to share. So for your own well-being and your dog's too, leave him on the floor, stop petting him, and don't look at him. Attach him to a Gentle Leader or buckle collar to avoid discomfort. When he does cooperate, use your clicker and treats to rally his enthusiasm.

The sooner you do this, the faster he'll give up his silent bid for control! Be strong. Think off-leash. Think of the slipper he chewed, the shrub he excavated or the neighbor he knocked over. If you can't convince him to walk with you, you'll never be able to persuade him to give up all his other darling habits. I know you can do it!

I have a young puppy. At what age should I begin leading?

Young puppies who have been properly acclimated to a leash will love to follow you around, but only for about five to 10 minutes because their attention spans are very short. (You can't do any leading with a puppy who isn't leash-trained.) Just remember that puppies under 16 weeks old can't pay attention for very long and are easily distracted.

Puppies, like babies, have five basic needs: eating, drinking, sleeping, eliminating, and exercising. (For a neat Puppy Needs chart, flip to page 234 in the Appendix.) Like a baby, they get frustrated when a need is not met. Here's the difference: Babies cry. Some puppies whine. Most get extremely mouthy and fidgety.

Wild and crazy energy spurts are normal in these little guys. What's the best thing for you to do at these times? Let your pup have freedom in an enclosed yard or kitchen while you stand aside and randomly toss toys for your puppy to chase.

Wild pups get nippy, and corrections only accentuate rough play (they think you're playing too). It's better to wait until they cool down before you attempt to reason with them. Also, consider nipping as a cry for help. If your puppy is telling you with his nipping that he needs something ("I gotta poop!"), pay attention!

How long should I lead my dog around?

That depends on a lot of things.

Age of dog. Young puppies cannot concentrate or sit still as long as older pups or dogs can.

Their behavior. Is your dog calm, restless, or off the wall? Manners buy freedom.

Your lifestyle. Are you around all day? You're very fortunate. You have more time to devote to the early stages of teaching manners than people who work. If you do work, your time will be more limited. Once home, you'll need to get out with your dog for some exercise and play, but when fun time's over it's time to lead (stationing is another option for keeping your dog nearby).

Your dog's personality. Sweet peas pick up structure faster than the comedians; trust me, I've had both. But don't let that frustrate you if you've got a more active personality under your roof. They learn, too. They just take a little more persuading. The greater the challenge, the sweeter the victory!

 Clicker Training

Throughout the book, I'll highlight how clicker training can be used in lessons and to aid in problem solving. To learn about clicker training, flip to page 57 in this chapter. If you choose to try a clicker, you'll discover that it's a fun and fast way to speed up your dog's understanding. By marking the moment your dog is good, he'll catch on quickly.

The whole thing sounds beautiful, but my dog thinks he's in a race every time I put him on the leash. How can I persuade him to walk without threatening my own safety?

Here's my solution:

1. Get a Gentle Leader on your dog. At the very least, a no-pull harness will help curb the pulling.

2. Introduce your dog to the clicker or the sound of the treat cup.

3. Go into a quiet room and secure your leash around your waist or hold half the slack of the leash to your body.

4. Walk forward. The second your dog takes off, call out his name, shake the treat cup if you have one, turn around, and move in the opposite direction. As you turn, look in the direction you want your dog to follow; if you look at him, he may stop moving or pull back.

5. It may take a few turns for your dog to pay attention. When he finally wises up and turns with you, click and treat.

6. Keep turning until your dog either alerts to his name or you collapse from dizziness (something I've done more than once!). Soon he'll be walking at your side.

Practice this exercise in areas with more and more distractions: in a busy kitchen, out in your yard and so forth. Once you've got the balance and coordination, use it on your walks. The next time your dog's radar picks up two gray tidbits playing in your neighbor's yard, call out his name and move in the opposite direction. Did he listen? Great — click and treat, and praise up a storm. If not, try again. And again. And keep turning until he puts your direction ahead of any distractions!

 Never Too Young to Lead

Young children can lead the dog by holding a short lead. It's fun to hold and can be released immediately. My car lead doubles nicely for this activity (find out how to order it at my website, www.dogperfect.com). I use the short lead in class to enable the kids to hang on and direct their dog while an adult holds onto the regular leash.

Can everyone belt around?

Everyone who can, should. However, use your good judgment. Pregnant women and children can wear the leash like a sash, provided the dog is not large enough to pull them down. I wouldn't suggest hitching your three-year-old to a Saint Bernard — or even to a Yorkshire Terrier. Do not lead your dog around if you're physically impaired or very pregnant. But if older children and/or other adults want to

The Story of Kibbles

Kibbles is a fun-loving year-and-a-half-old Cocker–Cavalier King Charles Spaniel cross rescued from the shelter by a loving family. Having spent a third of his life without a family, Kibbles can hardly sit still. There is even a pond in the backyard and two dog friends who stop by each afternoon to play! Heaven or what?

Kibbles is so busy taking it all in, however, that he doesn't pay attention to his bathroom habits. Wherever will do: upstairs playing dress-up with the girls, in the kitchen on a break from his nightly begging rituals, out on the deck if there's no incentive to leave the house or on the grass if the mood strikes him. He's not picky. He's not marking. He's not lazy. He's just clueless!

From the moment I met Kibbles, I was charmed by his sweet and eager personality. Before 10 minutes had passed, however, he trotted out on the deck, peed quickly, and ran back inside for some more attention. No remorse. No guilt. No understanding. This happens to a lot of shelter dogs. They think they can pee anywhere. Can you blame them?

Well, as soon as Kibbles and his family were introduced to the Teaching Lead method, things started to change. After showing everyone (including the girls, who wore the lead like a beauty sash) how to lead Kibbles, I went on to explain housetraining techniques. Until Kibbles was cooperating, he was to be led or stationed.

Not surprisingly, Kibbles took to the leading like a shadow to the dark and happily followed whoever was in charge. It was as if he had been waiting for a good leader all his life! Within just a few weeks, Kibbles had regained his freedom in the house and had learned to jingle some bells by the door in case his owners forgot to take him for a walk!

take part in the training, let them! Remember, dogs focus on a hierarchy, so it's best if everyone plays a part.

How can I get my dog to stop grabbing at the leash when I walk him?

Dogs love this game! Such a fun activity! I know — fun for them, not for you. First you must put an end to all those tug-of-war games. They encourage struggles for control, including the battle of the leash. Next, spray Grannick's Bitter Apple or rub Tabasco sauce on the lead. It has a vile taste that often discourages mouthing. If your dog thinks these are condiments (I had one who licked both right off my hand), then you must use a tougher tactic. Each time your dog goes for the lead, calmly and without eye contact, snap it firmly *into his mouth*. Let me repeat that: Pull the leash it *into* his mouth sharply, not out. I know that pulling the lead out is the more natural reaction; however, it only encourages a control struggle.

Want to know why you pull it in and not out of your dog's mouth? It's all about cause and effect. Dogs view our hands as mouths. Because we're holding the leash, they want to hold it too. For some dogs, it's a control issue; for others, it's more of a copycat reaction. When they do grab the lead, the human reaction is to pull it out. Most dogs interpret this as fun, not discipline, and so they grab it again. We pull the lead out. They grab. Grab-pull-grab-pull.

On the other hand, when the lead is pulled back into the mouth sharply, it doesn't feel so good. Although they may try it a couple more times, the behavior will fade if it brings neither play nor attention. It's more comfortable to leave the lead alone.

Into, not out. Don't forget.

How come I feel guilty moving on when my dog drags behind me or stops to sniff?

I don't know. Maybe you're the permissive type, concerned about your dog's feelings, needs and such. God bless you! But remember that your dog isn't human. He is more interested in figuring out the size of his territory and who organizes the walks than giving you brownie points for being nice. Unless you feel like sniffing a fire hydrant or marking your neighbor's bush, walk on.

Do I have to lead my dog around forever?

Of course not! Once your dog is responding to your verbal instructions and understands the rules (generally one to three weeks), you can start letting him drag the leash as you supervise. If your dog behaves, praise him. Help him find toys when he's restless. After you get a few days of good manners, try attaching a short lead. Slowly allow your dog more freedom, even when you can't be on his tail. Once he passes that test, he's a house-free dog. Congratulations to both of you!

Anchoring

Suddenly the phone rings, or you have to work on the computer or you're a kid and you've got some homework to do. What do you do with the dog? How do you teach your boy to quiet down when you're occupied? Off-leash, he would

---

🐾 Security Mat

To make your dog feel really cozy, put his mat and bone down before you relax. This is especially great if you're taking him to his veterinarian or on a visit. It's a little bit of home, a security blanket!

probably have you running around rescuing a favorite shoe or the defrosting chicken. Unfortunately, it's just that attention thing again. But I have the answer. I call it anchoring.

Whenever you're sitting down to answer the phone, speak to company, wait at the veterinarian's office, have a meal, watch TV and so on, sit on your dog's leash. Give your dog just enough freedom to lie next to you and offer him a mat, a favorite chewy and a friendly scratch.

Jodi Buren

In the beginning, expect a fuss. Your dog may whine, bark, paw or stare, which are all common attention-getting ploys. You must ignore him. Protests are OK, you just don't want to acknowledge them. Like people, your dog must learn self-control.

Anchoring teaches your dog to mimic your energy level.

A dog who is used to easily grabbing your attention and giving you orders may be more resistant to anchoring. Again, it's OK; no need for a correction — just don't pay attention to it. You're the leader, the director, and what you do is in the best interests of the group. A dog who can't quiet down gets left in the mudroom when visitors come to call. A dog who's hyper doesn't get invited on any social calls.

It may take your dog 15 minutes to settle down and chew his bone, but when he finally does pet him gently. Look at him calmly with the most loving eyes. If he hops up again, withdraw the attention quickly, but then return to soft, loving caresses when he settles down.

When I anchor my dog, he jumps on me. He's 95 pounds and a little hard to ignore. Help!

Remember the cardinal rule of anchoring: You must give thy dog a bone. A totally delicious bone. It's a displacement activity, like a coloring book for a child. Expecting him to sit there with nothing to do is like asking a three-year-old to sit still through church. That said, try this too:

1. *Close shop.* Fold your arms in front of your face. Tilt your head toward the sky and don't look down until your dog gets off you. Repeat as often as necessary.

2. *Side swipe.* Without looking at your dog, take the leash and swipe it to the side — no looking and no changing your body posture. No vocal correction is necessary, either. In fact, the attention would make matters worse. When you ignore, the leash corrects. Step in and praise when your dog

settles down at your feet. Your dog may try it again, so repeat your correction — perhaps a degree firmer.

3. *Spray away.* Use Binaca breath spray or a plant mister filled with water and perhaps a little vinegar. Without looking at your dog, spray a boundary between your body and his head. Do not look at your dog or spray right at him in revenge. The spray is a cause and effect correction: Jumping not only doesn't get attention, but this spray bomb explodes between both of you.

4. *Shorten up.* If yours is a real die-hard jumper, sit or step on a very short leash so that the jump itself will bring about a correction. Release some slack when he decides to lie down.

When I anchor my dog, he lies down but immediately twists around to lie on my feet. Is this acceptable?

Great question! No, it's not. He's bending the request. It's like my asking you to sit in the dining room and you go lie on the couch. Hello? Your dog needs to rest quietly at your side. Feet and head facing in the same direction. Every time he twists forward, say EXCUSE ME and bring him back to the starting point with your hands and/or the leash. You may need to do this several times, but he'll comply eventually. Just be persistent.

 **Slow Down**

Is your dog still out of control? You'll need to take it slower. Don't be discouraged, it's no big deal. Everybody's different in the dog world, too. I've had dogs who caught on in two weeks and others who took months. Be patient. Do some more leading before trying this experiment again.

Stationing

Imagine sitting with your family or friends enjoying a meal or a movie with your dog lying nearby chewing on a bone. It can happen, and in short order! The first step is to decide which rooms you'd like to share with your pal. Think about it seriously: If your dog behaved, what freedoms would he be allowed? The living room, bedroom or study? Next, decorate a nook in each room with a mat and a favorite toy or two. This is his play station. Just like we humans feel more comfortable knowing our place in a room, so do dogs.

Eventually, you'll be able to send your dog to any area in any situation by using a command such as SETTLE DOWN. I realize that for some of you this might sound like a fantasy, but trust me, it will happen. The key word is "eventually." First you must teach him the program.

STATIONING 101

Pick your areas. Pick a spot in each room where your well-behaved dog will be permitted. Make sure it's a safe space, off to the side, out of heavy traffic and clear of ledges, furniture legs and electric wires and outlets. This will be your dog's space and eventually he'll go there automatically, but for now you may need to secure him.

Decorate the stations. Create a familiar theme at each station. Similar bedding and chew bones will help your dog learn faster. Suddenly it's not just a spot on the floor, it's a play station!

Secure your dog near you. When you station your dog, give him just enough length of leash (about three feet) to lie down comfortably. Given too much leeway, dogs may pace, bark or worse, eliminate. There are two ways to organize your stations: Either secure a leash to something immovable near your station spot (so it's always there), or use your Teaching Lead as you go (take the clip on the hand loop, double the lead over and secure it to the bottom clip). Whichever leash you use, provide no more than two to three feet of freedom.

Show your dog the station. The first time you secure your dog, hang around. Sit down and scratch his ears. Show him his bone. When he's content, say WAIT as you walk away for no more than 15 seconds. If you come back to a hyped-up dog, ignore him until he quiets down. Pet a calm dog and you'll get a calm dog. Steadily increase the time of your departures. He may fuss a bit, but your preliminary steps will ensure him of your return.

Give your dog the command. Each time you bring your dog to a station, say SETTLE DOWN and point to the mat. He won't have a clue for awhile, but eventually it'll click. You'll be amazed when he starts doing it himself. Dogs, like people, are more cooperative when they understand what you want.

Give your dog attention. As you've probably discovered, the unsupervised dog often gets attention for being naughty. Poor thing, he can't help himself. On the other hand, a stationed dog doesn't have a lot of room to act up. Sure, he may bark, but if you ignore him that will go away. (For truly incessant barkers, other alternatives are discussed in Chapter 8.) He might roll around a bit and act kooky, but you can ignore that, too. How bad can he be with only a three-foot area, a mat and a favorite chew? Stationing encourages one thing: good behavior. So whenever your dog lies down to rest or chew, you can reinforce him with you know what . . . ATTENTION! Don't get too wild. Just go over (or send the kids) and happily give him some love and pats. Tell him he's a gem. You're so proud. You're so glad you found him.

You can have two stations or 20 — it's up to you. You can also have a car station and outdoor stations (great for barbecues and badminton games).

Here are some station ideas from my home to yours!

Bailey the Beagle

Bailey is an adorable eight-month-old Beagle. Although he is given a high-quality dog food (which he eats with gusto), he hangs around the kitchen table looking soulful and starved. This technique usually pays off with a few pats and an occasional tidbit, although both his owners would prefer that he lie down in the corner while they're eating.

Bailey also enjoys begging during formal dinner parties. His owners would like to take him along when they visit family and friends, but Bailey's table manners have placed him on the "B" list for most social affairs.

Bailey makes the "A" list

When I met Bailey, I discovered a very happy fellow who thought begging was just the right thing to do. How could something that resulted in attention and treats be wrong? I suggested that his owners create a station in the kitchen at least 10 feet from the table. As I predicted, Bailey barked during the first few meals, but his determined owners ignored him. Soon after, he began to settle down and chew his bone. Within a month, he was staying in his area off-leash. Getting consistent direction has helped Bailey make a successful transition from social outcast to welcome guest.

Family room. Since everyone wants to pet the dog while watching TV or playing Nintendo, you can create this station near the couch.

Dining room. Unless you like dog slobber with your ketchup, you can create this station across the room so that your dog won't be tempted to disturb you while you are eating. This one really impresses house guests and in-laws!

Kitchen. Unless you have a huge kitchen, you might want to station your dog outside the kitchen door. This way, he can watch all the preparations without getting underfoot.

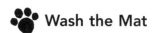

Greeting area or front hall. Dogs tend to get overexcited during arrivals. Left free, their enthusiasm can get in the way and is usually reinforced, unintentionally, by (what else?) attention. To avoid such hysterics and provide a better alternative, create a station in a corner of the greeting area. When the doorbell rings, instruct your dog to go to his place, secure him, give him a special toy and ignore him until he pipes down. The best of all possibilities is involvement without interference!

Bedrooms. Some of you may refuse the idea, but the truth of the matter is that your dog will feel safer and act a lot calmer during the day if he's kept with someone at night. This is especially true for dogs who are left alone during working hours. If your dog is older than four months and still needs confinement, station him at night in your bedroom.

Office. Some of you might be lucky enough to take your dog to work if he'd only behave. Now you've got a green light. Pick a spot by your desk, decorate it just like home and get to work!

Outside. If you're into gardening or you have kids who like to shoot hoops in the driveway and you'd be all for including the dog if he'd just calm down, you can help out by creating nearby stations.

In the car. It's safest to confine your dog while driving. It protects him the way a seatbelt protects you. Check out options for car containment in Chapter 2.

Wash the Mat

Are some of you neat freaks who wouldn't mind the dog if it weren't for all the hair, smell and dirt? I can relate. You might see a lot of paws in my house, but I do like a clean and pleasant-smelling home. Here's my suggestion: Keep flat, washable mats in each room and wash them frequently. You'll be happy and free of dog odor, and your dog will be delighted to have a place by your bedside.

What collar should I use to station my dog?

Don't leave your dog stationed to a slip collar or a metal chain. Secure the station lead to your dog's buckle collar, Gentle Leader or harness. (Some dogs get tangled in their harness. Observe your dog to make sure he doesn't.)

What if I have nothing immovable to station my dog to?

You have a couple of choices. Use a doorknob or a hinge. If your dog is small enough, move a piece of furniture near his station. If all else fails, get some eyehooks from the hardware store and screw them into a wall or the underside of a cabinet.

My dog won't stop barking on his station! Help?

If you've tried ignoring him for 10 minutes and he won't give up, you'll need to graduate to more active measures. Here are a few suggestions:

- Buy earplugs and wait it out. No joke!
- Consider a Gentle Leader. The nose strap has a calming effect, and gentle pressure to the leash shuts a dog's mouth naturally.
- Get a spray bottle or fancy long-distance water gun (the kids call it a super soaker) and discreetly spray him while you firmly say SHHH! He must not know where the water is coming from. Offer praise and attention once he calms down.
- If you've got a splitting headache, the baby's crying and your spouse is threatening divorce, very calmly remove your dog from the station and lead him by your side. The attention rule still applies. Ignore him until he calms down.

What if my dog panics when I leave him alone at a station?

It's common for young puppies to panic, so if yours does ease up on your routine and stay close until he feels more secure. If your dog is older, you must determine whether the reaction is really panic or simply a persuasive protest. Ignore the protest. If he's truly panicked, try to figure out why. Is he over-sensitive to weather changes or loud noises? Is he just needing a good romp and can't sit still? Did you feed him his last meal? Are the kids safe? Go down your checklist. If it all seems OK and he's still antsy, wait for him to take a breath and then go and sit with him. Encourage bone chewing, leaving his side only when he's sleeping. Pretty soon he'll get over it, whatever it is.

What if my dog chews the furniture or his station leash?

If you suspect your dog will chew his surroundings or his lead, spray anything he might test-chew with Grannick's Bitter Apple or another taste deterrent. If he's relentless, soak a couple of nylon leads in Grannick's Bitter Apple or Tabasco sauce. If all else fails get a short plastic-coated wire tie out and use that until he gives up on the idea.

Doggie Breaks

We all need breaks. You, me and your dog! Just how many breaks you'll need from this new teaching regime will depend on you and your dog. When considering these time-outs, your dog's age, size, behavior and temperament all come into play. Older dogs can concentrate longer than puppies can. Leading is great exercise for smaller dogs, but bigger ones need outdoor romps to burn off their energy. Those with livelier temperaments also need more diversionary play activities than passive dogs, who feel incredibly safe and calm next to your side.

Now for you. You'll also need a break. When you need a time-out from the Teaching Lead, you have several choices:

- Go out and romp together.
- Attach your dog to someone else.
- Isolate your dog temporarily in an enclosure or crate.

Optimally, you want to keep your dog with somebody, so the first two choices would be best, but avoid feeling too guilty if you must isolate him for short periods of time. As long as the isolation is not extensive, your dog will survive.

How long can I leave my dog stationed?

The amount of time you can station a dog depends on (you guessed it!) your dog. Age, energy level and temperament are paramount. Add time of day and weather to the equation. Puppies under 12 weeks can have stations; they just can't be attached to them. Older puppies and dogs can be attached to their stations, but, as common sense would dictate, young dogs need more breaks than older ones do. Time of day is also a factor. Is it nap time? You can expect more peace and quiet if you station your dog during nap time than if you station your dog during a peak energy time. In addition, rainy days usually mean less exercise, making it tough for active dogs to sit still for too long.

Do I have to leash my dog forever?

Of course not! Some dogs catch on to the SETTLE DOWN command so quickly that they're eagerly participating by the end of the second week. Others take longer, but what's the rush? Whether it takes a couple of weeks or months, once your dog learns this little trick, it lasts a lifetime. Mine were initially more cooperative when no one was around, but when I invited friends over it was not such a pretty picture. So for awhile I stationed when company was around. No biggie. Since my dogs are just like yours, you'll probably find yourself leaning on the leash from time to time, too.

CLICKER HAPPY TRAINING

If you've never seen or heard of a clicker, let me describe it. It's a small, rectangular plastic box with a metal strip inside that, when pushed, makes a distinct "click" sound. Although it may remind you of an annoying kids' toy, it's a phenomenal teaching tool. Here's why: The sound is sharp! It's distinctive. It's different from your voice. Always paired with a food reward, dogs quickly make the connection that the click is a real plus and getting the clicker to work becomes a top priority. For some dogs, it's an obsession.

Another influence of mine is animal behaviorist Karen Pryor; you can find her website listed in the Reference section of this book. She's responsible for bringing the clicker into the dog world. Originally, she used it to teach dolphins. Before that I believe it was used to train small Catholic children. I can always tell the adults who went to parochial school when I'm giving a lecture. A quick click brings them all to attention!

Think of the clicker much like taking a photograph: Capture the moment your dog does something good.

Jodi Buren

A clicker up close.

- Your dog sits for petting: you click and treat.
- Your dog pees in the right spot: you click and treat.
- Your dog walks next to you: you click and treat.
- Your dog comes when called: you click and treat.
- Your dog shakes paw: you click and treat.

Another cool benefit of clicker training is that it makes the teaching process more interactive and less purely instructional. With the constant feedback (click or not click in response to a behavior), a dog can try a range of behaviors (jumping, barking, racing in a circle) before he lands on the one that gets the magic click. From that experience he can easily learn that he gets the most attention by being calm and contained, rather than when being annoying.

To begin clicker training, get your hands on a clicker and start with the following exercise: Line up 10 treats. Click once as you simultaneously give your dog a treat and praise. Repeat this exercise 10 times. Before you finish, your dog should happily alert when he hears the clicker.

Now use the clicker to encourage him to sit. Keep the clicker in hand with treats available, and wait for your dog to sit. Don't tell him anything, just wait. Even if it takes two days, which it won't. If he jumps up or barks at you, cross your arms and look at the ceiling. If you've got a big dog with nails, wear a trench coat.

Pepper the Poodle

Pepper the one-year-old chocolate Miniature Poodle was trained with a clicker at five months old. Her humans kept the clicker and treats handy and when Pepper would sit for attention, chew one of her toys or play nicely with the children, she was often rewarded with a click and treat. As Pepper grew up, she'd test out other stuff, like barking and jumping, but it wasn't rewarded with anything — no click, no treat, no attention. So Pepper went back to the behaviors that made more sense, that kept the relationship interactive.

Don't despair if you've got a dog who is more addicted to misbehaving and ignoring you than Pepper the Poodle. Her family started when she was young, before she learned any annoying habits. Not only can the clicker teach your dog good behavior, it can help him unlearn the bad stuff, too.

If you've got a loud dog, buy earplugs. Just wait out the annoying behaviors (for other solutions, refer to Chapter 8) and ignore him. When he sits, click immediately, treat and praise, praise, praise.

Now start from the top. How long does it take him to sit this time? Are you sold? Most people look dumbfounded when their dog catches on, thinking their naughty dog must be stupid. But often they're wrong. The naughtiness may have been the only way to get attention. Show your dog another way and he just might surprise you. Make it a point to mark good behaviors, such as sitting for attention, and see what happens.

Now some of you are probably jumping ahead, thinking of using the clicker in the early morning hours to get your dog to come in the house. Stop right there! The clicker is only effective when used to reinforce a behavior; it cannot induce it. Although it's tempting, trust me on this one. Overclicking results in confusion. The formula is always one

Jodi Buren

Clicker fun!

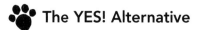

> ### 🐾 The YES! Alternative
>
> If the thought of a clicker doesn't appeal or it doesn't work for you, use a sharp word like YES! to mark the moment your dog does something right. It's quick and punchy, more pointed than a rambling "good dog, good dog, good dog," and, like the clicker, it will make your dog feel clever all over.

click, one treat — used to reinforce good behavior, not to induce it!

There are some situations where clickers don't work well. Here's a list:

A sound-sensitive dog. If the sound frightens your dog, you can try holding the clicker behind your back or placing it in your pocket. If your dog still freaks, use a word marker such as YES! to highlight the good stuff and give the clicker to a friend.

Around young children. They love the clicker too. A clicker in the wrong hands will bewilder your dog. If you're still determined to use the clicker, use it only when the kids are at school.

Dogs not motivated by food. Yes, they do exist. If you have one but notice that he's fixated on a ball or toy, you can use that as a reward after each click, or simply bag it and use YES! to mark good behavior with some very enthusiastic praise.

LURE TRAINING

To best understand lure training, think of your favorite thing on the planet: chocolate, money, a CD, GameBoy, whatever. Now imagine you're in my living room and I want you to come in the kitchen without using any words. Which would you prefer:

(a) I grab you by the shirtsleeve and haul you into the kitchen.

(b) I lure you (hint) by waving your favorite object.

Obviously, (b). That, metaphorically, is the principle of lure training. It's a fun and happy way to introduce new lessons to your dog. Essentially, you put the lure in front of your dog's nose and move it to guide him into doing what you want.

Most often the best lure for a dog is food. Some will do flips for a small grain of cereal, others need a more tempting goody. If your dog is either so food-oriented that he can't concentrate, or he couldn't care less about food, then try luring him with a favorite toy or bone.

Remember the rule of the lure: no hands. You can't give up and push your dog into position. It may stretch your creativity, trying to figure out how to get your dog to move into a certain position without touching him, but you can do it.

Below are some exercises you can practice. Bring your dog into a quiet room with some favorite treats or a toy. When luring your dog into any position, keep

Sweet Fiona

Lure training reminds me of a certain eight-month-old Jack Russell Terrier who wouldn't lie down. Her name is Fiona — such a sweet name. Fiona's mom claimed she would not lie down for anything. She'd tried pulling her front legs out from under her. I explained this would be like my yanking both of her legs out from under her. That explained Fiona's resistance.

She'd also tried using pressure points (which I'll teach you in the next chapter), but that didn't work either. Together we opted for lure training using a yummy snack that smelled like beef jerky.

Fiona showed us she'd do anything for the snack: sit, wave her cute little paw, walk on her hind legs, prance along at a heel — anything but lie down. That is, until her mom sat on the floor, bent her right knee so it was slightly off the floor, and lured Fiona under her leg. To get at the snack, Fiona had no choice but to lie down on the floor and crawl under the leg.

After several hundred repetitions (only slightly kidding), Fiona decided it wasn't all that bad, and now guess what she does when offered a treat? She goes straight down! She's even learned down tricks like roll over and crawl. Clever girl!

the temptation just an inch in front of your dog's nose and think what the movement would feel like if you were in your dog's paws. As your dog is moving into position, say what you want him to do.

Sit. Hold the lure in front of your dog's nose and slowly arch it back above his head. Stop and hold the treat steady above his ears. Say SIT as he's positioning himself. Say YES and reward the moment. Great job!

Down. Bring the lure from your dog's nose straight down to the floor in between his paws. Hold the object there. Some dogs position themselves better if you keep the treat still, however, others get it more quickly if you slowly slide the treat forward on the floor in an L-shape pattern. Reinforce your dog the moment he cooperates. Use the Fiona method (see "Sweet Fiona" sidebar above) if your dog is a refuser!

Come. Wave the lure in front of your dog's nose and say COME as you back up several paces. Bring the lure up to your eyes and encourage solid eye contact before rewarding him.

Heel. To teach your dog to walk at your left side, position the lure by your left leg. Reward him every few paces when he cooperates. As your dog catches on, increase the distance he must heel before he gets a treat.

Luring the DOWN.

TARGETING

Targeting is the latest craze. The goal is to teach your dog to go to a target, which can be anything from a coffee can lid to a book of matches, an index card or a paper plate. We'll use a coffee can lid for our example. Gather up some favorite goodies and practice before a meal. Here's how it works:

1. Place the lid on the ground next to you and wait for your dog to sniff or step on it.

🐾 Target Sticks

Target sticks are quite cool and fun, and they use the same idea as targeting. Imagine a metal stick with interlocking sections that can fold to fit in a pocket or be snapped together to extend three feet. (Think about an old-style car radio antenna.) If you can get your hands on a professional target stick, quickly do. Otherwise, start with a yardstick or a rolling pin.

Before using the target stick in lessons, a dog must learn to touch the end of the stick with his nose. Yes, his nose! It's not as hard as it sounds. Hold the prop out in front of your dog's nose. When he sniffs it, say YES or click and treat him. Keep presenting the stick and marking the moment he investigates it.

Once he catches on to this game, use the stick to lure him into many positions. For example, for DOWN, the stick would be brought from his nose to the floor.

2. Mark the exact moment your dog touches the lid with a sound marker (YES or a click), and instantly give him a treat. Continue as many repetitions as your dog will do enthusiastically. End on a high note.

3. As your dog catches on to your game, gradually move the lid away from you. Continue to work with food, rewarding each successful contact.

Targeting with style.

Once you know your dog is totally committed to this game, put a word to it, like TARGET. Say it each time your dog goes to the lid. As your dog learns other words, such as WAIT and DOWN, and even some tricks, you can mix them into this exercise. Tell your dog "target-wait-down-roll over." There's no end to the fun!

You may also use your target to help your dog with his lessons. For example, earlier in this chapter you learned how to send your dog to a designated area when you're eating or watching a movie. Targeting can speed up this process.

And don't forget your target can travel. It can be used to ease stressful situations, such as visiting the veterinarian, and can be use for other advanced activities like agility and pet therapy.

POINT TRAINING

One offshoot of target training that I teach all my clients is point training. It's invaluable! The long-term goal is to point your finger to direct your dog. It can be useful to direct your dog whether you're in the midst of a lesson, around your home or out and about. Your little index finger can make all the difference between your dog feeling lost and undirected and suddenly feeling like he's part of your team.

The target here is your finger. And, like target training, point training should be taught as a game. Use a toy or treat to start, although once your dog catches on, food isn't necessary. Of course, praising your dog and telling him how brilliant he is is a must!

There are three steps to point training. All involve helping your dog follow the point of your finger. Use a clear point of your index finger. It's as easy as 1-2-3:

1. *Instant gratification.* Hold a goodie in your hand and extend your pointing finger. Initally, exaggerate your pointing finger right in front of your dog's nose. When he hits your finger with his nose, mark the moment (YES or click) and give him the treat immediately. Continue to practice this, pointing within close range, until you see that your dog is catching on. Begin to slowly point in different directions. Eventually, point left, right, up, down, behind, and in front — he should follow that hand everywhere! And when he hits the point, treat him immediately.

2. *Delayed gratification.* Place your goodies in a snack pack or pocket, or on a countertop. Point at close range. When your dog goes to your finger, say YES! and/or click. Bring the treat from its location. As mentioned, move the location of the point as your dog catches on. You're still treating for every accomplishment, but now the treat is delayed and brought from a secondary location.

3. *Mental gratification.* Gradually phase out treating your dog for every successful point. Always mark the moment with an enthusiastic YES! GOOD DOG!

Now you can try to point your dog to his bed, and use your point to direct your dog up the stairs or off the couch. Guide your dog initially if he's confused. Pointing also works wonders for the obedience work in Chapters 4 and 5. Dogs love direction, and what could be handier than a point!

You can point here, there and everywhere!

Chapter 4

Starting Off on the Right Paw

Your mother was right, first impressions count! Starting off on the right paw is what will set the stage for all your future lessons. Want your off-leash dog to respond to COME? Then lay a consistent foundation each time your dog hears the word. If you're inconsistent with the basics, guess what? Your dog will never take you seriously with the more advanced stuff. It's not as difficult as it sounds. Really! I've set up this chapter to make it as simple, interesting and fun as possible. Let's begin!

THE POWER OF PRAISE

Who can argue? Praise just feels good. It feels good to get it; it feels good to give it. It's the universal motivator — and I haven't even begun talking about dogs yet!

Dogs are no different then we are. To see just how responsive yours is, go up to him whenever he's being good and tell him just how clever he is. Say YES and offer him some goodies. If you're using a clicker, this is the perfect opportunity.

When your dog is following the Four Paw Rule (keeping all four feet on the floor), going to the bathroom in the right place, licking your hand, listening to your direction on- or off leash, tell him he's brilliant. Don't miss a chance to praise, praise, praise!

Give it one week. Magically (it will seem), you'll see the scales of behavior start to tip. He'll calm down, he'll like the affirmations and so will you. Beautiful!

 **Chart It Out**

Make a YES chart. List all the behaviors your dog does right, from the simple to the complex. Aside from reminding you how good he can be, it will give you a chance to share the chart with family and friends. The more positive feedback he gets from everyone, the better.

Disney Makes a Choice

Disney is a 10-month-old Bichon Frise. A mop of white, curly hair, he's so cute he's almost edible. Loving the spotlight, if his family gets preoccupied he puts on quite a show to get their attention back on him. Pawing, barking and dancing on two legs are all part of his repertoire.

Lately, however, he had been running off outside, and the neighbors began to complain of barking when he's left alone (he hates to be left alone!). To help Disney, his family considered getting him a companion (fortunately they didn't — Disney wouldn't set a good example at this point). They also tried the discipline approach, yelling and correcting him, but that negative attention actually reinforced his misbehavior and left them feeling weighed down with guilt.

When they met with me, I could see that Disney thought the world of himself, and although he could get hyper, he had good attributes, too. The first thing his family did was make a YES list. Each time he did any of the following, he heard YES! and was rewarded:

Chewing on his bone

Playing with his stuffed duck

Sitting for his meals

Licking hands

Dancing on cue

Walking well on leash

Resting quietly

Not barking for attention

Waiting at the doors

YES Disney, I think you're great, too!

For a week the whole family focused on what Disney was doing right, praising him every single time. They ignored the bad behavior, prevented it or used the techniques discussed in Chapter 8. What a transformation a week can make! Disney's hyperactivity had calmed and he no longer felt confused. He understood what got attention and added extra gusto to each rewarded response. He was happy, and, just as important, his family was happy, too! The power of praise in action!

THE CONVERSATIONAL TECHNIQUE

When I was I kid, I remember taking a dog training class with an instructor who told everyone to practice twice a day for 15 minutes. This was not unusual or bad advice, and back when I was a kid, it was very do-able. Now that I'm a grown up, however, I can hardly find two minutes to brush my teeth. I found myself in the same predicament my clients complain about: New dog or old problems, who can find time to devote to organized lessons?

I'll tell you what I do now that I'm grown up. I use my training words throughout the day and I think of the words as giving me and my dog a mutual language — a consistent way to communicate with each other. By keeping the tone of the words clear and crisp, they sound different from my everyday chatter. I use these words conversationally all the time: SIT before petting my dog or giving treats, EXCUSE ME when I've got a dog underfoot, LET'S GO to change direction and NOPE for the naughty stuff.

By using specific commands conversationally all the time and focusing on what your dog is doing right, your dog will start picking up on what you want and (like magic) will start cooperating. Without taking time out of your day, you can teach your dog the Magic Seven.

A very Norman Rockwell moment.

THE MAGIC SEVEN

The Magic Seven are your start-up words. Knowing these words will give your dog a way to understand your expectations. (Imagine being a foreigner in a country where no one was speaking your language. It's the same for dogs.) We'll look at each word one at a time, but once taught you can intersperse them all throughout your day. Yes, your dog can learn seven words at once if you're consistent. And while you're introducing them, wear a snack pack to quickly reinforce your dog's happy cooperation. Here they are!

- SIT
- BUDDY (or whatever your dog's name is), LET'S GO
- EXCUSE ME
- BUDDY (or whatever your dog's name is)

- WAIT and OK
- NOPE
- SETTLE DOWN

The biggest motivating factor in training is you. To be a good teacher, you need to be consistent, clear and compassionate.

Be consistent. Use the same commands in every appropriate situation, and encourage everyone involved with your dog to do the same. If two people have different expectations, your dog won't know who to follow. **Be clear** in your communication. Use Doglish, not English, and stand confidently as you pronounce each direction clearly. And last, but not least, **be compassionate.** Praise a lot and reward with treats, especially in the beginning.

Sit

This command is one of my favorites. Why? Because once you start using it consistently, your dog will start doing it automatically. Without even having to be asked. Consistently-automatically. It's a wonderful thing.

Here's a quick exercise to teach your dog the wonders of sitting. Go into a quiet room with your snack pack or clicker and treats in hand. If food isn't a big motivation, bring a toy. Once your dog senses what going on, he may jump or bark for his goodies. Close shop: Fold your arms in front of you and look up. Instead of getting attention, it's actually being withdrawn. Wait it out. When your dog has calmed down, lure him into the sit position (without saying the command) by holding the treat just over his head and moving it back from his nose to his ears. If he jumps up, close shop again. Once he moves into the sit position say YES!, click and reward him. Now walk around the kitchen and each time your dog approaches, repeat the same exercise. Once your dog catches on, you'll notice that he approaches more often and sits automatically. GOOD BOY!

Practice this technique before

- Dinner
- Treats
- Tossing a toy or bone
- Petting
- Greetings
- Letting your dog outside, inside, down the stairs or out of the car

You can make SIT so user-friendly that your dog will actually look forward to hearing it. Think of it as the human equivalent to saying please, and use it each time you'd remind a kid to do the same. Your dog will think of SIT as the key to getting what he wants and will begin to respond without your prompting. Remember to:

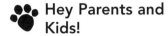

1. Be consistent! Say SIT clearly and encourage everyone to do the same.

2. Say it only once. Your dog understands sounds, not words. "Sit-sit-sit" sounds different than SIT.

3. Stand tall when you say SIT. If you're bending over, your dog might view your posture as indecisive or playful. Stand tall and be a proud leader.

4. If your dog doesn't listen, don't sweat it. Praise and position him gently. Yes, I said "praise." Even if

> ### 🐾 Hey Parents and Kids!
>
> If you have a big family, you'll have to help your dog out. Since everybody sounds different, life can get pretty confusing. When you give the commands, over-enunciate your syllables. Instead of using a blah SIT, bring the SIT to life by exaggerating the T sound: SITTT! Everyone will sound more alike. The dog will love the animation and respond better to the whole family!

he doesn't listen. Initially, it is important to create a friendly feeling toward new commands. For now, give the command once, then praise as you position your dog. To position him, use his pressure points. Tilt his head up by putting a hand under his chin, then squeeze the waist muscles just below his rib cage as you angle him back. Avoid pushing on his spine or hips.

James MacDonald

Sit is the "say please" position!

It's a motivational approach. It's positive. Your dog will want to get involved. And he'll equate sitting with getting attention. Finally, that attention equation is working in your favor!

Buddy, Let's Go!

Here is another favorite. It communicates the leadership concept passively. Your dog will learn to follow you as a trusting friend. On top of that, it's relatively easy to learn and teach. Start inside using a treat cup, jingle jar or clicker and treats for an off-leash lesson, and use your teaching lead for another exercise.

Off leash. Start in a quiet room. Use your treat cup or other temptation to encourage your dog to follow as you say his name (BUDDY), then LET'S GO! Praise the slightest cooperation. Gradually extend your distance and work into more distracting rooms like the kitchen or around other family members.

On leash. Go on a walkabout with your dog. Either hold the leash to your side (arms straight and relaxed) or secure it around your waist. Say BUDDY, LET'S GO! and start walking. That's the gist of it. Practice this once or twice a day for 20 minutes. Wear your snack pack initially to give your dog a bonus incentive. Where you go, your dog goes: dusting, phoning, laundering, whatever. . . . The take-home message: Dog follows the leader, the team captain. (That's you!) Whenever you change direction, say BUDDY, LET'S GO. And when you say LET'S GO, go. Leaders are busy, confident and inventive. You've got places to go, things to do. Your dog will have respect for you and want to follow your lead.

I know, in the beginning some dogs can be a handful. If yours is the racing-ahead type, consider the Gentle Leader as a teaching collar. Change direction every time he starts to get ahead. If he starts to forge ahead, say BUDDY, LET'S GO as you pivot in the opposite direction. Praise your dog when he starts to turn with you. If you're wearing a snack pack, slide a treat in his direction. Good dog, Buddy! Good dog.

Here's a human exercise! Take a look at these everyday situations and decide what your best option would be.

SITUATION LET'S GO #1

It's hot, you're sitting on the couch watching a rerun of *Star Trek,* your dog's leash is around your waist and suddenly you're craving mint chocolate chip ice cream. After five minutes of deliberation you decide to head for the freezer, but as you get up your Maltese, Max, has another idea. He hears the neighborhood children outside and wants to go check out the fun. You're still thinking ice cream, though. He's pulling you right; you want to go left. Which of the following three actions should you take?

(a) Immediately take Max out to see the kids.

(b) Pet him as you try to explain the situation, bribing him with a cone if he'll only cooperate.

Katie, LET'S GO!

(c) Walk with confidence into the kitchen, saying MAX, LET'S GO, with dear doggie in tow until he realizes that your way is the only way.

Did you guess (c)? Yeah!!! Options (a) or (b) would have communicated to Max that he calls the shots.

Did you miss that one? Here's another chance:

SITUATION LET'S GO #2

You're outside walking Sierra, your Samoyed. For a few moments all is calm. A nice walk. But suddenly another dog appears on the opposite side of the street. Sierra's a friendly gal and immediately wants to head over for a visit. She begins pulling you across the street. What should you do?

(a) Go with Sierra.

(b) Pet Sierra, telling her to settle down.

(c) Bring Sierra to your side, say LET'S GO and continue walking without hesitation.

Did you pick (c)? Yeah! Sierra needs to understand that she can't investigate every dog or person she sees. The other options support her leadership, in addition to communicating a mutual curiosity. Off-leash, she'd follow her impulses and be in serious danger from oncoming cars.

> ### 🐾 A Little More Freedom
>
> If you want to give your dog some freedom to explore, take him to a safe open area and let him go on a long line, as explained in Chapter 2. On his regular leash, however, a more civilized routine is in everyone's best interest.
>
> If you're a city dweller and your dog's walks are also bathroom breaks, he will need some time to take care of business. You can, however, let him sniff around and eliminate without letting him pull you around. When he starts to pull, say LET'S GO and move along in another direction. When he has finished his bathroom chores, it's back by your side for the rest of the walk.

Should my dog always walk on the same side of me?

Yes. Dogs, like people, are creatures of habit. In the beginning, he may get confused and wander back and forth from side to side. When he does, say EXCUSE ME and use the leash to bring him back to your left side.

I always thought neighborhood walks were my dog's time to sniff about. I've always let him pull me around. Is that wrong?

Nothing you do is wrong; you just have to decide what you want to communicate. Letting your dog lead you around the neighborhood teaches him that he's your leader and that the neighborhood is his territory. This can lead to a host of problems from barking at anything in his perceived "territory" to aggression with dogs and people.

I'm a fan of letting my dog free in an enclosed space (our backyard or at dog park) but I teach her to follow my lead when we're out taking a walk. Should she ever get out of the house, I can rest assured she won't go anywhere without her leader (that's me!). When you take responsibility for teaching your dog, you're assuming the role of team captain; your dog's leader. If you're inconsistent, your dog will develop inconsistencies too: COME! Ah — in a minute. SIT. No thanks, I'm busy. Maybe later.

LET'S GO lessons tell your dog that you accept the role of leadership with all its duties and responsibilities! Wherever you go, your dog must follow. Initially, it may not be his idea of fun, especially if he sees himself as the one in charge. But he'll dig your praise and soon be following along for the enjoyment!

Excuse Me

These words carry the same meaning for dogs as they do for humans. For dogs, however, they have more to do with hierarchy and leadership than with common courtesy. In dogland, it's a respect thing. Teammates watch out for their captain,

respect his or her personal space and keep the playing field clear. How they organize their space within a group determines who's in charge.

Ask yourself, how often your dog *naturally* watches out for you. How often does he automatically get up and move aside when you pass through? Once in awhile? Never? The rule is, from now on if your dog is in your way, say EXCUSE ME and move him to one side. No stepping over. No walking around. No changing direction. If he won't move, shimmy your feet beneath him or nudge him aside gently with your knees. Don't re-navigate an inch. If you do, your dog may question your ability to lead.

> ### 🐾 No Leaning, Please
>
> If you have an insecure dog who constantly leans on you, you're reinforcing his insecurity by allowing this or by soothing him. For him, the leaning creates a feeling of oneness. During stressful situations he should watch and mimic your sense of calm, not Velcro himself to your leg and assume you're just as afraid as he is. Confident dogs lean to assume possession and protection. This is also inappropriate; you're not a wimp!

Here are some other situations in which EXCUSE ME applies.

The leaners. Is your dog a leaner? I'm not talking about the occasional-lean-in-for-a-scratch fellows. I'm talking about the big timers — two pounds or 200, you know who they are. It's obvious. They sit in front of you and lean on your legs. Whether you're talking with someone, on the phone or pausing to catch a breath, they consider the opportunity right for a body press.

What's wrong with leaning, you ask? Isn't it affectionate? When it's mutual, yes. Consider yourself and someone close to you. Close contact is desirable at times, but if they have their arm around you every second it would be annoying and inappropriate. And what would you say to them? The same thing I'm encouraging you to say to your dog: EXCUSE ME!

The herders. The herders are just as obvious as the leaners. It's impossible to walk a straight line with these fellows. They like to get in front and lean in for a directional change. No go. Stay on course. And if you run into them . . . EXCUSE ME!

Hello?! If you wouldn't let a person lean on you, don't let your dog.

The blockers. These guys are very blatant about their intentions. They block the TV and stairways, and are known to position themselves in between loved ones in the middle of a hug. Sound familiar? These guys are taking the comedy thing a step too far. Out of the way chum . . .

Here are some more situations to think about. Good luck!

Situation **EXCUSE ME #1**

You're sitting in your favorite lounge chair speaking to a close friend on the phone. When you go to hang up the phone, you notice Quigley, your Golden Retriever, lying right in your path. Should you:

(a) Step over him.

(b) Bend over to pet him, then step over him.

(c) Say EXCUSE ME and then pet him if you're in the mood.

Did you answer (c)? Doing anything else would be subservient. You'd be communicating that your dog's in charge. Asking your dog to move may not seem like a big deal to you, but it communicates a lot to him.

Situation **EXCUSE ME #2**

Clarabelle, your big Rottweiler, notices you chopping salad in the kitchen. Immediately she seizes the opportunity to come over for a scratch. You brace yourself for the lean. As expected, she presses up against your thighs and looks up with her soulful expression. Do you:

(a) Pet her as you take a few steps back.

(b) Look down smiling and signal that you'll be one more minute before she gets her scratch.

(c) Bump her away from your body with your knees and say EXCUSE ME, repeating this until Clarabell respects your space.

You guessed it, (c). You're catching on to this leadership thing.

Will EXCUSE ME apply when my dog is constantly pressing his toys against me and putting them in my lap?

You need a big Steve Martin EXCUUUZZE MEE! Imagine a loved one using your back to write a note while you're in the midst of watching a movie — and without even asking. Hello?

First of all, don't pay any attention. No eye contact. No toy holding, tug-of-war, fond scratch beneath the ears until you get too fed up and annoyed. None of that.

Simply use your knee to push him aside as you say EXCUSE ME. Don't look at him; just do it. I had a dog I had to nudge away 32 times. How exasperating! But he caught on, and so will your dog. Just be patient. When he gives up and lies down next to you or drops the toy at your feet, toss the toy or pet him calmly. He's catching on!

Will this command help when my dog crosses in front of or behind me during a walk?

Yes. Every time he crosses over, take the leash and bring him back with EXCUSE ME. When he walks well, reward him. Also use this if your dog leans on you whenever you stop.

 **Aarrgghhh!**

If your dog is overtly dominant, growling or looking at you sideways when asked to move, avoid this exercise. Get professional help immediately! You've got an aggressive dog, and the sooner you address the problem, the better chance you'll have of remedying it. Push this character aside and he may bite.

Buddy

Your dog should get a rush of happy feelings when you call his name, especially if you want him to come to you when you call. If you pair his name with negativity: "no Buddy, bad Buddy, come here Buddy so I can clip your nails," hearing his name will make him feel glum. Instead, control the negatives and use your dog's name to forecast fun!

Clickers, food, toys and motion work magic in cementing a positive association for your dog to hearing his name. Try this:

1. Go into a quiet room with your dog off leash. Spend the first two minutes ignoring him, staying calm and busying yourself.

2. Stand tall and relax (the peacock position), then use a positive noise distraction (treat cup or jingle jar) as you call out your dog's name in a positive, strong voice. The second your dog looks to you, mark the moment and reward him!

3. Repeat the process from the top.

Is your dog catching on to this little name game? Super! Now practice it around your home in more everyday situations. Here's what I do. Put treat cups around the house (see Chapter 2). If you're using a clicker, place a clicker in each cup. Periodically shake the cup and call out your dog's name. Click or use a word marker, YES, to reinforce eye contact with your dog. Brilliant, isn't he?

You will begin to notice that when you call, your dog looks up, often running over to check in. Slowly space out the treat rewards, offering them on a more unscheduled basis. Still use the name game before all the daily positives, like mealtime, attention and play.

Uplift

If you have a small breed or a little pup, practice this exercise on a stair, step or table, or kneel in front of him. Continue to keep your back straight and use your finger to draw a line from his eyes to yours.

Sometimes my dog won't look up at me no matter what I do.

Make sure you're standing tall in the peacock position. Compromised postures can be seen as indecisive or as an invitation to play. Next, check your tone. Is it upbeat, directional and clear? If it's high-pitched your dog won't take you seriously. Did you start with food, or are you expecting your dog to listen just because? You won't have to use treats forever, but in the beginning they put a more mutual spin on things. If all else fails, put a leash on her collar and give her a quicktug as you say NOPE for the blow-off and YES for the check-in.

My dog jumps up and barks when I stare at him.

Don't stare at your dog. In Doglish, staring means you either want to play or fight. (How often do you stare at the people in your life?) A quick, attentive look is not a stare. That said, leave a leash on his collar and prepare to tug him aside and say NOPE when he starts to get excited.

My dog growls at me.

Get help! Avoid this exercise and see a professional trainer. You've got an aggression problem on your hands.

Wait and OK

A quick show of hands, please. How many of you have dogs who would plow you over if you got between them, the doorway and the great outdoors; have skillfully mastered the art of door dashing as you're greeting company; jump maniacally out of or into the car; haul you into every new experience or situation with the power of a charging bull?

Were your hands up for any or all of these situations? Embarrassed? Guess what? You're encouraging each situation by allowing such chaos. Yes you! It's time to reformat this routine.

First teach your dog WAIT (stop and focus) and OK (it's all right to move). It's permission training. These magic little words communicate your responsibility for new experiences and ownership of doorways and stairs. For your dog, it's impulse training — a self-control thing. Here's how to get started:

1. Pick any threshold in your home.
2. Hold your dog to your side on leash, stand calmly in front of the threshold and command WAIT.
3. If he tries to barrel ahead, say EXCUSE ME as you pull him back. Repeat WAIT.
4. Repeat the pullback as often as necessary until he pauses and looks up.
5. Encourage him to look at you by calling BUDDY (use his name, of course!) or making some clucking sounds. If you're using a clicker, reward him now.
6. Once he's checked in, say OK as you lead him through. Feet before paws.

Now you're ready for the big time! Go to the main entrance to your home. Prepare yourself as described in step 2, holding the leash back behind your body. Say WAIT just before you open the door. If your dog bolts, be ready. Give him a quicktug back behind your feet, say EXCUSE ME and repeat WAIT. When he does, say OK as you lead him through. If the doorway is a big problem area, go through five times in a row. By the end you'll be making real progress.

Reclaim your doorways, for safety as well as style.

Using **WAIT** in the Car

Once you've mastered using WAIT in the house, try using it in the car. Most dogs get pretty excited about a ride. Jump in, jump out. Yahoo! You're left holding onto the end of the leash for dear life. Another embarrassment. This can and should change. Aside from your personal humiliation, you're sending your dog the wrong message. Your permissiveness communicates approval. Now, do you really approve? I doubt it. Here's what you're going to do:

Getting into the car
1. Take your dog to your car. Instruct WAIT.
2. Open the door.
3. If he jumps, say EXCUSE ME and quicktug him back.
4. Instruct WAIT again.

5. Once he stops his shenanigans, say OK and in he goes.

6. When he's in the car, instruct WAIT as you shut the door, leaving his leash on for now.

Your job is half over. After waiting 20 seconds, try the following:

Getting out of the car

1. Instruct WAIT before you open the car door.

2. Open it just a crack. A centimeter. If your dog lunges, shut it and repeat WAIT!

3. Repeat this procedure until your dog stops lunging.

4. Once you're able to open the door, grab for his leash. (If you miss the leash, just put your dog in the car and start over. No big deal.)

5. Repeat WAIT as you brace him with a firm arm.

6. When he pauses, command SIT and release him with OK!

 Too Far in the Car

Some dogs take the car thing a bit too far. Allowed to jump in and out at will, they think the car is just another area of their domain. A fishbowl. These fellows can be quite bothersome. Jumping from seat to seat, barking like lunatics or face pressed against the window in an aggression response. Scary, effective (no one will come near your car) and attention getting. If this sounds too familiar, consider using a Gentle Leader, check out my suggestions on car restraint in Chapter 2 and suggestions on aggression in Chapter 8.

If this exercise was challenging and you can repeat it a few times without having a heart attack, do.

At this point your dog should perk up every time he hears you say WAIT. Start using it when you're out visiting friends or when you bring him to the veterinarian, groomer or dog school. In these situations, your structure communicates responsibility. A take-charge attitude from you will enable him to relax. Tell him WAIT at each threshold. Although he may protest initially, hold him behind you. When he calms down, say OK as you lead him in. It gets easier, I promise!

USING WAIT WITH COMPANY

We'll be covering this situation throughout the book. For now, WAIT is an essential part of your dialogue. Once your dog learns WAIT one on one, introduce it in distracting situations and around visitors. Here are two options when you're having company:

1. When someone visits, secure your dog in the front hallway (or wherever you greet guests) and tell him WAIT as you answer the door.

2. Keep him on leash as you go to the door, and instruct WAIT as you open it.

3. As you open the door, ask your company to ignore your dog until he's settled down. No eye contact, please. If he's stationed, ignore him. If you're leading, control his enthusiasm with the leash. Once he's bordering on normalcy, let him know calm dogs are always appreciated.

USING WAIT WITH FOOD

Is your dog a treat hound? Does he gobble food right out of your hand with no concern for your fingers? Not to worry — it's just another impulse thing. Line up 10 treats and bring your dog to your side on a leash. Fold up the slack so you're holding the leash near his collar, taut but not tight. Offer him a treat. If he lunges, pull him back as you say NOPE. Repeat WAIT in a clear, no-nonsense tone. You may need to repeat this message a time or two. When your dog pauses, offer the treat to him in a flat palm, saying OK. He'll catch on quickly. Once you've perfected this solo, test it out with loved ones and friends.

Some dogs snatch treats with their teeth. Here's a quick remedy. Take a stick of butter and rub it on the palm of your hand. As your dog is licking it off say KISSES. Do this often until the open palm becomes an obvious signal. Have friends, family members, little ones do the same, so the message transfers to all hands. Next, place a treat in an open palm and lower it quickly below your dog's chin. As he licks it off, say KISSES and praise him warmly. Each time he forgets and you feel his teeth, say NOPE as you withdraw the goodie. Each time he licks you, say KISSES proudly. YES!

No snatching — for toys or treats! Teach your dog WAIT.

Nope

Are you guilty of over-using the word NO? Does your dog think of it as an adjunct to his name? Do you have to shout it to be respected or are you getting no respect at all? Well, believe it or not, you're in the majority. Most people make this direction a lot more complicated than it needs to be. And the poor dog winds up thinking NO is interactive, not instructional.

Since most dogs have already heard NO and aren't impressed, change the word to NOPE. It's a little softer and sounds different enough.

Now, think about what it is that you're trying to accomplish. Want a hint? With NOPE you're shooting for impulse control. NOPE, chasing cars is not cool. NOPE, don't chase the cat. NOPE, don't jump on the children. NOPE says "not now" or "that's unacceptable" or that's "not in the interests of our team."

To teach your dog the concept of NOPE, you'll need to interrupt his thought process. Before we go into the conversational application, practice this exercise (with your dog on leash):

1. With your dog in the next room, place a plate of cookies on the floor.

2. Holding his leash, approach the plate.

3. The very second your dog notices the plate, tug the leash back and say NOPE! Now tell the cookies they are bad. You read right: Look at the cookies, stamp your foot next to the plate and say "bad cookies" without looking at or involving your dog.

4. Continue walking your dog as if nothing big happened, praising his focus on you.

5. Walk by the cookies again. If your dog shows any interest whatsoever, repeat the procedure.

6. Play this game tomorrow — with some cheese or steak, perhaps!

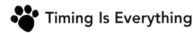 Timing Is Everything

Imagine you're in a country where you don't speak the language. You're at a café jotting a note when someone races over shouting something you don't understand, snatches your pen and leaves in a huff. Would you have a clue what made them angry? Probably not. After all, writing notes is a normal human behavior.

A little while later you're looking for a pen and, as you reach out to get one, you're interrupted by a person making a clear sound — still in a foreign language. You instantly pull away from the pen, at which point he looks angrily at the pen, making it clear you should find another.

Which person communicated that you shouldn't take the pen in the first place? The one who caught you as you were reaching for it, right?

Jodi Buren

Catch the thought and correct the object, not the dog!

Pretty soon, your dog will see a plate on the floor and turn his nose toward the sky. *"I don't see anything!"* Now you're ready to start using NOPE around everyday distractions. Try it with one of your snacks. Keeping your dog on a leash, sit in a chair. Have an Oreo, a potato chip, a rice cake, perhaps. If his nose shifts in your direction, tug the leash back and say NOPE! Do this without making eye contact. Give him one of his own dog toys, saying GET YOUR BONE. Whenever you discourage one thing, encourage something else! Although food is always tempting, you're not teasing your dog. He must learn that not all food is his. He'll be more pleasant at dinner time, calmer during the kids' snack time, a welcome party guest and a fine addition at neighborhood barbecues.

Once you've got the food thing clear, try using NOPE whenever your dog is too attentive to the countertops. If he's off leash, stamp your foot as you say NOPE! Perfected that? Now it's time to hit the road. Whenever your dog barks at a bicyclist, a jogger, a friend from the neighborhood or a car, give his leash a quicktug as you say NOPE! Immediately refocus his attention with LET'S GO and praise him.

THE LEASH SNAP–NOPE CONNECTION

Some people forget to say NOPE when they tug the leash. Although the short-term effect is very good, this lesson has no long-term off-leash value. Once the leash is off, you ask, how can you contain or discourage your dog? That's why teaching the term NOPE and pairing it with a leash tug is so important. Done

Self Control Is a Picnic

In my grade school (beginner dog training class), we have a picnic party. Everyone brings some food and we all sit down on the floor and feast. The dogs are all on leashes and everyone gives their dog a bone but then stays focused on the human crowd. If a dog rushes in for food, he gets a quicktug and NOPE. Try having a picnic on your floor (dog on leash) and teach your dog the true meaning of self control.

together, they begin to mean the same thing. Your dog will eventually associate the word NOPE with the leash tug, so when the leash is off, a simple NOPE will do.

What do I do when my dog has already snatched the chicken off the dinner table?

Forget it. Yes, I'm serious. Once he's got the chicken, it's gone. Think back to the pen example on page 80. Correcting a dog once he's in the act of eating makes about as much sense as shouting at your friend while she's writing a sentence. Neither is going to have any idea what you're trying to communicate. A dog might wonder, "What are you mad about? My chewing? The way I slobber when I eat? My grunting sounds? What?" Or, upon closer examination, he might be interpreting your reaction as prize envy. That whatever he found is super valuable so he better hide or gulp it. I know it's hard, but let it go.

Does the same attitude apply for stolen laundry?

Yes, the same attitude applies.

My puppy loves to grab everything on the ground. Is this safe?

I wouldn't go so far as to say it's safe, but if you pay too much attention, you'll be reinforcing the activity. Obviously, you should observe what goes into your puppy's mouth, although if you make a big fuss each time he grabs for something, he might interpret your fast motions as prize envy (that what he found has a lot of value) and start protecting, or worse, swallowing his finds.

Instead of making an issue out of your puppy's curiosity, try to encourage him to share his treasures by putting this positive spin on it: Each time he grabs something, find a treat cup and say "what did you find?" When he comes over to you, offer him a tasty snack in exchange and say "thank you for sharing." Soon he'll feel less confrontational and will be more open to sharing his treasures: the grab-n-show, instead of the grab-n-go. Although some may think it's pure bribery, I'd rather have a dog showing me his finds with his tail wagging than destroying something.

Settle Down

Teaching SETTLE DOWN is like teaching a child to sit still at the dinner table. It's all part of life. If kids don't learn manners, they end up with the ferocity of a young Helen Keller. (By the way, one of the best movies to watch if you're serious about dog training is *The Miracle Worker*. Are you siding with her parents or with her teacher? Three cheers for Annie Sullivan!) Kids have to learn to sit still, and so do dogs.

I love SETTLE DOWN. It's conversational and civilized. I'll expand on the joys of its application momentarily. For now, you must go through the teaching process:

1. Pick a 15- to 30-minute block of time. You can be watching TV, helping the kids with their homework (doing your homework, if you are a kid), working on the computer, eating a meal or whatever.

2. Place your dog's lead on his buckle collar, Gentle Leader or harness (not his neck training collar), and bring him to this area with a familiar mat and a chew toy.

3. Place his mat and toy on your left and instruct SETTLE DOWN, as you point to his mat.

4. Sit on the leash, offering him just enough freedom to lie on his mat.

5. Ignore your dog until he quiets down, and then only give minimal praise to avoid exciting him.

6. No, I'm not joking. Ignore him until he relaxes. Because he's with you, he'll feel included and part of the program.

7. At the end of your time, release him with OK! You can give him a treat, get down and hug him, whatever — that was a big deal!

Initially, this exercise can be a real bear. Some dogs whine because they're a little confused. Others fidget in protest. Some dogs have a problem giving up control. In any case, the lesson is not about them. It's about structure. After several days they calm down — provided no one gives in.

Giving your dog a play station really calms things down.

Jodi Buren

Once you've mastered using it in controlled settings, try using SETTLE DOWN in more stimulating situations — around family gatherings or during mealtimes or visits from company. No problem? How about when you're visiting friends or your dog's veterinarian. Directing your dog with SETTLE DOWN is impressive and purely functional. It's not only leaves you feeling more in control, it lets your dog relax too.

I'm not totally clear. Why must dogs learn to settle down?

Good question! There are several reasons. The first goes back to when the leader wolf would make one sound to send all the pack members running for cover. They trusted his direction. They never questioned it. It was a survival thing. They stayed put until he made another sound indicating that all was safe. Your sound is SETTLE DOWN. Someday it may be a life or death thing; for now, it's about being a good leader and organizing your team. You want your dog to be still, and he must. Why? Because it's in the best interest of your group.

In addition, this exercise teaches self-control. Dogs are born with it and use it naturally around mom, but they often lose it when brought into their human homes. Humans tend to be too permissive with young pups. This exercise brings the self-control back. It helps check dominant dogs and notifies the more submissive types that someone's in charge. What a relief!

What if my dog won't lie down?

Some dogs totally resist the concept of being put into a submissive (down) position. If yours growls or snaps, do not proceed with this exercise; you need professional help to offset present or potential aggression. On the other hand, if your dog is just stubborn, sit on the leash and ignore your dog until he settles down on his own. He'll look bewildered, but eventually he'll chill. When he lies down, make sure there's enough slack for him to lie comfortably at your side.

Should I keep him on the leash the whole time?

Initially, yes. If your dog gets up, you won't have to bat an eye — the shortened leash will correct him automatically. He'll be perplexed for a moment, then he'll lie back down and chew his bone. After a couple of weeks, you'll notice his cooperation and you can loosen your controls. If he slips back, don't feel too bad — just get the leash out and sit on it again!

OK, here is a situational puzzle:

Situation SETTLE DOWN #1

Emma, your Border Terrier, is going to see her veterinarian. For the past two weeks you've been practicing the Magic Seven with great success, although you've never had lessons away from home. When you get to the hospital, Emma is very excited, but she must wait her turn. Do you:

(a) Pick her up.

(b) Repeat SIT 15 times, eventually positioning her.

(c) Bring Emma's mat and toy into the waiting room, placing them and her at your side, command SETTLE DOWN as you sit on the leash and wait your turn.

What did you guess, (c)? Congratulations! Although picking her up would have been the easiest solution, she would have felt more threatened and defensive. Whether you have a little dog or a big dog, you want to encourage good, ground-level coping skills.

All of the commands we've discussed are your Magic Seven! Remember to use them conversationally throughout the day. Good luck!

UNIVERSAL DISCIPLINE

There is one Universal Discipline. One that works on every dog. Granted, it works to varying degrees, but it works. What is it? It's the cold shoulder; simply put, ignoring your dog. Too often, dogs perceive discipline as play or confrontation, and the attention is so desirable that dogs learn to be naughty!

 Developing Constants

Dogs love to hear special words throughout the day, and they can learn the meanings of a lot of sounds if they're repeated often. Come up with a list of constants — words to identify routines you repeat at least three times a week. Here are some from our home to yours:

> INSIDE
>
> OUTSIDE
>
> CAR
>
> BONE
>
> UPSTAIRS
>
> IN THE KITCHEN
>
> KIBBLE TIME
>
> GO FOR A WALK

Borrow from this list and add to it. Your dog will feel psyched and connected when you say your constants, and you'll be nothing short of amazed!

I can already hear voices of protest. And I'd agree, you can't always turn the other cheek. We'll cover the more serious infractions in Chapter 8. But there are many times you can and should ignore your dog. More than you'd imagine. Here are five examples.

The Passive Director

These guys thrive on attention and when they're not getting it, they feel insecure. To alleviate their stress, they demand attention. However, if you respond, what are you reinforcing? That's right, their insecurity. You're also following their direction and giving up your leadership role, which leads to more insecurity. More stress. You don't want to do that.

When your passive pooch is pawing, whining, head-butting, staring, barking or hiding under your legs, ignore him. Yes, ignore him. I know it may sound cruel, but if you coddle an insecure dog, you get a more insecure dog. Stand tall, relax, be a pillar of serenity and he'll calm down. He'll start looking at you in a whole new light. And when he does, reinforce that with — what else? — your love and attention!

The Active Director

These guys like to remind you of their smarts. They try many of the same ploys as their passive counterparts, but they calculate their successes. It's a different approach — much more demanding. And if you pay attention to these characters, you're reinforcing their dominance; the idea that they direct you. You don't want to do that either. So use the same tactic as for the passive director dogs: ignore them. They'll be more persistent and more annoying, but remember their motive and be strong.

The Grab-and-Go

Dogs think this is a riot. . . . I grab a sock. Show the household. Wait in my ready position until someone notices! Then I fake left. Dart right. Dodge for the table. Under the legs. Up the stairs. And for the big finale. . . I'll hide under one of the beds. The little comedian! It's quite addictive. Meanwhile, the entire household has been disrupted and everyone is racing around like crazy, yelling or laughing at the entire scene. Take-home message: A great game!

Relating? Let me make a suggestion: When your dog starts baiting you, leave the room, the house or the yard. Shut all the doors behind you. Dogs hate this. Yours will wonder where you went and forget about the game.

If he's got an object you can't ignore, however, avoid making eye contact with him initially. Wait a few minutes and then go find your treat cup. Act like you're shaking out biscuits for yourself. If he comes with the object in mouth, thank him. That's right, "thank you for sharing." If he comes without the object, still reward him and refocus him on something else, leashing him only as a last resort. Rescue the object later when he's not watching. Corrections, after all, are a form of attention.

The Noise Maker

These guys love the spotlight, and if they're not in it you're going to hear about it. I've read a zillion techniques for remedying this situation and found that nothing works better than a patient dose of the silent treatment. Whether your dog is stationed or crated, if you give him attention when he's barking, even negative attention, you're reinforcing his behavior. Now, wouldn't you rather have a quiet dog? Of course you would, so pay attention to that! (Tip: Buy yourself some earplugs while you're doing the silent-treatment bit.)

If the ignoring thing is just not going to happen, try a Gentle Leader attached to a long line. Pull the line and say SHHH as you continue to give him the cold shoulder, until he's quiet. And last but not least, you can try a quick dose of the SHHH spray. Get a long-distance water gun or a plant mister or a stream spray. When your dog pipes up, discreetly spray his body from a secret location. SHHH!

The Runaway

I don't recommend off-lead activities for untrained dogs. Invariably, they'll wander off and figure out how much fun it is to stay just out of reach. This is tremendously annoying and counterproductive to future off-lead work.

The reality, however, is that your dog may get away from you before his off-lead training has begun. The kids may leave the door open, he could jump out of the car or his leash could break. There are two options for these emergency situations:

If you have a treat cup, use it.

1. Run away from your dog quickly while calling out to get his attention. I've been known to bolt in the opposite direction, shrieking like a baboon to get a dog's attention. You can hop in the car, run inside, hide behind a tree or whatever. Just disappear! Dogs find this fascinating. If he follows, praise him profusely, even if you're mad.

2. If your dog really takes off, follow him quietly. Shouting is equated with barking and reinforces his excursion. When you finally get him, praise him. I know you're mad, but if you discipline him he'll never trust your approaches.

Right now, teach your dog to come back to you in a yard or field while he's on a long line. Shake the cup as you run from your dog (holding the line if necessary), saying BACK TO ME. This fun game can be used in emergencies, too.

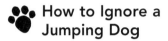

How to Ignore a Jumping Dog

It's difficult, I know. Although I list other remedies in Chapter 8, try this little activity for now. When your dog jumps, close shop: Fold your arms in front of you like a pouting child and raise them to your eye level. Stare at the ceiling. Dogs hate this. Once he stops jumping, let your arms down but continue to deny him attention until he has completely settled down. This technique also works wonders when you're coming into the house after running errands or school. Encourage everyone to use the same approach and the message will spread like fire.

Let me get this straight: I should ignore my dog instead of correcting him?

Yes — for the minor attention-getting routines. I know, hitting a dog over the head with a saucepan is more tangible, but aside from the fact that it's cruel, it's still attention. As tough as it may be, give my "ignore it" suggestion a try for one week. Pretty soon you'll be a believer, too.

What should I do about unsuspecting visitors?

Friends and family can help out — letter carriers and spouses' bosses not included. When someone arrives, place your dog on his leash and either hold or station him by the door, as outlined in the WAIT section of this chapter. Refocus his enthusiasm with a favorite toy, and either ignore or correct any jumping with a quicktug of the lead and SHHH! He gets no attention until he's calm. After he's settled down, bring him to the company, instruct SIT and praise calmer interactions.

PLAYING WITH YOUR DOG

Dogs, like people, learn so much through the rules of play. Certain games encourage interaction and respect, which is good. Others encourage confrontation, which is not so good.

Good Games

Good games encourage positive interaction and teach your dog something you want him to learn. And what could be bad about learning while you play?

SODA BOTTLE SOCCER

This game is played with empty plastic bottles (paper label and cap removed) or a couple of balls. Kick them around — you don't even need to set up a goal.

Always use more than one object, as much to avoid kicking your dog as to keep your dog focused on what you have (not what he has). The rules for this game: no hands! It's a great energy release for both dogs and kids! (Once the plastic container is punctured, discard it.)

Two Ball Toss

Preliminary to fetch, this game not only encourages a good retrieve, it also communicates that you're the one to watch. Take two of your dog's favorite toys. Toss one, and when your dog runs to it cheer him on: "You're brilliant!" When he turns to show it off, praise him again, but then promptly bring out the second toy and play with that. Ignore him until he's at your feet on all four paws begging for your toy! If he's calm, encourage a SIT and toss the toy in your hand. Pick up the other toy and start from the beginning.

A clicker is another invaluable tool for teaching your dog to retrieve. Keep clicker and treats handy and when your dog returns with a toy, show him the treat and click and reward as he releases his toy.

Hide and Seek

Most dogs don't like to lose sight of their owners. When your dog is sniffing around on his long line or in an enclosed area, call out his name while shaking a treat cup. When he looks up, race away and hide behind something (tree, house corner and so on). When he finds you, give him a big hug! As he catches on, hide before you call out his name.

Toy Along, Tag Along

This one is great for smaller dogs or young puppies, and is a real hoot to watch. Tie one of your dog's favorite toys to the end of a short leash or four-foot rope. Tie the other end to your ankle. Now walk around!

Treat Cup Name Game

Your dog can learn your name too! Take two treat cups and two people (you and Joan). Stand six feet apart. Send your dog to Joan saying GO TO JOAN. When Joan hears her name she shakes the cup and calls your dog. When your dog finishes the treat, Joan will send her back to you. Stretch the distance and introduce hiding in increasingly more challenging spots.

Swing Toss

This is a phenomenal energy burner! Take an empty half or full gallon plastic milk jug. Remove the paper label and cap. Slather the opening with peanut butter or cream cheese and tie the jug handle to a five- to 15-foot rope. Go out in a yard or

The treat cup name game!

field and swing the toy around. Let your dog chase it, pounce and catch it. By releasing all that predatory energy, he'll be a lot less inclined to hang from your bathrobe or chase the kids. (The spread around the inside and outside lid is to prevent tug-of-war and encourage licking. Don't forget to let your dog win sometimes!)

Bad Games

Bad games teach your dog a lesson you would prefer he didn't learn.

TUG-OF-WAR

This game makes dogs think the struggle for leadership is still on. It's too confrontational and bad if they win. What an ego booster! They'll soon start challenging you for the leash, biting down harder during play and even trying to pull the socks off your feet!

ROUGHHOUSING

Another confrontational event. Some dogs don't take it too seriously. Others do. They think it's a challenge to their identity. They may growl or mouth too excessively; if not with adults then with children. Keep pushing them and they may snap, even when you're not playing. It's best to avoid wrestling altogether.

TEASING

Seems pretty obvious, but you might need to remind the kids. Sometimes kids tease the dogs to get attention. Sound familiar? If you see this happening, try to pay more attention when your children are interacting peacefully with your dog. If the children's interactions are inappropriate, give them a choice to either stop or to put the dog in a quiet room until they feel ready to play nicely. It's not only better for the children to be given the ability to make the right choice, it's much nicer for the dog. No creature likes being teased!

Chapter 5

Basics for Your
Best Friend

OK, I'm going to come right out and say it: Your dog doesn't know too much human stuff. Oh, she's intelligent all right, but she's still a dog. She doesn't sit around contemplating complex sentence structure and vocabulary. She'll know plenty as soon as you teach her, but for now it's not making a whole lot of sense. Take a look at this example:

OWNER: *"Daisy, come. Come on, please. Come. Come. Right now. I'm running late. Please come — I'll give you a biscuit. Biscuit. Biscuit. Come on, Daisy. Daisy. Ugh!"*

DAISY: *Doesn't she look ridiculous? I think she'd be happier over here rolling in this sweet scent with me. Why is she running at me? She looks scary. Uh-oh, I better run back, fake left and stay away. This is funny.*

OWNER: *"Sit. Sit-sit-sit. Really, she's obedience-trained. Daisy, stay. Get down. Stay. Stop jumping on the nice man. Stay. Stay. Sit-sit-sit."*

DAISY: *A visitor! My favorite time of the day. I'm so excited. When I jump, everyone moves and pays attention. How fun! Jumping must be good.*

OWNER: *"Daisy, heel. Heel. Heel."* (Arm wrestling and choking dear Daisy into position.)

DAISY: *I don't understand what's taking my breath away. I feel like I'm being strangled. I want to get away. "Heel" must mean something bad.*

Jodi Buren

Dogs see the world in a whole different way.

You see? Your dog may be the most intelligent dog in your town, but she can't understand how to respond until you teach her properly. The best methods for learning provide a calm environment, a totally cool teacher and lots of positive reinforcement. Good teachers take their job seriously and know the learning process is gradual. They liven up each lesson with enthusiasm, clear directions and heartfelt praise for even the smallest success. They know they can never overemphasize good behavior. They encourage much more than they discourage.

Teach your dog how great she is for doing things right and bad behavior will lose its allure. In this chapter, you will teach your dog five more words:

HEEL

STAY

DOWN

COME

STAND-STAY

 **A Shared Vocabulary**

Although your dog doesn't understand human language, she will recognize the sound of a word when it is repeated and linked with happy moments. Think of these commands not as giving you the power to control your dog, but as an opportunity to talk with her.

Then, in the Game Gallery section of this chapter starting on page 132, you'll find tricks and games that excite the magic of learning.

I have always had a problem with the word "training." It sounds so militaristic and forceful. A few years back, when political correctness was sweeping our silly nation, I joined in by changing the phrase "dog training" to "teaching your dog." Teaching is more friendly — something to do *with* your dog, not *to* her. Showing your dog the plan instead of forcing your will upon her. It's a process that brings kisses, tail wags and mutual understanding.

Think of each word you teach your dog as representing a human phrase. Because dogs can't decipher the complexities of our language, you must speak each word clearly and encourage everyone to do the same. You'll soon find out that your dog loves her lesson times, and why? Because she's getting all your attention and learning words that help her feel connected to you.

These commands are the basics — they're nothing fancy or showy; perfectly adequate for your family dog, your best friend and your companion. I've listed each in the order that you'll teach them. I know, COME is your top priority and it's almost last. Each lesson, however, relies on the ones before it and COME is complex, so don't rush ahead. Breathe deeply and have lots of patience!

In the previous chapter, you built a foundation of understanding between you and your dog. You taught your pal the Magic Seven commands. In this chapter, we'll be extending her vocabulary by using a similar approach. Conversational and friendly.

Each new command has three levels of learning:

1. Tell and show

2. Ask and appreciate

3. Request and enforce

> ### What Kind of Teacher Are You?
>
> Be the type of teacher you would want to have. Would you want a teacher who shuffles, mumbles and yawns in the midst of a lesson? Or one who sparkles, says new words with crisp excitement and walks with an air you couldn't turn away from?

Don't worry! It's not as complicated as it sounds. Breaking it down makes lessons easier and encourages success at each level. Here's a quick explanation using the SIT command as an example:

Tell and show: At this level assume your dog is a blank slate. You'll say SIT as you lure her to sit or position her gently.

Ask and appreciate: Sooner or later she'll start beating you to the punch line. Now you can use SIT around everyday situations, positioning your dog if she is too distracted. Your praise and rewards encourage her cooperation.

Request and enforce: After your dog recognizes her word, use it everywhere! Phase out food rewards but never forget the power of your praise.

How quickly you move from one level to the next will depend on your dog. Some learn faster than others, just like people. Approach the initial stages of training slowly, even if your dog is a certifiable genius! Simple training steps build success, which creates an addiction to learning.

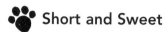

With each new command, you'll practice "tell and show" only during the lesson. Your lessons should last no more than 5 to 10 minutes and should end on a high note: a jackpot of goodies, physical attention, a game or a walk. After you've practiced "tell and show" for a few days, you can move on to "ask and appreciate," bringing the new word into everyday situations. As one command graduates from lesson time to everyday use, the next word can be introduced. Confused? Cross-eyed? It will all make sense in a minute. Let's begin!

HEEL

HEEL says to your dog, "I'm the leader, follow me!" I like to teach it as a command of position, not just for walking control. HEEL directs your dog to be at

Mary Bloom

your side. Standing at your **heel,** to be exact. Eventually, you'll be able to HEEL around any distractions, to call your dog to your side, and to calm your dog around company. No, I'm not kidding! It can happen. With the right training approach (one that takes into account your dog's personality and encourages her individuality), anything is possible!

Aside from the stylish look, walking your dog suddenly takes on new meaning. For you, it's just plain relaxing. Good exercise with a friend at your side. For your dog, the concept of having a leader to make executive decisions takes a load off her mind. She can look around calmly, hang with the one she loves and leave all the stressful decisions to you!

Shayna knows the HEEL position.

Tell and Show

It's a pretty picture. It embodies the concept of togetherness. HEEL lets onlookers know you are mindful of your dog's inner world and willing to be her

guardian. After all, someone has to lead, and this lesson teaches your dog that you're willing to take on that responsibility. Your dog is following your heels, with your head and her feet aligned. If you're walking, so is she; when you stop, you stop together. Symbiotic. Simple.

When introducing this command, pick an area free from distractions. Outside is fine as long as you avoid heavy stimulation. Inside will do, provided you can clear an area large enough to practice in. A quiet setting is key to a successful lesson.

Strap on your snack pack or put some treats in your pocket with a clicker, if you're using one. If your dog is treat-crazed and you'd rather not use treats, that's OK; use a toy or just praise lovingly.

Just One

How many ways were you taught to sit in a chair? No, it's not a trick question. How many? Who said "one"? You're right. There's only one way to do it. And who taught you? Right again. Your parents/guardian taught you. Now guess how many ways there are to be at heel? One. Just one way. And because you're the parent, you must teach that. Dogs, like kids, will test lots of ways. They'll sit backwards, behind you or twist around to face you. But, like a good parent, you'll be consistent and reinforce the one correct position.

Once you pick your area, pattern a circle. Not a square, rectangle or triangle. A circle, nice and round. The diameter will depend on your dog. Small dog, smaller circle. Big dog, bigger circle. Got the circle in your mind? Bring your dog to the edge, face in a counter-clockwise direction (dog on the inside of the circle), and say DAISY, HEEL as you either lure your dog into a sit or position her at your side. Yes, HEEL, not SIT. Teach your dog HEEL as a position next to you, either walking or sitting.

Before you begin walking, check yourself. Are you relaxed? Standing tall? Looking confident? OK then. Adjust the training collar either under the dog's chin for the Gentle Leader or right between your dog's ears for neck collars; keep the collar relaxed with no slack in the leash. To keep your dog walking in the proper position, relax your arm at

Hold the leash the way you would hold a child's hand.

your side. (If need be, review leash holding techniques in Chapter 2 and the LET'S GO exercise in Chapter 4.) Deep breath!

Now you can begin:

1. Say HEEL as you step forward.

2. Walk around the circle at an upbeat pace, keeping your left arm relaxed at your side.

3. Use quicktugs to keep your dog's attention. Encourage all focus with praise, and if you're really coordinated, with a treat.

4. Before you stop, slow your pace and say SHHH.

5. Keep your arm back, exaggerating the last step by tapping your heel to the floor.

6. Remind HEEL as you lure or position your dog into a sit at your side. (To position her, transfer the leash to your right hand along your left thigh and guide her into position with your left hand.)

For the first few days, practice six trips around the circle. This should take no more than a few minutes. Keep your pace steady even if your dog stops dead or races forward. You're the leader, the pacesetter. You control the rhythm.

As your dog catches on, add pace changes and turns to your normal routine. You can use a lure to help your dog follow along or just exaggerate your body language, marking each successful transition with a reward and praise.

Fast pace: Start normally and then increase your speed. Cluck to encourage your dog's focus. Trot like a horse to encourage interest. Before you stop, slow to a normal pace.

Slow pace: Start normally and then slow your pace. Like a snail. A tortoise. Lengthen your stride to encourage your dog's focus.

 ## The Quicktug

When you're moving along with your dog, she may lunge forward or sway to the side. Common stuff, but your quick response is paramount is keeping the HEEL on track. Muscling her back into position will only create an instinctive pull-against-resistance reaction. White knuckling (holding the leash so tight your knuckles bulge) has the same effect. Instead, relax your arm and issue a quick-tug (faster than a quick tug) — a really, really fast quicktug with your elbow. It's the sound of the correction and the suddenness of the tug that discourages your dog from leaving your side. When your dog is back at your side, remind HEEL and praise her cooperation with YES! The good feeling she gets at your side is what will keep her there.

Turns: Start normally and then remind HEEL as you pivot away from your dog. Not a U-turn, just a pivot. Slap your left leg and bend your knees to encourage your dog's focus. Turn with your head, throwing your voice in the new direction to encourage your dog's interest. Walk in the new direction several paces, then stop.

Keep these practice sessions short, up-beat and consistent. End on a high note and make it special with praise, treats and a favorite game.

In summary:

1. Pattern a circle, keeping your dog on the inside.

2. Using the words DAISY, HEEL, place your dog in a sit at your side and stand confidently with your arms straight and relaxed.

3. Start with DAISY, HEEL and walk in an upbeat fashion.

4. If your dog drags or bolts, do not change your rhythm; start out using treat cups or other incentives to jolly your dog along as you keep calm.

5. To stop, slow your pace and tap your heel to exaggerate your last step. If necessary, use food or a toy to lure your dog into position, or use your left hand and position your dog into a finished sit.

Reading this on paper, it all sounds pretty simple. But initial problems are the rule rather than the exception. Don't feel bad. I once tripped over my dog in the middle of a four-way intersection. Quite embarrassing! If you're having trouble, go though this checklist:

* Are you standing tall? A bent body posture encourages play.

* Is your arm straight or bent? Are you relying on your biceps or triceps? Straight arm and triceps win. If your arm is bent, you're muscling and pulling your dog in front of you in your attempts to control her. Relax and straighten your arm. Corrections come from a quicktug of your elbow. If your dog is super strong, hold the leash behind your back with both arms.

Ready? Set? I'm the leader, follow me!

- How's that tone? It must be directional, not whiny, playful or angry.

- Are you looking at your dog while you're walking? You're sending a mixed signal. HEEL says you're the leader, that you'll protect your dog and be her guardian. Avoid looking to her, as it seems you need direction. Keep your focus on the world around you.

- Some dogs get too stimulated when touched or fed. If this sounds familiar, hold off interaction until the lesson is over. Just a quiet word of praise will do.

- Get a straight sit. If your dog sits crooked, chances are she's focused on something else. And if that's so, your lesson is compromised. Encourage focus from start to finish.

Do dogs get confused when HEEL is used for SIT?

I honestly don't know. Food rewards make everything less confusing, though. Most dogs pick it up with a couple of repetitions. In the long run, it's best to teach the word HEEL as a position next to you, not strictly a walking exercise. HEEL says, "sit by my side if I'm not moving and walk at my side if I am." Initially, if your dog is totally clueless you can say HEEL-SIT-HEEL when you stop. Then, wean her off the word SIT in a week.

My dog refuses to sit straight. What should I do?

Lure her into 10 straight finishes with a wall on her left to prevent swinging out of position: As you stop, bring a treat or toy from her nose back above her head. If she's still pulling her tricks, determine whether you might be playing an unintended role. Are you giving your dog too much slack or pulling the leash forward when you stop? Are you staring at her waiting for some miracle of knowledge to descend? If you're not the problem, consider your dog. She'll fall into one of three categories:

1. The confronter: This dog turns to face you. She's more interested in play or resistance than in your leadership.

2. The daydreamer: This one's likely to sit on your heels or face in the opposite direction. She's interested in everything *but* you!

3. The Velcro dog: Preferring to stick to your calf, this dog is either insecure ("Did I do it right? Please tell me you love me!") or dominant, wanting to obliterate your decision-making abilities and bring the focus back to herself.

If you've got a confronter, don't get offended. Brace your arm behind your body as you stop to discourage forward motion. If that doesn't work, hold the leash at your side with your right hand and slide her into position with your left hand. Get her into a proper finished position before making eye contact or praising. If your dog thinks this is all a game, you can try a Leg Back: As your dog shimmies in front of you, grasp the base of the lead with your left hand, step back on your left foot and rotate her into position by bringing your leash behind you in an arc. Do it swiftly and praise your dog when she's sitting straight.

Blessed are the daydreamers. Of course, if you let their lackadaisical attitude slide, it leads to the off leash "ho-hum" and the "in-a-minute" routine when you call. To prevent this part-time philosophy, either bump her off your legs with a push of your foot or sidestep to the right and quicktug the lead to your left hip. If she should topple over, help her into position. Praise her once she's sitting straight.

Velcro dogs — now there's a common issue. Unfortunately, if it's not addressed it can lead to a canine hip check or being plowed into when you're out playing. It's a respect-the-leader's-space issue. If your dog is insecure, letting her Velcro herself to your leg keeps the insecurity alive. If it's dominance, a whole host of other unpleasant behaviors await you — especially when your dog hits full maturity (16 to 36 months). Repeat after me: "No Velcro. No Velcro." When your dog leans in, simply bump her off you with your leg (the very one she's leaning on) and say EXCUSE ME. If she's really determined, she may lean in 50 times; just keep bumping. When she sits straight and without leaning on you, use a sound reward (either a YES or click) and a treat.

Can I ever let my dog lean against me?

Of course you can — so get that silly sad look off your face! When your dog is calm and you feel like a big mutual hug, go for it! It's a lot like hanging out with someone you love. The mutual cozy is great. But if this person tried to hug you in the middle of an important meeting, it would be too weird. When you're having a lesson or are busy with something or someone else, that's instruction time. No leaning. When you feel like interacting and your dog is feeling cuddly too, don't hesitate.

When I train in the grass, my dog gets very distracted.

Try pavement. Save grass work for the second stage of training.

I think I have the most powerful, the most pain-insensitive dog in the world. None of the collars make much of an impression.

Consider the Gentle Leader or a no-pull harness. The designs of both limit the pulling and are gentler on both your bodies. Whatever the collar, you need what I call the tush push! Slide the leash around your back and grasp it with both hands together. Keep your arms straight and relaxed against your backside. Now, as you're walking bend your left knee down and push with your tush. This puts the strength of the tug on the trunk of your body rather than your arms. In class I sing a jingle: "Put your right foot out (way out), bend your left knee down, do the tush-push back, and bring your dog around." When your dog walks well, mark that moment. YES!

> ### My dog refuses to heel. Every time we start out, she begins to paw and jump at the leash. It's like we're in battle!

Hmm . . . Either she's getting more attention for her theatrics than for behaving correctly, or you're holding the leash too tight and she's choking. Make sure it's not you: If you're guilty of muscling your dog, change to a more humane collar or get a lesson from someone in the know. If it's your dog, she has to be redirected. Whatever you do, don't give up. HEEL is the foundation for all your dreams of being out and about with a fabulous dog. Try the following:

- Don't fight back. Carry a snack pack (with treats, a clicker if you've got one, and Binaca breath spray or Grannick's Bitter Apple). When your dog walks well, click and treat. You can never overemphasize the positive! When your dog acts up, get your Binaca or Grannick's Bitter Apple spray out and, as you ignore her, spray a boundary around your body. The point is not to aim and shoot at your dog, but to make the effect of her wildings a nasty-smelling spray and a lack of your attention. Be discrete or she might try to attack the spray bottle!

- Don't give her any attention, negative or positive. Negative is the worst, because it's perceived as confrontational play.

- If your dog acts up again, ignore her and continue walking calmly. If she won't relent, repeat the same spray boundary routine.

- Don't forget to mark the moment your dog walks well. Say YES! or click and treat. Good dog! Finally . . .

Ask and Appreciate

By now your dog should perk up at the word HEEL. Begin using it in everyday situations and to teach your dog to come to your side (HEEL) from a distance. Work at this stage for a week or two, depending on your dog's level of cooperation.

Slowly increase your work around distractions. No living-room-on-Monday-and-Main-Street-on-Tuesday attempts, please! As you progress to more distracting environments, don't forget your snack pack, filled with positive stuff like treats, toys and a clicker (if you're using one).

For starters

- Practice during your daily walks.
- Practice some patterns indoors as you move from room to room.
- Give the HEEL command as you walk to and from the car.

Hands-free HEEL: As your dog improves, try heeling hands-free. Secure the leash around your waist and let go of it. Slap your leg with your free hand and keep your posture and pace relaxed and upbeat. If your dog begins to stray, use a quicktug of the lead and continue on.

Call back to HEEL: This is really handy. Your goal is to call your dog to your side, regardless of where she is or what's going on. First you'll need to teach her one-on-one. In a quiet room, practice this exercise four times. Treats or a toy are optional, but I always recommend them — it makes learning fun:

1. Stand four to six feet behind your dog and call her name.

2. When she looks at you, show her the reward and take a few steps backward to excite her to come to your side. (If you're not using food, keep your dog on leash so you can guide her.)

3. Say HEEL and slap your left side as she moves toward you.

4. Lure her around you, stepping back as she walks around your legs and forward as she comes to your side.

5. Once her body has completed the turn, encourage a straight sit (guiding with the lure or positioning), then reward her. Well done!

6. Let her return to normal activities immediately. You don't want her to think HEEL is a life sentence!

There are two ways your dog can walk around you and stop at your side: around your right side or around your left. Which side you pick will depend on your dog. Try both to see what works best.

To rotate around to the **right,** take the leash or the lure in your right hand as your dog approaches. Step back and transfer the leash (or lure) around your back to your left hand. Draw your dog up against your left side and finish with a straight sit. To rotate to the **left,** hold the leash or the lure in your left hand as your dog approaches. Take a giant left step back as you direct your dog into position. End by stepping forward, finishing with that pretty sit, then treat and praise!

Luring to your side. Around you go!

> ### The Physics of the Feet
>
> When you're teaching your dog to rotate around to your side, don't stand still. Think about how your dog must move to get into position and guide her by stepping back or walking forward.

Once you've mastered the call back solo, practice the same sequence outside on your long line or Flexi-leash. Initially, call your dog back to your side from 10 feet, then 15 feet, then 20 feet away. Cheer her on as she comes toward you and help her into position when she reaches you.

The leg slap: Dogs are very sensory-oriented. They love sound and motion. The leg slap adds a little zing to the call back. As you say HEEL, slap your left leg.

You can also practice this exercise inside. Say HEEL before offering dinner, pats or treats. Lure her into position and reward her enthusiastically!

One more great application: Try it when you're sitting in a chair. Say HEEL as you slap the side of your leg. Help your dog move into position and pet her lovingly (treats and toys work great here too). Eventually, you'll be able to call your dog with a leg slap and have her settle down when company is visiting. Quite an accomplishment!

Request and Enforce

You've been a patient teacher. Your dog is a great student. You've both put your time in and now you can really reap the benefits. Begin to use the HEEL in normal, everyday situations. Here are some examples:

- When you are walking in town, HEEL reminds your dog to stay focused on you.
- When the letter carrier arrives, HEEL tells your dog to stop barking and check in with you. Eventually, she'll do it automatically — the perfect watchdog!
- On your walk, HEEL helps contain her impulses as joggers, cars and other animals pass by.
- In the evening, HEEL calls her to your side for a pat.

Add to the list. The applications are endless!

At this stage, enforce your direction. If your dog chooses not to listen, say NOPE as you give a quicktug reminder. Don't forget the cardinal rule: "When you discourage one behavior you must encourage another." After saying NOPE, remind your dog to HEEL and praise her cooperation. If she looks at a passerby, say NOPE! If she keeps sniffing when you call her to your side, say NOPE! If you instruct HEEL when there is a guest in the house, but she decides not to listen, say NOPE! Issuing a quicktug with NOPE ensures that someday the word will stand on its own — with or without the leash. And after each NOPE, remind her HEEL. Good for both of you!

I've taught this command for a solid month. Sometimes my dog still ignores me.

Patience, dear reader. She's testing to see whether you mean what you say. Like kids, dogs want to know whether we're paying attention to them. If your dog ignores you, quicktug the leash, say NOPE and reel her in. Enforce your expectations every time. Soon she'll trust that you mean what you say.

Off lead, my dog totally ignores me. It's so frustrating!

Who said anything about off-lead? This chapter is about conditioning on-lead control. Now, about the frustration. We've all felt it. Yes, even me. However, don't let your dog know. She won't understand frustration. Your tense body posture will be interpreted in one of two ways:

1. The active personalities see the tension as a play posture. The old catch-me-if-you-can!

2. The quiet personalities are confused. They get frightened and either cling to you seeking forgiveness, or they won't come near you.

In either scenario, getting frustrated doesn't reinforce your leadership or bring your dog back to the planet earth. If your dog should slip away, walk into the house or get into the car. Most dogs get curious and will follow you. Or else simply stand calmly until your dog returns. For now though, your best bet is to keep your dog leashed!

When I'm sitting and call my dog, she has a hard time rotating into position.

Most do. Remember the physics of the feet. Move your feet backward as your dog comes toward you and forward as she circles around, to help her maneuver into position.

STAY

The word STAY says, "Contain yourself, ignore all distractions and stay focused on me." I'm sure some of you are rolling your eyes, thinking, "My dog never sits still, especially when she's excited." In this section she'll learn — you both will. Eventually, you'll be able to use STAY to steady your dog around distractions, calm your dog during greetings, settle your dog during mealtimes and even get your dog to stop and STAY when she is running away from you.

Yes, it *can* happen. Fairy tales can come true. But you must take it slowly! By approaching this command one level at a time, you're ensuring maximum success. You'll build a positive association and enhance your dog's trust in your direction. Trusting dog, confident owner. A beautiful equation. Are you ready?

Tell and Show

When teaching this command, select an area free from distractions. Indoors is best. Bring your dog to the area with the leash tied around you or folded neatly in your left hand. Slide her neck collar between her ears or the Gentle Leader under the left ear. Since your dog is most familiar with the SIT command, we'll start with the SIT-STAY. Eventually, you will be able to get your dog to stay in any position.

First, get yourself ready:

1. Bring your dog to your left side and say SIT.

2. Check your line-up — are both your head and feet facing in the same direction? Human toes in front of dog toes? You're the teacher, so stay in front.

3. Hold the leash above your dog's head at about your hip level. If you're using a Gentle Leader, keep the nose loop below your dog's ear.

4. Keep the leash taut but leave the collar loose and comfortable.

Stand confidently when leaving your dog in a STAY.

This is your start and finish position. I'm a real stickler on order when introducing a new lesson. Think of it this way: If you were teaching a young child to count three numbers, would you scatter them on a page or line them up neatly with a line underneath? You'd line them up, of course. Same concept here. Start and finish at your dog's side, feet ahead of paws.

Keep your lessons upbeat and short: five to 10 minutes. Remember, cheerful happy teachers are fun. Now, try the easy eight:

Take your dog into a quiet room, direct SIT-STAY and . . .

🐾 Flashy Signals

Flashy signals are eye-catching and encourage visual focus. Your dog will learn to watch and listen for you — paramount for your off-leash aspirations. If you're handling your dog on your left side, signal with your right hand. Make a flat palm, holding your fingers together like a paddle, or extend your index finger in a point. Each signal should flash from your dog's nose. Signal together with your verbal direction:

SIT: Scoop upwards from your dog's nose to your eyes.

STAY: Quick-flash your signal in front of your dog's nose.

OK: Sweep your hand straight out from your dog's nose as you step forward, adding lots of energy and praise for a job well done!

1. Pivot six inches — I repeat, six inches — in front of your dog.

2. Pause five seconds, return (feet ahead of paws) and release with OK!

3. Pivot six inches, pause 10 seconds, return and release. OK!

4. Pivot, pause, and then march — yes, march — in place. Don't look into your dog's eyes — too stimulating. She'll think play.

5. Pivot, pause, and then start walking side to side very slowly. Stop in front of your dog, return to her side and release!

6. Pivot, pause, then make funny sounds. Barnyard noises will do: moo, neigh, meow, quack! Just for a few seconds, then return and release with OK! Remember: No eye contact!

7. Pivot and pause for 15 seconds. Return, pause, praise and release.

8. Go for the big hug. Job well done!

Who's wondering about steps three, four and five? Let me explain. Your goal is a solid stay regardless of distractions — marching bands and cattle herds included. To reach this goal, however, you must start small. And the best way to do that is to be distracting yourself.

Once you've got the six-inch stay down to a science, it's time to increase the three D's: distractions, distance and duration of your departure.

Distractions: Intensify your distractions *gradually*. Hop around, twist and shout, sound off like a wild orangutan. As you're letting your imagination run wild, look over your dog's head. Staring at her while making a fool of yourself is too intense. Also, practice walking around her in a circle. This short disappearing act may be too much to handle. If she can't hold still, place your free hand on her head as you walk behind her.

Duration: Increase the time from 10 seconds to 20, to 40, and on up. Vary the exercises so predictability doesn't reign.

Distance: Go slow with the distance. Initially, as you move away, keep the leash angled up for a quicktug if your dog thinks to follow. At each distance, introduce the distractions slowly.

Practice your lesson once a day if time is limited, or up to four times a day if your time allows. Keep the lessons short, punchy and fun — no more than 5 to 10 minutes. End with a jackpot of treats and some solid loving time!

USING TREATS AND TOYS

During lessons, keep things moving along and use your voice, hand signals and body language to keep the lesson lively. I've found that treats or toys shorten a dog's attention span when used between exercises. This is not to say that you shouldn't use STAY interactively throughout the day when playing or treating your dog. Here's how it goes:

1. You're holding a ball (or treat) above your dog's nose.
2. Your dog can't wait for you to toss it. She jumps. You pull the toy up and away. No go.
3. Next time you hold it out, she sits as still as a statue. You say STAY and count to three.
4. As you toss the toy (or treat) you say OK.
5. Next time you count to five, or you hop or you squeak like a mouse while she's waiting.

Get it? If you're using a clicker, STAY lessons are quite fun. Take your dog into a quiet room. Do several SITs, rewarding each with a click and a treat. Now introduce a short STAY. Speak clearly — leadership tones. STAY. Signal too if your hands are free and you're super coordinated. Pause three seconds and then say OK as you click and treat. Great! Increase the duration and add distractions as your dog catches on.

Can you repeat the STAY command?

Yes. Whenever you're introducing a new distraction or if your dog is getting fidgety, give one quick, perky reminder. Avoid the run-on STAY, however: STAY-STAY-STAY-DAISY-STAY! That's confusing.

My dog does the STAY part really well, but she breaks when I return.

Hmmm . . . that generally happens for two reasons. One, she's anxious when you leave her. Or two, when you come back to her side, you're standing behind her and she's got to move to watch you. Keep your feet in front of her when you return. If she's got separation anxiety, don't make eye contact until after the OK, and hold the leash taut above her head so that you can pull it up when she moves.

What do I do if my dog gets up?

Very calmly and without a lot of fanfare, reposition her in the same spot where you left her. If you chat to her about it, blow it off or let her sit wherever she feels like it, breaking the STAY got more attention than concentrating and doing it right.

What if my dog lies down?

Go to her calmly, cup your fingers under her neck collar and lift her back into position (big dog owners, bend those knees!). Avoid hauling her up by the leash if she's on a neck collar — serious choke! Also try clapping above her head and say UP, UP. If you see her thinking about lying down, tug the leash up and remind her SIT.

Help! My dog keeps jumping on me!

Quite a comedian. First of all, stop looking at her and don't laugh! Also avoid pushing her away, because pushing is considered confrontational and fun. Use the lead to quicktug her off and back into position. Gaze calmly above her head and relax. Staring, shoving and tense body postures make dogs jumpy.

My dog growls. What should I do?

You need professional help! You've got a budding aggressor on your hands.

How do I know when to move on to the next stage?

When you can act like a goon and sound like a monkey with six feet between you and your dog and she doesn't get up, you're ready to move on.

 Bracing

Should life throw you a heavy distraction, such as an adoring visitor, brace your dog. Hook your right thumb pointing down (toward the ground) onto your dog's collar, fanning your fingers out across her chest. Place your left hand on your dog's waist, placing pressure on the waist muscles with your index finger and thumb if she starts to squirm.

James MacDonald

Bracing up close.

Ask and Appreciate

Now it's time to test your teaching skills. Here are three quick exercises to see how well your dog understands STAY.

The tug test: Instruct STAY and pivot two feet in front of your dog. Remind STAY as you give a very slight tug or put gentle pressure forward on the lead. If your dog starts to get up, step toward her as you signal and remind her STAY. (Don't worry about confusing your dog — she won't think the gentle pressure is a correction. The STAY command supercedes the pressure on the lead; pressure on a lead can come from many actions that aren't corrections, and you don't want a dog to automatically respond to it.)

Situational set-ups: Set up everyday situations. For example, if your dog gets crazy when she hears the doorbell, you can rig that situation. Ask a friend to ring your doorbell or stand close enough to the door to ring it yourself. Tell your dog SIT-STAY. If she gets excited, pull up on the leash and say SHHH before reminding her to STAY. Once she behaves well in this little game, ask a helper to surprise you. Leave your dog dragging her leash and have your friend ring the bell five times at 20-second intervals. Each time remind your dog to SIT and STAY. Then, if you can, have your friend disappear and come in another entrance. This deconditions the doorbell excitement ritual.

You can set up any situation and use it to practice: cyclist on the street, kids running by, food temptations, the dishwasher being loaded — you name it!

Disappearing act: Position your dog three feet from a corner of a wall or hallway. Command STAY and pivot to face her. Remind STAY as you disappear behind the corner for five seconds. Upon your return, avoid direct eye contact with your dog and remind her to STAY. As you continue practicing, increase the duration and distance you hide. This exercise enhances your dog's focus when you're not there to watch.

How did you do? Don't feel badly if your dog didn't pass each test on the first try. Bringing a lesson into the real world can be like teaching it from scratch!

Start using the SIT-STAY command around low-key distractions. Need some examples? Use a SIT-STAY when you

- Sort laundry
- Make the bed
- Tie your kid's shoelaces

Add to the list! Be creative; remember to give your directions like a team captain and use those hand signals. Eventually, just a hand signal will be enough.

I tried using STAY the other day when I dropped a carton of milk. It didn't work too well.

Good for trying. You get an A for effort. Now set up the same situation (with an empty milk carton this time). With your dog on her leash, drop the carton and tell her SIT-STAY. By setting up everyday mishaps you can be more attentive as your dog is learning, and your efforts will carry over the next time life throws you a curve ball.

I tried that doorbell thing and my dog went nuts!

It sounds like the doorbell was too much for your dog. Try with a lower-level distraction: opening and shutting the door, or a knock perhaps. If your dog's a real jumper, consider handling her on a Gentle Leader.

My dog pops up the minute I disappear around a corner.

Don't worry. Hide yourself a few body parts at a time. A leg, another leg and an arm; a leg, an arm and a shoulder; and so on.

My dog mouths my hand as I reposition him.

She's protesting the reposition or trying to turn the lesson into a game. Make sure you're not choking her. Otherwise, carry on and ignore the protest. Yes, ignore the protest. Attending to it would be perceived as interactive or confrontational. At the very least, quicktug the leash and say NOPE as you carry on. If she doesn't stop, or she gets more dominant in her protest, hire a professional dog trainer.

When I go to reposition my dog she cowers, although I've never mistreated her. What's that about?

I don't know. Did you rescue your dog or get her from a shelter? There may be some history there. Could you be hovering over an already-passive dog? Try kneeling or bending to the side of her as you reposition her. You'll look less threatening. Perhaps you're correcting prematurely or marching over in an angry fashion? I'd cower, too. Ease off. Calmly position your dog.

How do I know when I'm ready for the Request and Enforce stage?

It's an inner feeling. You'll just know. Your dog will cooperate willingly, looking at you with eyes that say "I know that."

Request and Enforce

Continue working on your leash. Off-lead applications are discussed in Chapter 7. Begin incorporating the STAY command into normal activities. Here are some handy applications for everyday use:

- When you're meeting a friend or helping someone with directions
- When you're putting the kids on the bus: "No, you can't go with them!"
- As you're signing for a package
- To calm your dog before tossing a ball

Add to the list!

Now that's a classy greeting!

Most dogs break their commands when they're first exposed to intense distractions. I know, you've been working so hard. Your dog should reward you with complete attention. The key is to stay calm when your dog is over-stimulated. Don't get bent out of shape. Your reaction must depend on your dog's mindset. Yes, her mindset. Is she breaking your instruction because she's confused or nervous, or is she just blowing you off?

If it's the first two, don't make a fuss. It would make her more confused and nervous. Quietly take her back to her original spot and remind her STAY. If she keeps breaking, she's telling you that you're asking too much. Slow down; pressure strains cooperation.

If she's blowing you off like a teenager, looking perhaps as though she's never met you before, that's another story. You can't play the sympathy card here; your dog will just laugh. To handle this:

1. Look to the ground as you go to your dog calmly.
2. Pick up the leash.
3. Give it a quicktug as you say NOPE.
4. Return her to the original spot.
5. Position abruptly, no sweet pats, and don't let her eyes fool you!
6. Re-command STAY, without making eye contact.
7. Go back to whatever you were doing, giving your dog verbal assurance when she's calm.

If your dog keeps breaking, the situation may be too much for her to handle. Try an easier setting.

What's the difference between WAIT and STAY?

Great question! They are brother-sister commands, with only impulse control in common. WAIT is a spur-of-the-moment direction — it says "freeze!" You would use it, for example, to stop your dog momentarily when a car passes. The STAY command is more formal. It begins as a stationary command, like SIT, and ends in a formal release. You would use STAY if you stopped to talk with a friend.

My dog scootches forward when we're around heavy distractions.

Ahhh, the old scootch routine. Clever, funny and very creative on her part. Still, it won't fly. She's trying to have her dog biscuit and eat it too. Calmly give a quick-tug of the leash and tell her SHHH. If she absolutely can't sit still, she's sending you a message that you're asking her for too much.

My dog dashes from me when I go to reposition her.

Is your dog off-lead? If so, there's your problem. We'll get into the off-lead stuff in Chapter 7. If she's on-lead, then perhaps you're approaching her threateningly or correcting before you reach her. This reaction would concern any dog. Otherwise, you must determine whether your dog is anxious (in which case you'd reposition her calmly) or defiant, in which case you'd:

1. Hang your head low as you calmly walk towards her.
2. Gently grasp the dog's lead or collar.
3. Say NOPE as you return her to her original spot.
4. Remind her STAY.

If your dog keeps breaking, you may need to return to the Ask and Appreciate level and hone your skills.

DOWN

This word asks that your dog lower herself into a totally relaxed, totally submissive, totally vulnerable position. Some dogs are less than thrilled with this. COME? No problem. STAY? With grace. But DOWN? That can be a whole other story. Why? It's a trust issue. For starters, your dog must believe you can protect her in this vulnerable position and that you have her best interests in mind. Once your dog learns this and trusts your judgment, she'll more or less do anything you ask. DOWN is that important.

Teaching this command is often less than poetic. Most dogs resist at first. The more positive and rewarding you make the lessons, the less overwhelming and easier they will be to digest. Treats and a clicker are great ways to introduce your new idea, but phasing them out eventually is a must. A dog who lies down for cheese and only cheese has missed the point.

Are you ready? Remember, it's a three-step process — and nobody's rushing you!

Tell and Show

There are two ways to go about introducing this word to your dog. One involves pressure points, the other involves a hands-off lure. Some of you will select one approach and swear by it; others will try both, mixing and matching as the situation demands. Generally, I mix and match, although certain dogs (due to age, temperament, size) demand more of one approach than the other. The one constant: the signal, a point to the floor. If you missed Point Training at the end of Chapter 3, go back and review it. You'll find it comes in handy when teaching your dog to lie down.

LURING THE DOWN

The luring rule: no hands-on positioning! You must be creative and thoughtful as you encourage your dog to move herself into the DOWN position. Luring requires yummy treats and/or favorite toys. And to be most effective, use a sound marker — either the word YES! or a clicker.

Just follow that yummy snack!

Take your dog into a quiet room. If you're using food, hungry is better, so practice before a meal.

Hold a snack or a toy between your thumb and middle finger, extending your index finger in a point. Hold it in front of your dog's nose, and just as she reaches out to sniff it, drop your hand to the floor. Hold off saying DOWN until she gets the gist of what you're trying to get her to do. This way DOWN is paired with a sense of accomplishment, not confusion.

If a miracle happens and she goes right down, mark the moment with YES or a click, and give her a treat. If your dog thinks twice (and many do), draw the lure from her nose to the floor again, then once more — but this time stopping and holding your point halfway down. If your dog follows at all, say YES or click and treat. Continue this partial reinforcement until she'll follow the lure down all the way.

Once your dog will lie down three times in a row, start saying DOWN as she's moving into position.

If your dog absolutely wants nothing to do with this lesson, you may need some props. A chair or low table or even a bent leg will do. Take the toy or treat and lure your dog under the obstacle. The instant your dog is down, whether or not she's even aware of it, say YES or click, then reward her enthusiastically.

PRESSURE POINT DOWN

What's a pressure point? Take your left thumb and place it in the area between your dog's shoulder blades. Steady, gentle pressure here should relax your dog's back, lowering her into the DOWN position. If she still resists, gently lift one of your dog's front legs and move it forward. If she won't budge, consider using a Gentle Lead head collar to guide her head down gently.

Now that you understand the idea, go into a quiet room and practice five DOWN exercises in a row.

1. Instruct SIT and kneel at your dog's side.

2. Quickly draw a line from your dog's nose to the floor with your hand in a point. You may tuck a treat or a toy into your signaling hand to get her attention in the beginning.

3. If your dog won't move, place your thumb between her shoulder blades and the other hand on her leg, if necessary.

4. Gently lift her paw forward as you press between the shoulder blades — the shoulder blades, not the neck.

5. Say DOWN as your dog relaxes into the position. Wait three to five seconds before you pet your dog, then release her with OK and reward her warmly.

My dog growls when I'm positioning her.

That's not a good sign! Go to the phone immediately and get help from a professional dog trainer or behaviorist. You have a dominant dog who may bite when confronted.

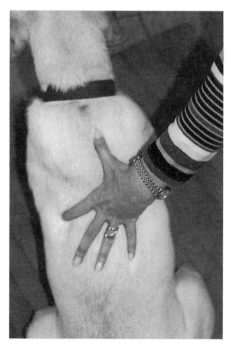

Lift one paw gently. Apply steady pressure between the shoulder blades.

I have an 18-week-old puppy. How can I stop the mouthing?
My corrections seem to make it worse.

First of all, don't correct! It turns the DOWN into a challenge game. Your dog is anxious. Let her know that there's nothing to fear by simply ignoring her. Yes, ignore her. Let your hand go limp, stare at the wall in front of you and ignore the situation until she settles down. This communicates security and leadership.

If the mouthing is excessive, get a Gentle Leader. This reduces the nipping tenfold and a small pull will close your dog's mouth. Also, luring works wonders for young puppies and does not involve using your hands. Start there!

My dog rolls over when I give the DOWN command.
How can I get her to stop her clowning?

She's trying to play her way out of her lessons. Whatever you do, don't pet her belly — this will turn your directions into a game. Stare at the wall (not your dog) and wait it out until she's upright. Pause for a few seconds before you release her, praising her warmly with your voice — not with a belly rub!

My dog goes right down, but she's back up
again just as quick. What do I do?

As soon as she's down, either hold the treat in your hand and count to five or rest your hand on her shoulder blades. Release with OK and the treat after she relaxes for several seconds.

Should you command DOWN more than once?

No. It's like the SIT command. If you keep repeating it, it becomes a different sound. Repetition blurs clarity!

How do I know when to go on to the next stage?

When your dog starts responding without your help. That might be four days or four weeks. Your dog will let you know.

Ask and Appreciate

Your goal at this level is to be able to say DOWN from a normal standing position. I call it the Standing DOWN. If you stay at the first level too long, your crouched body posture will be part of the cue and the Standing DOWN will seem like an entirely different exercise. So to master the art of the Standing DOWN, you'll first need to learn the Straight Back DOWN.

THE STRAIGHT BACK **DOWN**, WITH FOOD

Kneel on the floor or sit in a chair, keeping your back straight. With your lure in hand, point to the floor as far as your hand will reach without bending over. Your dog may simply try to grab the treat. Hide the treat in your hand and wait it out. No DOWN, no treat. Your dog may get frustrated and start barking. No DOWN, no treat. She may jump on you and nip at your clothing. No DOWN, no treat. Eventually she'll lie down, and when she does, YES! or click and treat. Good dog!

Once your dog is going down with style, phase out the treats. It's a two-step process: Line the treats up on the counter. Point to the floor and say DOWN. Your dog may sniff your hand like "where's the treat?" Just keep looking at the floor. When she lies down, say YES or click and reward with a treat from the countertop.

Now treat every other time, or every third time. Mix it up — sometimes two treats in a row, sometimes no treats. Treat one time, toy another. Keeping the rewards a mystery is nothing short of fascinating. (Remember, the clicker is always paired with a treat. If you're not going to treat, don't click!)

THE STRAIGHT BACK DOWN, WITHOUT FOOD

Same set-up as the one before. Either kneel with a straight back or sit upright in a chair. Point to the floor and say DOWN. Your dog may give you a sideward glance, like "huh?" Without the floor tap, it's just not the same. Hold the point and look at the floor (not at your dog — she doesn't know what's going on). If, after a few seconds, your dog is still baffled, position her with shoulder blade thumb pressure, lifting the paw out only if necessary. You'll begin to notice that only slight pressure is needed to persuade, then none at all.

Straight back, even in a chair.

STANDING DOWN, WITH FOOD

Now on to the Standing DOWN. The rule here: Keep your back straight. If you must lower yourself initially to help your dog with the visual cue, either kneel or crouch. Your goals are normal body posture and the everyday use of this direction.

1. Take your dog into a quiet room, stand at her side and instruct her to SIT.

2. With a treat in hand, back straight, point at the floor and say DOWN. Stare at the floor.

3. Wait it out. Your dog may try a lot of other tricks to get you to give up the goodies, but no go.

4. Once she lies down, say YES or click and treat. Good job — both of you!

Stand tall and relaxed, and no treats until your dog lies all the way down.

The rule of partial DOWNs: If your dog offers some version of DOWN, initially you can reward her efforts. After 10 partial DOWNs, hold out for the full position.

Phase out pointing with a treat in hand. Point, say DOWN, and when she responds take a treat from your pocket or from the counter and give it to her. Eventually, vary the treat-per-DOWN ratio, making the food rewards surprising and unpredictable!

Standing DOWN, Without Food

1. Go into a quiet room with your dog on a leash.
2. Stand calmly at her side and instruct her to SIT.
3. Say DOWN as you point to and stare at the floor.

If your dog is clueless you can bend your knees to bring your point closer to the floor, but remember to keep your back straight.

Pause a few seconds and then kneel to position her.

If, after three days, your dog is no closer to cooperating, try the Gentle Slide:

1. Tell your dog to SIT; pivot so you're facing her side and very discreetly slide her leash under your left foot. (Hold the end in your hand.)
2. Stand straight and point to the ground as you say DOWN.
3. If your dog doesn't budge, gently slide the leash (like a lever) under your foot until you feel gentle resistance from your dog's neck or head. Stop sliding now!
4. The point of the slide is not to force your dog into position, but to impart a slight pressure and encourage cooperation. If she doesn't get that, use her pressure points to position her.
5. After she lies down, pause then release with an OK.

When your dog catches on and no longer needs reminders to lie down, you're ready to add some distance with your DOWNs. Once your dog is responding at your side, pivot six inches in front of her and . . . .

1. Discreetly slide the leash under your foot or use a target stick (see page 62).

2. Lift your arm above your head. Point swiftly to the ground as you say DOWN.

3. Pull the leash gently, if necessary. Press her shoulders downward if she is reluctant.

4. Pause, praise (using a marker sound and treats, if that's your habit) and release.

Once your dog is responding well at six inches away, try it from one foot away, then two feet, four feet, six feet and so on. You're on your way!

Now bring the DOWN command into everyday situations, such as before meals, toy toss time and petting, at night while you're watching TV or reading, or when your dog comes over for a well-earned kiss. When it's a new distraction, stay by her side initially to ensure success.

How many DOWNs should I practice at each lesson?

From 3 to 10, depending on the age, breed and temperament of your dog. Some breeds could review the lesson all day (Golden Retrievers, other sporting and working breeds), while other dogs are bored and fidgety during the three repetitions (a certain Jack Russell Terrier named Mad Max comes to mind).

Should we practice DOWN-STAYs?

Absolutely! Once your dog lies down willingly, you can practice DOWN-STAYs. Do your drills in the same way as you do SIT-STAYs.

My dog scootches forward when I command DOWN from a distance. Should I discipline her?

No. Scootching is a sign of separation anxiety. Corrections only intensify it. Return to a distance she's comfortable with and work back slowly. If the scootching continues, try the following Sarah trick:

1. Pivot three feet in front of your dog. Just before you give the command, step forward on your left leg (keeping your back straight) and command STAY. Your left toe should be right in front of her paws.

2. Quickly command DOWN with a big hand signal.

3. When your dog responds, bring your foot back and stand straight three feet away. Return to release her with OK.

4. As your dog begins to feel more comfortable, lessen the step forward until you are standing straight at the three-foot distance. When this is a success,

stand five feet in front, stepping forward if necessary to give the illusion that it's still the old three-foot distance. Then lessen that step forward until you're standing straight at five feet away from your dog.

Request and Enforce

Once your dog understands your expectations, use the DOWN command to calm her whenever a situation becomes chaotic or to settle her whenever you feel it's appropriate. Here are a few situations that come to mind:

- When company is visiting
- At the veterinarian's office
- When there's a sudden change in the environment
- Outdoors, when she gets over-stimulated; start small (squirrels) and work up to big (deer)

Add to the list!

It's still an on-leash request at this point, so if you know life is going to get hectic and you want to practice a DOWN, let your dog drag a leash around (under supervision only!). At this level, introduce the concept of NOPE if your dog ignores you. By this time, your dog has a positive association to the DOWN command. Since she understands what you're asking, NOPE lets her know you don't accept being ignored. She must learn to filter your directions from all other distractions.

UNDER

The word UNDER tells your dog to lie down under your legs or a table or chair. Teach it at home first, but then use it anywhere. Initially, treats or a toy are a must. Here's how it goes:.

1. Place a chair in the middle of a room.
2. Fold the leash up neatly in your left hand. Hold a goodie in your right hand.
3. As you sit on the edge of the chair (leaving enough space under your legs), lure your dog under your knees with the goodie as you point and say DOWN UNDER.
4. Transfer the leash to your right hand and guide her into a DOWN position under your legs.
5. Initially, release her immediately with the treat. After the fourth successful UNDER, say STAY, offering a chewy if you've got one handy.

You've done your first UNDER! Once you've mastered this command at home, try it on the park bench, at a barbecue, when visiting a neighbor or in your veterinarian's waiting room!

We learned the SETTLE DOWN command in Chapter 4. What's the difference between SETTLE DOWN and DOWN?

You use the DOWN command when you're requesting an immediate response. SETTLE DOWN directs your dog to a certain location, such as a mat or bed.

My dog scootches around on her belly when there's something stimulating. How do I correct her?

Use a quicktug on the leash and say NOPE. She's testing a variation on the theme. If she keeps it up, wait until she's

Service dogs know UNDER, and now yours can too.

totally out of place, act astonished and reposition her sternly with SHHH!

My dog doesn't listen when other dogs are around. What should I do?

This is a good NOPE moment. Praise her for staying focused on you. Another great option is to join a dog training class. It's a lot of fun, great socialization and very helpful if you have the right teacher. Ask around your neighborhood and/or call your veterinarian. Gather up some choices, then view ongoing classes before you select the one for you.

My dog is very fearful at the veterinarian's office. Should I force her DOWN?

This situation calls for the UNDER direction. Under your legs it's safe and cozy, and you're in front so you're the protector.

COME

At long last, the command you've been waiting for! A quick poll before we begin: How many of you, after calling COME once, have ever:

- Repeated yourself
- Chased your dog

- Brought out the dog treats
- Followed and captured your dog and then gotten angry

I hate to tell you this, but you're actually teaching the opposite of COME. Your intentions are genuine, I know, but by repeating, chasing, bribing or following, your dog is getting the message that COME means run. The real trouble is not the behavior itself, but your response to it. Bribing your naughty dog with treats, calling the command 50 times or chasing her as she explores the neighborhood is what's really getting you into trouble. You're communicating that COME is the start of one big game. Fortunately, you can clear up the confusion, although it will take some time and concentration from the both of you. Don't worry too much, though. I've made the steps easy to follow and the lesson motivational!

Imagine a friend calling you into the kitchen when you're busy reading the mail or watching TV. This friend calls to you first in a squeaky, happy voice. When you look puzzled, the friend starts to get demanding, repeating the word COME over and over and over: COME, COME, COME, COME, COME! Eventually she runs at you and grabs your shirt sleeve. Will this give you a warm, fuzzy feeling? Are you going to invite this friend to spend more time with you or less? I'd bet less.

For dogs, COME is just like that. Their immediate, untrained impulse may not be to drop everything and run to you joyfully. On the other hand, teaching a happy response to this all-important word is very do-able. It just takes an extra dose of creativity, enthusiasm and patience. Are you ready and willing? Let's begin!

There are a few rules before we get started:

- Use COME sparingly. Over-used, it loses its magic.
- Don't chase your dog if she doesn't respond! Practice on-leash so you can stay cool if she decides to bolt. We'll discuss off-lead applications in the next two chapters.
- Surround the COME with positives. Keep the lessons upbeat and use COME whenever you're offering something good, like attention, food or toys.
- Never call your dog to come for something negative, such as isolation, getting her nails clipped or a reprimand. If you must retrieve your dog for grooming, isolation, discipline or something else she doesn't like, find her and escort her calmly. Don't associate COME with unpleasantness.
- If your dog runs away, don't correct her! I know the frustration and panic of marching around in the middle of a cold, wet night calling your dog, but corrections only erode trust. And trust is the first ingredient in a reliable response to the COME command.

- Use a different command to bring your dog inside. Coming in from outdoors is a big drag, right up there with being left alone or ignored. Instead, pick a command like INSIDE. Start using it when you're coming in from a walk. When you step in the door, make a fuss using food or toy rewards to speed up the positive association.

Tell and Show

COME says, "check in with your leader please!" The key word here is *leader.* Once your dog trusts your direction, she will actually want to stay focused and check in, whether you request it or not. I'll assume you've mastered the leadership thing. Now it's time to teach your dog that checking in actually has a word associated with it: COME!

You'll actually start teaching COME backwards, teaching the last step first. COME will take on new meaning for you both: togetherness not separation.

THE COME FRONT

When you call your dog from a distance, you're asking that she drop everything and run over to you, no questions asked. Most dogs aren't inclined to do that. When a dog doesn't respond, the impulse is to either repeat the command or get angry — which certainly does not enhance their impression of this word. And so it goes: A dog quickly learns COME means to stay as far away as possible. Fortunately, I have the perfect remedy. Start teaching COME as a place near you, not away from you. This exercise will help your dog fall in love with COME, perhaps for the very first time.

1. Start inside with few distractions. With a treat or toy in hand (or in your snack pack), walk in front of your dog while she's standing calmly.

2. Show her the reward and point from her face to your eyes as you say DAISY, COME. Encourage eye contact before marking the moment with YES or a click and give her a goody.

3. Ideally, she should be sitting in front of you, looking up. That's what COME asks of her: the classic check-in posture. If she looks up but doesn't sit, reward her the first few times, then either lure her into a SIT or position her gently. Always finish with her looking up to you.

4. Once she's positioned, give her a big hug!

Repeat your COME Fronts throughout the day — whenever you're offering something good.

Repeat this exercise throughout the day, whether you're offering a treat or a toy, to ensure that your dog's first association with the COME command will be immediate, rewarding and fun!

How much time will it take for my dog to learn this new definition of COME?

I wish I could tell you! Every dog is different. Some get it in a few days; others, in a few weeks. Be patient and positive. You want your dog to love hearing you call her.

What's the difference between the COME and HEEL commands?

A specific spot. The HEEL is next to you; you and your dog are aligned, heads in the same direction, facing the world. COME is a more of a checking in position out in front of you, looking up at you. HEEL allows mutual attention to a situation, like someone coming to the door. COME requires full attention on you — good for when the neighbor passes with a dog. COME, as you've probably guessed, is harder. It takes more concentration.

🐾 The Natural COME

I start teaching this command as early as 12 weeks. Here's the deal: Wearing a snack pack, treats and a clicker (if you're using one), go outside with your dog on a long line or in a fenced enclosure. Each time your dog walks within a couple of feet of you, say YES or click and treat. You'll begin to notice your dog is checking in more often. And why? Because the check-in has not been demanded, it's been reinforced.

For dogs who are more reluctant to check-in, do something to excite their interest. Play with their favorite toy or a stick, or shake their treat cup and pretend to be eating the snack yourself. Do all this without looking at or talking to your dog until she checks in. Once the check-in becomes a habit, begin to say COME as you give your dog her reward, reinforcing your togetherness.

*My dog sits crookedly and actu-
ally shimmies to my side.*

Straighten her out calmly by luring her
with a treat or toy, or gently guide her
by grasping the collar under her chin.
Say YES or click the moment she
focuses up!

Ask and Appreciate

Once your dog has positive associations with COME, start practicing
around distractions. This is a big deal.
Dogs are perceptive. They (and us)
like to keep track of their surroundings. COME says shut everything off
and focus on you, only you, and for
that your dog must buy into your leadership hook, line and sinker. At first,
even dogs who respect their people and know their COME Fronts inside and out
may have a hard time concentrating around distractions. Don't get discouraged!

> ### 🐾 The Human Element
>
> There are three elements to remem-
> ber when you call your dog. First is
> your voice. Nothing too high-
> pitched or frustrated, please. Be
> clear and directive, team captain
> style. Next is your body language.
> Stand straight. Bent postures are
> confusing to interpret. Imagine a
> friend calling you while he was all
> hunched over. You'd think he lost a
> contact lens or had a backache. And
> last, but most important, look at
> where you want your dog to end up:
> at your feet! Staring at a dog can
> overwhelm him, as well as reinforce
> the separation. Your dog will usually
> end up where you are looking.

Progress to low-level distractions and increase the distance from which you call
her. Here are some ideas:

- In front of the TV
- In the backyard
- In front of the kids
- During mealtime
- In a quiet hallway or the garage; attach the Flexi-leash and increase your
  distance slowly

Set aside five minutes a few times this week for some formal training. Go into a
quiet room. You may use a treat or a toy to help your dog learn your expectations.

1. Practice three regular SIT-STAYs. Return to your dog's side and release her
   with OK!
2. On your fourth STAY, walk out to the end of the leash and pause.
3. Vary the duration each time to avoid predictability.
4. Next, call DAISY, COME! as you sweep your arm across your chest.
5. As your dog comes to you, scurry backward (reel in the leash if necessary).

6. When she gets near your feet, point from her face to your eyes (you may use a lure here).

7. Encourage eye contact by standing tall and making kissing sounds.

8. Release her with OK!

Practice this exercise three times per session. That's all. More is stressful.

Also, do a few regular SIT-STAYs between each COME. If you don't, your dog will break her STAY early to please you. Sweet thing!

Pretty soon, your dog will run to you, sit automatically and look up for approval. No magic, just good old-fashioned conditioning. You've reached the goal. Congratulations!

CALL BACKS

How do you increase the distance from which you call your dog? With call backs. Go into a large, quiet area (a hallway or garage) with your dog on or off leash. Take treats and any other teaching props, such as a toy or clicker. Keep this time short and upbeat.

Call your dog back when she least expects it.

1. Stand no more than four feet behind your dog, lure in hand, and call her name, DAISY.

2. As she turns to you, sweep your arm across your body and say COME.

3. Take a few steps back as you hold the lure out in front of your body.

4. When she's standing in front of you, quickly draw an imaginary line from her face to your eyes, just as you did in the COME Front exercise.

5. Mark the moment she sits in front of you, gazing up: Say YES or click and treat. Awesome!

6. Practice this twice, then take a rest.

I can't get my dog to stop turning toward distractions.

Stubborn. A hard nut to crack. Perhaps she's not convinced you're the true leader. My advice is to stick with it. Don't lose. You must communicate there's only one way to COME, and that is to sit directly in front of you. Practice the following in a quiet room to encourage your dog's attention and success.

1. Leave her in the STAY.
2. Pause at least a minute (building up her anticipation).
3. With a straight back, deep voice and gigantic sweeping signal, call your dog, DAISY COME!
4. Point to show her where she needs to be and reward a straight sit, positioning or luring the dog if necessary.

Work up the distraction chain slowly. If she's too stimulated, practice in simpler situations for awhile. There's no rush. It's not a race. And whatever you do, don't get frustrated! Frustration kills enthusiasm.

Request and Enforce

The biggest mistake people make in teaching COME is over-using the command. Too much calling and your dog will resist. Think back to the example of someone calling you. If you responded and they had nothing positive to say or do once you got there, you'd be less likely to come the next time they called. If they called every five minutes, after awhile you'd just ignore them.

Dogs are no different. When the day finally arrives when yours understands the COME command, avoid using it all the time. It's like crying wolf — no pun intended. If you want a happy response to COME, make sure it's necessary, infrequent and rewarding.

Set aside 5 to 15 minutes at least three times a week to work on a formal lesson. Leave your dog in a SIT-STAY and vary the request to COME by increasing your distance, varying the angle you are calling from or hiding before calling. Although COME is the word of the day, sandwich each exercise between a couple of regular SIT-STAYs. If you don't, your dog may start anticipating COME. And

Other Ways to Say It

Don't forget your other words that can bring your dog to you: INSIDE when you want your dog to come indoors; LET'S GO when you want her to follow you; and HEEL when you want her to stay at your side.

since you can't correct a dog who's coming to you, you're stuck. Avoid the problem by working a few SIT-STAYs between each COME command.

Next, set up a temptation in the middle of the floor. It could be a person, food, toys — whatever. Stand near it and call your dog. If she can't resist, say NOPE and quicktug the leash. When she gets back on course, praise her with a strong, solid YES!

DEVELOPING YOUR DOG'S CONCENTRATION

Once your dog knows, really knows how to COME, start developing her concentration. Her sense of right response, wrong response. Cheer the right response, YES! Issue a quick correction from a distance, then, after the negative, redirect your dog with COME and reward her. You're a hero!

1. Take your dog into a busy room (kid's playroom, a room where a family member is on the phone, wherever).

2. Stand four feet behind your dog and call out her name, DAISY.

3. If she looks to you, mark the instant with a YES or click and treat, and leave it at that. Repeat her name. If she doesn't pay attention, quicktug the leash and say NOPE. The moment she looks to you, praise her.

4. The third time you call her name, say DAISY and when she looks to you, COME, then wave your arm across your chest and run backwards.

5. When your dog reaches your feet, finish in COME Front style (with her sitting and looking up). Say YES or click and reward.

Proof your dog. Will she come if she's distracted by things on the floor?

🐾 A Fun Quiz

Look at the following examples and decide which command you would use in each situation: HEEL, INSIDE, NAME or COME.

1. The ice cream truck pulls up across the street. Although you don't have kids and you're a little busy trimming the hedges, half the neighborhood empties onto the street. When your dog starts running toward the crowd, you command _____ to discourage his focus on the situation.

2. You're walking your dog on his Flexi-leash at the local park. Suddenly you and your dog notice a squirrel. You command _____ to bring his focus back to you.

3. Someone arrives at your door asking directions. You command _____ to keep your dog under control but focused on the situation.

4. It's 11:30 P.M. Your yard is fenced, so you've let your dog out to relieve herself. You use _____ to bring her in.

Here are the correct answers:

1. and 2. COME. This tells your dog to stop paying attention to external matters and to focus on you.

3. HEEL. This tells your dog to stay cool but keeps him involved in the situation.

4. INSIDE. This word means only one thing: When you get your tail in this door, you'll get a treat and a whole lot of loving!

Practice around different everyday distractions. Outside, extend your separation using the long line or Flexi-leash. If your dog's attention is divided, say NOPE and quicktug the leash. Praise her enthusiastically when she focuses on you: YES! Then use the COME to call her in.

Use COME in two of the following situations daily:

- When your dog is distracted on a walk
- Around food that's either on the table or on the floor
- If the kids are getting too wild
- When the neighbor is jogging by

You can add to the list. Remember, the second your dog looks to you, say YES! If she blows you off, NOPE!

My dog comes when I call her, but she's so excited that she jumps all over me!

Your dog reminds me of one of my students. Cooper is a big, blocky yellow Labrador Retriever whose enthusiasm could knock you flat. When his owner calls him, we all duck for cover, other dogs included! It's a positive problem, though, so don't worry too much. To tone down a reaction such as this, try the following:

1. Command in a calmer voice.

2. As your dog comes, lean forward with your arms outstretched like those guys who direct airplanes into the gate. (This blocking posture slows a dog down.) Stand as she approaches.

3. Say SHHH as she gets closer. Bring your fingers from her face to your eyes.

4. Stand tall and mark the moment she's sitting square with praise and treats.

My dog stops three feet in front and veers to one side, licks my face or tinkles.

You're probably bending over. You're in her way. Try leaning back when you call. Bent postures communicate play, confrontation or submission. Straight postures communicate confidence.

My dog comes too fast for me to reel in the leash.

Another positive problem with an easy solution. As soon as you've said your command, scurry backward. This will give you added time to reel in the leash.

My dog looks so depressed when I call her.

Either you're commanding too harshly or not enthusiastically enough. Use a strong voice, not a cross one. Also, increase your animation; make it seem like more fun. Say COME and really run backward or kneel down with your arms open for the big effect. Never call your dog for something negative. One more thing to ask yourself: Are you bending over your dog to call or to praise her when she comes? If you are, you may be inadvertently scaring her. Every dog is different, and if yours finds your size or enthusiasm scary, find another way to communicate your approval.

My dog comes on the Flexi-leash, but then veers past me.

Are you fudging on the finish? Remember the structure of this command? Your dog must return to you, sit in front and look up. Remind her with a few beginner COME Front exercises. When she's cooperating, go back to your Flexi-leash and correct her if she races by with NOPE and a quicktug. Guide her into the proper position with a lure or a leash, mark the proper eye contact and praise as usual.

When I say COME, my dog looks at me like she's too busy to be bothered.

Kind of amazing to see the thought process. Just quicktug the leash, say NOPE and encourage her with praise.

If there's a distraction, my dog will walk sideways and sit on my feet to keep focused on it.

Clever dog. Trying to please everyone. Not exactly what the teacher had in mind! When your dog takes her eyes off you, sidestep away from the distraction as you quicktug the leash and say NOPE! Praise her when she's back on track.

STAND-STAY

This exercise is great for wiping muddy paws, grooming and helping you get up off the floor. Fortunately, it's easy for both student and teacher to master.

STAND-STAY With Treats or a Toy

1. SIT your dog and hold the lure in front of her nose.
2. As soon as she catches a whiff, bring the treat straight forward in front of her nose (your eventual signal).
3. As she moves into a standing position, say STAND and hold your hand still for three seconds.
4. YES or click and treat. Good job!

Once your dog learns STAND, introduce STAY. Gradually increase the time she must stand to 10 seconds. Then begin to use the flat palm signal from your SIT-STAY exercises. Proceed as you did in that section. Punctuate the ending with a YES or click and treat.

STAND-STAY Without Treats

1. Kneel down on the floor next to your dog.
2. Place your right hand, palm out, on your dog's buckle collar or Gentle Leader.
3. Slide your left hand under your dog's belly.
4. Say STAND as you prop your dog into a standing position.
5. Relax your right hand and slide your left hand to rest on your dog's thigh.
6. Pause two, three, four, five . . . and release with OK!
7. Increase the time to one minute, introducing the STAY.
8. Gradually stand up from the floor. Now you're ready to let go.

James MacDonald

STAND-STAY comes in especially handy when it's time to groom your dog or wipe muddy paws. Your dog may need a little help at first.

9. Prop your dog into position. Remind STAY and slide your left hand away from your dog. Now slide your right hand away as you rise up to a standing position yourself.

Slowly increase the distractions, duration and distance your dog can control her impulse to move.

GAME GALLERY

Playing with your dog is just plain fun — a tail-wagging good time! By using your command words in these games, you keep the communications flowing. (The games are listed alphabetically, so sift through the list and find the ones most appropriate for the lesson you're working on and the dog you're playing with.)

GAME GALLERY INDEX

Game	Command
Fancy Fetching	GIVE
Four-Footed Fax	GO, COME, and personal name
Happy Heel	HEEL
High Five	SIT and PAW

Game	Command
Jumping Jimminy	HEEL
Paw Please	SIT and PAW
Puppy Ping Pong	COME and personal name
Quick Down	DOWN
Rollin', Rollin', Rollin'	DOWN
Simon Says "Speak"	SPEAK and QUIET
Sneak-n-Seek	COME
Sniff-n-Snarf	SIT-STAY and HEEL

Fancy Fetching

I have to admit, I've got a fascination with fetching. The concept of throwing something as far from myself as possible and then having it returned is pretty mind-boggling. First, you'll have to judge whether you can teach this game to your dog. Some dogs love the concept; others will look at you cross-eyed for suggesting such a ludicrous activity. They're all different. If you notice your dog likes to chase and return to you with objects (although she might prefer playing keep-away), try this game:

1. With some snacks in hand, take your dog into a small, quiet room.

2. Show her a favorite toy or a small folded section of the newspaper (if you plan to teach her to bring in the paper). Move it playfully in front of her face. When she takes it, praise her enthusiastically. (If she doesn't take it, gently squeeze behind her canine teeth and pop it in her dropped jaw.). If she holds onto it, say BRING as you scratch her head and act very pleased. (If she doesn't hold it, brace your hand under her jawbone to help her hold onto it, praising all the while.)

3. Next, say GIVE, placing your open palm under her jaw. If your dog does not release the toy, use one of these three approaches:

   Say GIVE and offer a treat. Let the toy drop into your hand. If you're using a clicker, this is the ideal situation! Click the instant your dog releases the ball.

   If you find having treats on the scene is over-stimulating, check your treats at the door. As you say GIVE, calmly reach your thumb and forefinger around the top of your dog's muzzle, behind her canine teeth. Squeeze gently until the toy is released into your hand.

   If your dog knows GIVE and is being stubborn, try the treat and click method to see if you can cajole her. If not, leave a leash on during this game.

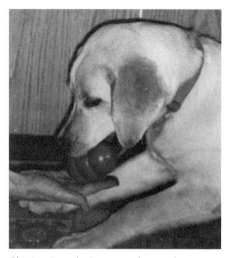

Sharing is a choice your dog makes, not a tug-of-war struggle.

If she slips away or ignores you, quick-tug the leash and say NOPE. Repeat GIVE, then NOPE again if she still resists your request. Repeat this exchange until your dog gives you the toy. When she does, praise her warmly.

Once she's got the picture, take the game into other rooms. If she gets distracted, attach a leash to direct her. As you say BRING, run back away from her clapping. When she gets to you say GIVE and praise or click and treat. If she refuses to share, encourage the release by squeezing her jaw gently or with a quicktug with the leash: NOPE.

Now you can take the game outside, attaching a long line or using a Flexi-leash if needed to direct her.

Four-Footed Fax

Puppy Ping Pong and Fancy Fetching are prerequisites for this game. Once you've mastered those, you can teach your dog to carry important messages to people in your house. Give her a note and say BRING IT TO MARY. Once your dog has mastered this, you can graduate to other objects. You can send her to BRING the newspaper (using a command like BRING THE PAPER) or teach her to return those sneakers someone left in the kitchen (BRING IT TO BOB). The recipient should enthusiastically praise every correct delivery.

Happy Heel

Although chasing your dog is a big no-no (it makes you look like a follower, not a leader), encouraging her to chase you is totally acceptable. Use this fun time to encourage an enthusiasm for heeling.

1. Get treats or a toy and show them to your dog cheerfully.

2. When she comes over to investigate, say HEEL and help her align herself at your side.

3. Holding the treat or toy in your left hand, say DAISY, HEEL and move forward happily.

4. As she follows, praise her enthusiastically. Stop often to build her success rate.

5. As you slow to a stop, help her sit at your side. If you're using a clicker, now's the time! Toss her a treat or toy after each stop.

Don't expect perfection, especially at first. You're striving for enthusiasm and fun, and if you get that you're doing great!

High Five

Paw, Please is a prerequisite here. Is your dog super paw-expressive? Well, it's time to employ those talents. From PAW you can teach her HIGH FIVE and WAVE.

High Five: Slowly rotate your extended hand from a flat position to a lifted one. As you rotate your hand into the high five position, say PAW-HIGH FIVE until your dog gets it. Use a clicker or say YES and treat to mark the exact moment your dog's paw hits your palm. Good job!

Wave: Ask for PAW, but at the last minute pull back and say WAVE! as you wave your hand in front of your dog's nose. The idea is to get your dog to imitate your movement. Praise her as she does it. Use food and YES or a clicker to encourage your dog's understanding.

HIGH FIVE, Ginger. You're the cleverest dog in town!

Most paw-expressives are so addicted to this behavior that they'll do it any time, anywhere, no treats required. Soon, your waves will get a quick reply!

Jumping Jimminy

This motivational game is fun to practice by yourself or with the kids.

1. Create a low jump by resting a broomstick on two objects of equal height. (Rolls of toilet paper or cereal boxes make good props.) Place your jump in a doorway, so your dog can't cheat and go around it.

2. Let your dog sniff the setup before you begin. Use a treat cup to encourage your dog to follow you.

3. With your dog either off leash or wearing a short leash, take her back several paces. As you trot to the jump, say OVER and jump together. (If your dog is startled, walk over the jump together several times, making it as low as necessary.)

4. Praise and treat your dog. Make a big thing of it!

🐾 Keep It Low

Puppies need time to develop. If yours is under a year, keep the jump height below the elbow.

5. Jump back and forth together several times before you stop.

6. After two days, encourage her to take it on her own. Run to the jump with her but stop short as you say OVER! Reward her, then call OVER as you encourage her return.

7. Increase the height of the jump as your dog gets the hang of it. Don't push her though; one-and-a-half times the height of your dog's shoulder is the absolute limit.

Paw, Please

Some dogs are so predisposed to pawing that you're probably wondering how to teach NO PAW, but we'll get to that later. For now, kneel or sit in front of your dog (treats handy, if they're not too distracting) and ask her to SIT. Stretch one hand out and with your other thumb press your dog's shoulder muscle gently until she lifts her front leg. Say PAW when her paw touches your palm and mark the moment with YES or a click and treat. As she catches on, mix your PAW requests into your day. Isn't she a clever dog?

If your dog won't stop pawing you and you've had enough, let her know. Say NOT NOW as you shoot her a sideways glance then ignore her.

Puppy Ping Pong

This game is a blast! It teaches COME to all family members, in addition to helping your dog learn everyone's name. For this fun exercise, you'll need at least two people and at least as many treat cups. In this example, John and Mary are the people and Maverick is the dog.

1. John and Mary stand or sit 10 feet apart.

2. John tells Maverick, GO TO MARY as he points in her direction and withdraws his attention from the dog.

3. Mary shakes her treat cup and, as Maverick runs to her, calls MAVERICK, COME.

4. After a few seconds of praise, Mary points GO TO JOHN and withdraws her attention.

5. John shakes his cup, calling MAVERICK, COME, and praises him as he comes.

6. After the dog goes back and forth a few times, end the game with hugs from everyone.

Quick Down

This game is super for all those hard-to-get-down dogs out there. It makes the DOWN command more like a game. Here's how it goes:

1. Call your dog over, a yummy treat and/or clicker in hand. Ask her to SIT.
2. Brace your legs in a play stance.
3. Dart a short distance across the floor, stop short and say SIT, luring her to you with a treat. If you're clicking, click the instant she sits. Praise wholeheartedly.
4. Repeat this procedure three times: dart, SIT, dart, SIT, dart, SIT.
5. During your next dart, say SIT and suddenly . . .
6. Say DOWN as you drop to the floor treat in hand, slapping the floor playfully.
7. Release with OK and lots of treats and praise!

Rollin', Rollin', Rollin'

If your dog's the athletic type or just spends a lot of time on her back, this game is a real showstopper. It puts a whole new spin on DOWN.

1. Call your dog in and put her in a DOWN-STAY.
2. Scratch her belly until she's leaning to one side.
3. Hold a treat in one hand and use it to draw an imaginary circle around her head by bringing it from her mouth line back toward her ear.
4. Slowly circle the treat backward over her head.
5. Initially, she may need some help to follow the treat with her body. Guide her to roll over by gently pushing her leg to the other side.
6. Initially say ROLL OVER as she completes the roll. Mark the moment with YES or click and treat.
7. Gradually coach her roll from a kneeling position, still hands on, to a straight back hands off, using an exaggerated signal and yummy treats to help ease the transition.

Rolling one, two, three!

Simon Says "Speak"

Does your dog love to make noise? Does she bark when she's happy, excited or when she doesn't get her way? Is your biggest question not how to teach voice lessons, but how to find her off switch? Actually, it might be easier than you think. Start with your dog's passion (barking), then teach her quiet control.

Most barking dogs think their barking is beautiful and very much in demand. After all, they bark at the letter carrier and he disappears. Surely that means they have scared him off! And when they're lonely, a bark brings company — you. Bark at the door and the family starts yelling (yelling in Doglish is barking), so now it's a concert.

Teach SPEAK:

1. Psyche your dog into barking (by ringing a doorbell or standing out of reach).

2. When she starts barking, look at her alertly, praise her and say SPEAK! (Click and treat, if that's your habit.) For some added encouragement, add a fun hand signal such as snapping your fingers.

3. Once she's caught on, encourage barking throughout the day for positive things: a walk or a meal. If she speaks out of turn, just ignore her.

Teach QUIET:

1. Psyche your dog into barking. Look into her eyes and use your SPEAK signal.

2. After a few barks, say QUIET as you avert your eyes, then stand tall and clap your hands sharply.

3. If she stops, mark the moment (YES or a click) and offer her a treat. If she doesn't stop, wait it out. No eye contact or interaction. When she's quiet, mark the moment and praise her warmly.

Practice these words throughout the day, varying which one you reinforce. Sometimes SPEAK, other times QUIET. Have your dog SPEAK-QUIET two or three times before rewarding her. She'll be so proud of this new trick, and so will you!

Sneak-n-Seek

This game helps your dog learn to respond to the COME command. Once a day, grab your treat cup or clicker and do the following:

1. When your dog is in another room, poke your head in the room, shake your treat cup and say DAISY, COME!

2. Run out of sight, clapping your hands and cheering her on.

3. Kneel down, click and treat when she gets to you and fold her into your arms for a big hug! (SIT is not a requirement here.)

Sniff-n-Snarf

Dogs love this game. In addition to helping them perfect their responses to the STAY and HEEL, canine detective school and finding lost treasures is fun no matter what your species! Long term your dog's talents can come in handy when you lose your keys or the TV remote. But first, let's start with food.

1. Wearing your snack pack or holding some treats, take your dog into a quiet room.
2. Say SIT-STAY and take out a treat.
3. Hold the treat in front of her nose and say SNIFF.
4. Remind your dog to STAY as you toss the treat three feet in front of you. (Use a leash if she can't hold still.)
5. Pause, varying the duration from two to10 seconds.
6. Encourage your dog to look up, either by calling her name or clucking, and say FIND IT! as you point to the treat.
7. The second she reaches the treat, praise her enthusiastically!
8. When she finishes her treat, say HEEL and help her back to your side.
9. Repeat this game five times.

Playing strengthens all bonds.

Jodi Buren

Increase the distance you toss the treat in front of you. After you've succeeded at 15 feet, try hiding the treat around the corner. Your dog will probably be a bit confused. Help her by getting on the floor and act like you're sniffing; she'll catch on quickly. Make the hiding spots more challenging as she does.

Once she's mastered finding treats, teach her to find other objects. Your keys, for example. Tell her to SNIFF, then place them three feet in front of you. Instruct FIND IT. When she does, click and treat. You'll be hiring her out for detective work in no time!

Chapter 6

Out and About

The biggest reward for all your efforts is the freedom it gives you to take your dog everywhere. He'll be a welcome social guest, a plus at parades and picnics and an additional fan at after-school sporting events.

GOING PUBLIC

Before that dear dog of yours can accompany you anywhere, you'll need to do some preparatory training. That means going on practice runs to selected areas so that you can devote all your attention to your dog. Eventually, it will seem effortless and your dog will truly be welcome everywhere, but your first trips out may be a real shock. You'll feel self-conscious, your dog will be too distracted to listen and you'll feel compelled to tell everyone you see that he's in training. How do I know? I've been there.

Are you wondering, "If it's such a nightmare, why bother?" There are three reasons:

1. It gets easier.
2. A well-mannered dog is fun to share.
3. It broadens your dog's horizons. You'll be the one looking confident in new, unexplored territories. And the initial effort will yield a lifetime of shared experiences.

Although your first day might be on the chaotic side, it really does get easier. I promise! Keep thinking of the first time you tried something new — driving, tennis, a computer game. It felt awkward, right? But if you stuck with it, you're probably an expert by now. Going out with your dog is the same. The first outing with your perfect-at-home pal may feel more like his first day of lessons.

Even I had the first-outing blues with my Border Collie mix, Shayna May. As I bent to tie my shoe, she enthusiastically jumped at a total stranger and I fell flat. Ouch!

But that first day passed, and Shayna learned that manners were expected everywhere, whether greeting the meter reader or children in the park. Your dog, like Shayna, will come to understand that house rules apply everywhere. The compliments you'll receive on your well-trained dog will more than make up for your initial embarrassment. Just remember, I didn't start out with perfection, and you may not, either.

The bottom line when you're out: Your dog needs direction. He needs a plan. If you don't have one, he'll be left to make his own decisions. And that might mean jumping on strangers instead of focusing on you or chasing cars rather than standing at your side. So take charge!

Now that you know going public requires some effort, I'd like to help simplify the process, from getting into the car to a restful ride home. I'll walk you through it step by step. Before we begin, keep these universal rules in mind:

- From start to finish, be your dog's guardian, his protector and leader. Stand confidently in front of your dog: paws by heels! You lead and he follows.

- Keep your dog on lead. No fancy stuff or showing off. Too many dangers!

- Use lots of encouragement. Cheerfulness is contagious. Bring your snack pack with treats, and a clicker if you're using one.

- Keep the communication flowing. Your words provide structure and security.

- No eliminating in public. Take care of that activity close to home, in areas you've designated. (But bring a poop pick-up bag just in case!)

- Know when to say NOPE — to your dog and to other people.

It's all about continuing your emotional connection with your dog. When he's out of his familiar environment, he needs extra direction to feel connected and safe. Use your words to communicate direction, like a good team captain should. One of you has to be the leader, the guardian and the protector — and I say it's you!

On a field trip with my class to the Bedford Village Library.

CAR MANNERS

The first step in shaping your perfect-in-public partner is getting him to your destination with your sanity intact. If some of you are chuckling, it's no wonder. Some dogs are less than cooperative in the car. Pacing or jumping from seat to seat and barking at passing strangers is no way to start an outing.

To correct this problem, think of the situation from your dog's point of view. To him, your automobile is a window seat with legs. His own little fishbowl. And while passing other cars, pausing for bicycles and braking for squirrels is part of your normal routine, it pushes his chasing and territorial instincts to their max. Not to mention his sense of balance. Whether he barks or bounces, the predator whizzes away. Conclusion? He's victorious. The champ! Not only

The ride structures the experience.

do they run away, but they run fast! You haven't even gotten out of the car and your dog's already pumped up. See where the problem starts?

First, structure the car experience to help your dog feel less out of control.

1. Create a pleasant area for your dog in the car. I suggest the back seat or cargo area for safety reasons. Decorate this area with a mat and a toy or bone. Secure a leash to contain your dog, as described in Chapter 2. Crates or gates are other options.

2. Say HEEL as you lead your dog to the car.

3. Open the car door and pause — WAIT. Prevent your dog from jumping in the car until you say OK.

4. Direct your dog to his spot, saying SETTLE DOWN as he gets inside. Secure him to this area and instruct WAIT again.

Now you can proceed. Things always go more smoothly when they're organized.

ONCE YOU GET THERE

Getting your dog out of the car calmly is as important as the ride there. Again, from your dog's point of view, the situation is pretty exciting . . . new sights, smells and faces. Don't take it personally if he doesn't acknowledge you or listen to your direction at first. Getting him out of the car in a contained manner is the challenge at hand:

1. Before you open the door, instruct WAIT.
2. If he jumps forward, catch the car lead, say NOPE and tug him back.
3. Re-instruct WAIT and pause until he's calm.
4. Put on his leash and say OK as you let him out of the car.
5. Immediately instruct BUDDY, HEEL, bringing him next to your side with a quicktug or by luring him with a treat.
6. Instruct WAIT as you shut the car door.
7. Direct BUDDY, HEEL, as you set out on your new adventure.

Now you've arrived! Instantly, your dog will probably have one of two reactions: the socialite or the shrinking violet.

The Socialite: If your dog's a socialite, his head will be twitching a mile a minute, he'll pivot toward every new stimulation and pull to investigate every person and blade of grass. These guys are so passionate about exploring everything new that they often don't know which direction to turn next. First, try centering your dog with a treat or toy. Lure his attention, calling out his name, saying YES and clicking with rewards if he focuses on you. Next it's time to HEEL, which let's your dog know he can chill — that you'll be the leader and filter out the extraneous stuff.

SIT-STAY is important too, since it's all about impulse control and containment. Sometimes stillness is not a priority for a dog (like an over-excited child), but hold your ground. Brace your dog if you have to (see "Bracing" box on this page), but enforce SIT-STAY. All his activity reflects apprehension. Provide a calm and confident example, speak clearly and follow through.

If an admirer approaches, ask yourself if you're ready to handle the situation? Can you control your dog's enthusiasm? If not, thank the person but pass on the meeting for now. You don't want your dog jumping on anyone or scratching or scaring a child, even by accident. Take all commands back to the introductory stage, no

Bracing

To physically brace your dog, point your right thumb toward the ground, slip it over his collar and fan your fingers out across his chest. Use your left hand to hold his waist (see page 109).

If your dog is pulling, resisting or choking on a neck collar, consider using a Gentle Leader. This collar braces your dog's head, putting pressure over his muzzle and scruff: two acupressure points his mother used to teach him to calm down.

matter how well you're doing at home. Initially, practice only HEEL, WAIT and SIT-STAY.

The Shrinking Violet: For this type, the experience of being out away from home may seem overwhelming. His tail may disappear under his belly, his body may lower and, when stimulated, he may try to hide behind you.

These are not naughty behaviors: Your dog is a unique creature and is allowed to see the world in his own way. But you don't want him to be so fearful that he is always awash in stress. And how you choose to react will shape his future. Bend to soothe your shrinking violet and you're affirming his worst fears. Since I can't let you do that, I've come up with a better plan.

It's so tempting to soothe! You've got to keep reminding yourself that your dog is not human. Say to yourself over and over: Soothing reinforces fear, soothing reinforces fear. Instead, stand confidently and direct your dog with HEEL and STAY, bracing if need be. Familiar sounds ease anxiety.

Deflect any admirers until your dog is feeling safer. Use your treats and clicker to encourage your dog to focus on you. If your dog is too scared to follow directions, just position him without losing your patience. A frightened dog is convinced the world might end

 Too Much Attention

Be prepared to attract some attention when you go out training. Some people, like myself, delight in dogs and love to talk to people who share the same passion. If people ask to pet your dog and you don't feel ready to handle the situation, you can reply politely, "Thank you for asking. I've just begun training, though, and we're not ready yet. Catch us in a week or two!"

in a moment. Do whatever it takes to bring his attention out to you (treat cups, jingle jars, clickers, whatever) and use your words to communicate that you'll be there as guardian and protector, come what may. (If your dog is still too scared, go home. Call a trusted professional trainer and get some help.)

HEEL! Are you joking? He does it great at home, but he's wild when we go anywhere else!

The first rule is to stay calm. If you get hyper with your dog, the whole outing is a wash. Next learn the Tush Push and Side Step. Since you can't seem to hold onto your dog with your arm, let's use your body!

Tush Push: Put your arms behind you and grasp the leash with both hands together, resting your straight arms on your backside. If your dog forges ahead, bend your left knee and push back with your tush. To get the maximum push, put your right foot out, bend your left knee down and push back with gusto. When your dog lands back at your side, say YES and HEEL. Use praise and treats to encourage his focus initially.

> ### 🐾 Let Him Go, Then Say NOPE
>
> For safety as well as respect reasons, your dog should be more focused on you (his leader) than the environment, especially when you're out and about. A clue: Your dog's ears are his antennas. Watch them and you'll know what he's thinking about. If they're relaxed back or flicking quickly to catch a noise, he's still focused on you. If the ears are riveted forward, his attention is likely elsewhere. Stop walking momentarily and let your dog continue out the length of the leash. When he reaches the end of the leash, quicktug back and say NOPE! Direct him back to your side by calling his name and HEEL. Praise him for walking with you!

Side Step: If your dog is riveted on something to your left or right, take a giant step away from the distraction and quicktug your dog back to your side. When he's there, praise and reward him. And keep moving as if nothing happened. You're the leader — there are places to go and things to do!

My dog starts barking the second I let him out of the car!

Your boy is either worried or too excited. In either case, bring him behind you the moment he gets out of the car so he knows he can depend on you. Use your SIT, STAY and HEEL words to let him know what he's supposed to be doing. Review the Gentle Leader collar option. On your first trips out, practice in the back of an empty parking lot. If your dog's woofing because he's unsure, remind HEEL as you move steadily, keeping him focused on your rhythm. If your dog's the type who wants to take on the world, try the Surprise Spray. Pack a container of Binaca or a plant mister to use in your training. When he starts barking, discretely spritz *above* his nose (not at it) and say SSHHH. Be secretive about the spritz, because you don't want him to know where it is coming from: His bark brings about a surprise from the environment, while you have all the answers and the treats to reinforce his good behavior!

My dog is so afraid, he freezes and won't move. I've never seen him this bad.

If he's terrified, get some help. Try coaxing him forward with his favorite treats and praise, but if he refuses to eat, follow my first suggestion.

GREETING PEOPLE

Stop shaking. This doesn't have to be a hair-raising experience. Just keep your head on straight and remember everything that I've taught you. I have faith in you!

Before I talk you through the procedure, though, please read over the following points. If you identify with any of them, please follow my specific instructions and skip the rest of this section.

- If your dog is having aggression problems, the only person you must introduce your dog to is a professional trainer with a specialty in aggression rehabilitation. How do you find such an expert? Ask your veterinarian. It's better to be safe than sued.

- If you notice your dog getting nervous or tense around unfamiliar people, join a dog training class or work under private supervision. Don't push the issue alone.

- If you don't believe you can get your dog to change, you won't. Hire some extra training help to build your own confidence!

When meeting people, you should greet them first.

If you're still with me, here are five rules to follow when that dog of yours makes his debut:

Rule #1: Make sure your dog is familiar and comfortable with the setting before attempting to share him with anyone. Don't greet people on your first day out!

Rule #2: Feet ahead of paws! Correct all attempts to scootch forward.

Rule #3: Tell admirers what you're doing. "We're learning our greeting manners."

Rule #4: Keep more focused on your dog than on any admirers. Praise all his good behavior.

Rule #5: Have faith in your own knowledge. Just because everyone has advice doesn't mean it's right. "I don't mind if he jumps" doesn't hold water. *You* mind. Period.

Now for the actual greeting. Drum roll, please! How you handle the situation will depend on your dog, but you will always set the example. If your dog is overly enthusiastic, you'll need to tame his expressiveness. Keeping him focused on you is the key.

Handling the Socialites:

1. Ask people to wait just a second until your dog is calm.

2. Enforce a SIT-STAY, keeping your feet ahead of his paws.

3. If he's too excited, kneel down and brace your right thumb over his collar to prevent any upward motion.

4. Brace his waist with your left hand.

5. And now, if the person is still standing in front of you, they can meet and greet your beloved dog!

6. Remind STAY, and don't let up your containment until the person is gone.

Remember, even Lassie wasn't born trained! Whew — what a workout!

Handling the Shrinking Violets:
You'll need a totally different approach if your dog is more passive.

1. Place your dog in a SIT-STAY and kneel down at his side.

2. Put your left hand on his waist and, with your right hand, pet him under his chin, keeping his head up.

3. Ask your greeter if she wouldn't mind giving your dog some treats. If you use a treat cup or clicker, the sound will condition a positive reaction to new people.

4. Another cool trick is to hold the person's hand in yours and let your dog sniff them together.

My dog is more sensitive to men than to women. Sometimes he growls at them.

This problem generally results from either inappropriate experiences with or lack of socialization to men. Whatever the cause, make sure you use your dog's favorite treats for the introduction. (If the man is visiting your home, place your dog on his leash during the man's arrival and follow the same directions.) Try this approach:

1. Instruct your man friend to avoid direct eye contact with your dog.

2. Do not force the situation. Be friendly and calm, setting a good example.

3. Casually place a trail of treats to the man, with a pile of goodies on his shoe. Praise your dog as he follows the trail.

4. Ask the man to kneel calmly while continuing to avoid direct eye contact.

5. Offer the man some treats to hold and praise your dog if he takes them. If you're clicker training, click as your dog moves toward the man.

6. The man should continue to offer your dog fistfuls of treats as he gets calmer.

7. Eventually, when your dog initiates the interaction, take the man's hand in yours and pet your dog together.

If the apprehension doesn't subside, get professional help and avoid men until you do.

My dog is suspicious of children and my husband and I are planning to have kids. What can I do?

If the problem doesn't improve with the following suggestions, find a private trainer who has experience with this problem. To socialize your dog with children, try this:

1. Walk around the perimeter of a playground to get your dog used to the noise and motions of kids. Practice your HEEL and SIT-STAY to remind your dog that you're confident in this situation and that you'll direct him. Use your clicker and treats to liven up the outing. Do not let the children approach.

2. Act like a child with your dog. For example, poke him or pull his ear like a child would do, squeal in a high-pitched voice and stare at him at his level by kneeling or crawling. Use treats to link up a positive association. Once he's socialized to these behaviors, he'll be more accepting when the children do them.

3. If your dog is nervous around babies, borrow a friend's baby blanket (for the aroma) and wrap a doll baby in it to carry around the house, including your dog in all the fuss!

4. Condition him to the sound of his treat cup or jingle jar, and take it with you when you're around kids. Let the kids take it and reward your dog. If he's enthusiastic, you can let him take treats gently from the children (see "Kids and Dogs" in the Appendix, page 234). Have a child use words like SIT and DOWN to lure your dog with food.

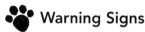 **Warning Signs**

If your dog tenses up, his eyes grow cold or he starts to growl, do not work him around children until you are under the supervision of a professional trainer. You don't want you and your dog to be another statistic. Dogs who bite children are often euthanized by court order.

GREETING DOGS

Are you shaking again? Envisioning your dog hurling himself at the end of the lead? Well, wake up! You're just having a bad dream.

Seriously, though. If you've had some stressful encounters in the past, try to put them behind you. Bad memories cloud your control. Wipe the slate clean and have faith in what I've taught you.

If you see a dog when you're out and about, don't approach the dog initially. First, get control of your end of the leash:

1. If your dog acts stimulated, quicktug and remind him to HEEL. Praise and reward him for focusing.

2. Continue walking, picking up your pace to keep it interesting.

3. Don't look toward, approach or follow either your dog or the other dog. Any eye contact would convey interest.

4. Your dog may continue his shenanigans, but don't worry. Just speed up and keep balancing a quicktug for pulling with praise and rewards for staying focused on you.

5. Remember: Keep him behind you, leaders must be in the lead!

6. Once you have your dog under control, decide if you want to approach the other dog. If you do, keep your dog at your side and greet the other owner (making certain the other dog is friendly) as you tell your dog WAIT. Then release your dog with OK, GO PLAY!

7. When playtime is over, call your dog back to your side with BUDDY, HEEL, and move on.

What if someone approaches me?

If you're not in the mood or your dog is too excited, just say, "No thanks, not today." If you're game, however, get your dog in control behind you, then release him with an OK, SAY HELLO! Call him back with BUDDY, HEEL, when play-time is over.

What if we're approached by an aggressive dog who is off lead?

I love this question. When approached by an aggressive dog, do not turn or make eye contact with the dog and prevent your dog from doing the same. Correct any confrontational attempts your dog makes as you hightail it from the scene. The aggressive dog is protecting what he considers to be his territory. If you leave without confronting him, he'll stop the chase immediately to reserve his fighting energy for a more threatening foe.

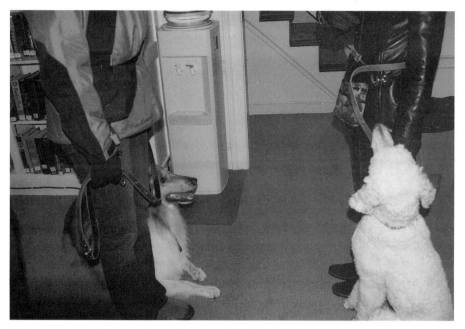

Make sure your dog is calm and in control before releasing him to play.

ENTERING BUILDINGS

Pick a building you might visit with your dog: the veterinarian's office, a hardware store, a pet supply shop, your kid's school. Your dog's behavior in those buildings will depend on one major factor: Who enters the building first. If your dog leads you, he's in charge. If you lead your dog, you're the social director. And as such, you'll need a plan!

Taking for granted that you're going to run the show, let's consider the following situation: You arrive at your dog's veterinarian. As you bring your dog out of the car on leash, say BUDDY, HEEL, and slap your left leg to direct him. Walk towards the building, confidently, checking if your dog is more focused on you than on his surroundings. If he's distracted, quicktug the leash and remind him to HEEL. When he's focused, praise and reward him enthusiastically.

1. At the door hold the leash behind you (dogs sense when they're going somewhere new) and say WAIT. Open the door.

2. Say SHHH if he starts getting excited and let the door close.

3. Pause before you open the door again and say WAIT.

4. Don't proceed until he has settled down.

5. Recommend WAIT as you open the door.

6. If your dog pulls forward, quicktug him back and say NOPE.

7. Pause again until your dog is calm. Say OK as you lead him through!

My dog is always cautious when entering new buildings.

That's a pretty normal reaction. Don't pet or sweet talk him — you'll be reinforcing his anxiety. If you bend over to soothe him, your compromised body posture makes you look weak. When your dog shows fear, you must show confidence. Take along some treats to cheer your dog up as you approach the building. When you get to the door, hand out a treat for standing still. Use a SIT-STAY once you enter the building to center your dog's focus. Use BUDDY, HEEL, to proceed. Attitude is everything and confidence is catching.

CURB ETIQUETTE

Curb control not only looks nice, it's safe. Applying our usual psychology, some structure is in order here!

1. As you approach the curb, your dog should be at your side.

2. At the curb, instruct him to WAIT.

3. If your dog continues moving forward, quicktug the leash and say NOPE. Once your dog is by your heels, repeat WAIT.

4. Say OK as you lead him across and remind BUDDY, HEEL in a happy, confident voice.

Should I instruct a SIT-STAY if we're forced to wait at the curb?

That's up to you. If your dog is fidgety, then, definitely, yes. The SIT-STAY is very grounding. Good application!

GRATES AND OTHER SCARY OBJECTS

Dogs see the world a little differently than we do. Take your average grate, for example. Standing five feet above it, our binocular vision separates out the spaces between the bars and it seems harmless. To a dog, who has much less perspective and no template for such a thing, grates looks pretty scary! The holes mesh together and it looks more like an abyss.

Bearing this in mind, also remember that your dog is very much a creature of habit. At home, he takes comfort in consistency. Even a new piece of furniture or a houseplant can throw off his sense of stability. If you've ever seen this, you've probably noticed a cautious stance, worried eyes, an avoid-approach pattern and eventually a full-length-stretch-to-sniff investigation. (Unlike humans, dogs "see" a new object by smelling it; with their noses, not their eyes.) After a couple of days, the new thing will be absorbed into the dog's mental map and seem like old hat.

When you go out, there may be unfamiliar objects that spook your dog. How you handle the situation will be based on your dog's reaction. If he's afraid and you try to calm him, your body language and voice will communicate fear, not confidence, and he'll grow more and more wary. If he bucks to avoid it altogether and you force him, he'll be likely to refuse anything new.

On the other hand, if you act confident about the new object, your dog will have more respect for your courage. Give your dog some slack as you inves-

Safety and good behavior all rolled into one!

tigate the scary stuff. He'll watch you and be impressed. After seeing that no harm came to you, he'll follow your lead and feel pretty smart about overcoming his fear.

What About Those Bags?

One fall evening, I was walking my Labrador Retriever, Calvin, when suddenly we came upon some leaf bags blowing in the wind. Mr. Confidence himself suddenly crouched in fear, ran behind my legs and started woofing at the unusual sight. Instead of petting him, I let the leash go slack and walked forward to investigate the bags by myself. Slowly he crept up, paused, stretched his body long with his nose extended, and then pounced on the bags as if to say, "I wasn't afraid of these dumb old bags anyway!"

You can help your dog overcome his fears.

My dog refuses to walk over grates.

Bring your dog at your side toward a grate. Let the leash go slack and go sit by the grate, treats in hand or in your snack pack. Sitting with your back to your dog, pretend to eat his snacks or play with his toy. When your dog comes to join you, reward him calmly. It may take weeks before he'll walk over a grate, but your efforts will be worth the reward. If you absolutely have to walk over a grate with your dog, do it and do it quickly. No eye contact, no silly voices, just say BUDDY, HEEL and move quickly across the area. Worrying about your dog's reaction will only increase his anxiety, and some things just can't be avoided.

My five-month-old puppy has developed a fear of people in uniform.

I can relate to that. I still get a little nervous about uniforms myself! To help him overcome his fear, act very friendly toward uniformed people. Put your puppy on his leash, instruct HEEL and let him greet the person from a safe place by your heels. Ask this person to shake a treat cup and reward your pup's enthusiasm. Put peanut butter on their shoe to encourage your puppy's approach. Use a click and treat any time your puppy is showing confidence. If the person is especially cooperative, ask them to kneel and avoid eye contact until your dog has thoroughly sniffed them. Another great trick is to rent a uniform from a costume shop and dress up in one yourself.

IMPRESSING YOUR VETERINARIAN

I'll let you in on a secret: Veterinarians love a well-behaved dog. It makes their job a lot easier. To impress yours, do the following:

1. Walk your dog in at HEEL. Use WAIT at all doors.
2. Bring his favorite mat and toys for the waiting room, instruct SETTLE DOWN.

3. While waiting, place the mat at your side and give your dog his favorite chew.

4. Instruct WAIT as you go into the examination room together, to keep him focused.

5. Place your mat on the examination table (your dog will feel happy and secure, and there's no clean-up). Use peanut butter or cream cheese to keep your dog busy and cheerful while he's being examined.

My dog is very suspicious of receptionists and growls whenever one approaches her.

Set up a practice run and ask the receptionist to meet you outside. Give her your treat cup to shake and ask her to kneel without making eye contact with your dog. When your dog approaches, have the receptionist reward with treats. Repeat this procedure at the threshold of the office and once more inside.

My dog gets on the seat next to me and looks threateningly at everyone who passes.

What is he doing on the seat? He's not a person! By letting him sit at your level, you're encouraging him to assume a protective role. Instead, put him under your legs or on a mat and ignore him. If he growls, quicktug him back and tell him THAT'S UNACCEPTABLE. Then, direct him with SIT-STAY and praise all cooperation. If you're still having problems, refer to Chapter 8 or call a professional trainer.

GOING FOR AN OVERNIGHT VISIT

Taking your dog with you on an overnight visit can be a lot of fun. Or it can be a disruptive nightmare. It's all up to you. Yes you! Here are some basic guidelines for your predeparture planning.

- Pack your dog's favorite mat, bed or crate.
- Snack pack and treats are a must! Use them to reinforce everything your dog is doing right.
- Don't forget some favorite chewies or toys to help your dog displace any tension.
- Bring the props for a familiar game, such as canine soccer or fetch. Everyday games help your dog feel connected.

- Leashes are important; you don't want your dog to get lost. Bring a regular leash for everyday stuff and a long line for a supervised romp. (If you're going on a long visit, get an ID tag with the local phone number.)
- Bowls, food and water are obvious necessities.
- Last, but not least, bring a radio. Yes, a radio; it drowns out any unfamiliar sounds and soothes his anxiety while you're out.

When you arrive, if you're going to do any heavy greeting leave your dog in the car with the radio playing. Overly enthusiastic hellos can start things off on a hyper note.

Use your words to stay connected: HEEL for walking on leash, SIT-STAY for greeting, WAIT at the doors, SETTLE DOWN to direct your dog to his mat and toys.

 **Mozart, Please**

When you turn on the radio, try to find a classical station. Hip-hop or heavy metal can be a little jarring!

Go to your room and set up your dog's sleeping station or crate while you keep him busy with treats and a chew toy. Then set up the radio next to his area.

If possible, avoid leaving immediately. After setting up the bedroom, walk around the outside perimeters of the room and play a familiar game. End with an upbeat five-minute lesson, using your clicker and treats to keep the focus on you and the mood happy.

When you must leave your dog, place him in his area calmly with a chew toy and turn on the radio. Make sure you depart calmly (no overly theatrical guilt-trip scenes, please) and arrive in the same fashion.

My friends have two dogs. How should we introduce them?

Bringing your dog into another dog's home can spark a fierce territorial reaction. Have your friend and his dog meet you at a neutral location instead, such as an empty playground or a field — at the very least, outside the house in a yard or on the sidewalk. When the dogs meet, let the leashes drop. If you're concerned your dog will bolt, attach a long line rather than hold the leash. Many dogs feel trapped when the leashes tighten, causing an aggressive response where one may not be warranted. Expect a lot of threat bluffs, such as growling, mouthiness and mounting. It's natural, so don't overreact; your interference might prompt a fight. Stay calm and observe closely. The dogs must determine a hierarchy, and once that's accomplished they'll settle down. If you're certain a fight has begun, separate them calmly with their leashes or pour a bucket of water over their heads. If you're at a loss and there are two of you, you may try to pull them apart by grasping the base of their tails. As a general rule, don't handle fighting dogs, especially when you're alone.

We are staying at my in-laws and they have two young children. What's the best way to introduce my dog?

Bring your treat cup and jingle jar! When you arrive, let your dog out and calm him down before meeting and greeting anyone. Have the kids shake his treat cup, direct him with familiar words and reward him.

If you anticipate or sense any aggression, do not socialize your dog with the children. Seek professional help immediately!

My dog barks every time I'm out of sight.

Poor thing! He's frightened. Whatever you do, avoid discipline, as it will heighten his fear. Next, do a quick lesson with food and praise as his rewards. Run through a few practice departures. Station your dog on a mat, turn the radio on, leave a chew and a toy and tell him WAIT as you leave for a couple of minutes. If you come back to an anxious dog, ignore him until he settles down. When he does, praise him warmly and offer a treat. Continue making short departures until he stays calm.

When you must leave, contain him (in a crate, gated room or station) with familiar toys and blankets, and don't forget the radio. If he's anxious when you return, ignore him until he's calm. It will only take a few minutes, I promise!

Chapter 7

Your Off-Lead Companion

Having a well-trained off-lead dog is definitely all it's cracked up to be. But as you work toward off-lead control, you'll be put to the test. Yes you! The hardest thing to control won't be your dog, it will be your temper. To be a good off-leash teacher, you have to stay cool. Frustration kills trust. Think of you, your dog and the leash as a three-part equation. You and your dog have relied on the leash for guidance. Once you start letting it go, one third of the dynamic is missing. It's a given that your dog's behavior will be affected. But if you get impulsive or lose your cool, your dog will learn to stay away when the leash disappears.

Keep your dog in a confined area while you practice. If she should sass you and run off, you'll be able to disappear calmly and not worry about her safety. Remember, a graceful departure does not equal defeat. When you first drop the leash, your dog may get distracted, not out of spite but from excitement. If you fall into the trap of chasing or correcting your dog, she may remain unfooled by or skeptical of your off-lead control forever.

Remember that all the exercises in this chapter assume that your dog already knows the basics you taught her in Chapters 4 and 5. If she doesn't, back up and make sure you both feel comfortable with those skills before you try any off-lead work.

OFF-LEAD PSYCHOLOGY

As you work through the following lessons, continue to encourage, praise and reward good efforts. Off lead, your dog will be a little confused; the tool you have used to guide her is missing! Encourage every attempt to look to

> ### 🐾 The Big Goal
>
> The goal of off-lead training is not to have a dog who will stay with you, it's to have a dog who *wants* to stay with you!

you for direction and she will feel safe and trusting, not nervous and out of control. Snack packs and sound markers (YES or the clicker) should still be used, especially in the early stages.

🐾 Your Mindset

We humans are a control-oriented bunch. We want our dogs to come when called, stay calm in exciting situations and control their fun-loving, mischief-making impulses. But off-lead, dogs think "play, explore, chase!" They are either terrified of or unimpressed by human frustration.

Teaching off lead takes a lot of concentration, self-control and focus. And I'm not just talking about your dog! To be a good teacher, look at the situation through her eyes. By understanding her perspective, you'll be able to perk up the exercises in this chapter to encourage her participation. Once you know when to animate your exercises and when to stand firm, you'll have a dog who stays close and follows your direction in no time!

As for you, keep these three suggestions in mind:

1. **Detach:** When you first start weaning your dog off lead, you may feel like you're taking steps backwards. Your dog may not respond as quickly. She may look at you with a clueless expression, like she's never met you before or doesn't understand you. Don't get disheartened, tense or flustered. Off leash is a transition for your dog, too, and it's natural for her to hesitate. Don't take it personally. I know, detaching yourself is more a meditation exercise than a dog training technique, but if you get impatient, you'll seem high-strung. Dogs (like people) like fun, confident leaders. The calmer you are, the cooler you are, the more confident you will seem. Detach. Although you may think all your effort has been a waste of time, it hasn't.

A voluntary check-in. YES!

2. **Watch that eye contact:** Eye contact communicates control. If you look to your dog more than she looks to you, her perception is that you need a plan. To avoid this disaster, make sure you work in a confined area so that you can ignore your dog when she disobeys or tries to get your attention. A graceful retreat is not a failure.

3. **Fall back:** Well-mannered, off-lead dogs don't develop overnight. Like everything else, it's a process. If you or your dog is having an off day, practice on leash. If there's too much excitement or stress, on goes

the leash. Using it helps control the situation while simultaneously conditioning more appropriate behavior. There's no right or wrong, good or bad; no "have-to" in the journey you're on with your dog. The leash is like holding a person's hand — and we all could use a little hand-holding when life gets distracting.

NEW EQUIPMENT FOR LEARNING RIGHT

Off-lead behavior won't emerge overnight. Like everything else, it's a step-by-step process. What follows are the tools you'll need to increase your dog's focus, but don't get itchy fingers. Just because she behaves well on her Flexi-leash one day doesn't mean she's ready for an off-lead romp the next. Take your time. It's gradual. Step by step.

I'll explain how to use each piece of equipment in this chapter. While the exercises are explained separately, you can use the equipment interchangeably.

- **Long line:** This line can range in length from 25 to 50 feet. You'll use this for distance control with the WAIT, HEEL, DOWN and COME commands. You can buy a commercial line, or use a clothesline and a heavy-duty clip. Tie a big knot in your long line that you can step on or grab if your dog darts away.

- **Flexi-leash:** This retractable leash is invaluable for advanced work, but it is generally not strong enough to pull a dog away from a dangerous situation (depending on the size of the dog, of course). So for safety reasons, don't use it on the street or in areas with traffic.

- **Tree station:** You will be attaching this line to a tree to practice long-distance STAY control. Buy a long canvas leash, or make your own out of clothesline and a heavy-duty clip.

- **Indoor drag lead:** I explained this one on page 46. It's for inside control, and should be 4 to 10 feet long.

- **Short lead:** This training tool should be long enough to grab but short enough that it doesn't distract your dog.

Attach all lines to your dog's buckle collar or Gentle Leader — *not* her training collar.

USING THE LONG LINE

If I had to pick just one off-lead teaching tool, the long line would be it. Depending on your dog's size and speed, the line should be from 25 to 50 feet and made of a light nylon or cotton mesh. Clip it to your dog's collar when she's in an enclosed outdoor area and allow her to roam freely while you walk around,

basically ignoring her. Remember, the less you look at her, the more she'll look to you. Look interested in other things and she'll show interest in you.

The Check-In

Each time your dog walks within two feet of you, say YES or click and reward her. Soon you'll notice that she checks in often — and not because you're screaming for her, but because she makes the choice. If your dog doesn't come over to you, pick up a stick or toy and play with it. She won't be able to resist. Mark and reward her arrival.

Name

When your dog is poking around, moderately distracted, pick up the line and call her name, DAISY! If she doesn't respond, quicktug the line. When she checks in, say YES! End it there. If she returns to you, reward her, but the return is not mandatory. Checking in is a must!

Wait

Use this to teach your dog to stop in her tracks. When your dog is moving away from you, stand next to the long line, say WAIT and step on the line. The moment your dog pauses and looks back to you, say YES and release with OK.

Sit

When your dog is at a distance, how can you enforce the SIT command? When first giving this cue, use a treat or a toy. Start with WAIT to get your dog to pause at a distance, then SIT, then toss the toy as a reward. If your dog doesn't listen, don't get mad. Calmly go to your dog and position her. When she does respond, mark it enthusiastically with one strong YES!

 Don't Forget the Rewards

Off lead, your dog will suddenly have a whole host of new distractions, new possibilities and new freedoms. Scents drift in the air. Sounds that were shadowed by your voice suddenly take on new clarity. Just because you spent weeks articulating the basics, don't overestimate your influence. If your dog loves food or lives for a toy, bring it with you when you're starting out. Sound markers (YES or the clicker) help cheer your dog on.

Long line freedom, long line control.

Down

Once you've got SIT, mix in a DOWN from time to time. Make it a prelude to a toss of the ball or a treat. Same rules apply: Give the direction once, and if your dog doesn't listen, position her.

Although you may have told your dog NOPE for ignoring a direction on her regular leash, avoid saying it in the early stages of off-lead work. The transition is stressful enough.

Come

Remember the COME Fronts from Chapter 5? Saying COME when your dog is close to you teaches her that it means togetherness, not separation. Well, back we go for the first few lessons! Each time your dog is close, stand tall and signal her attention to your eyes as you say COME! Reward her and let her go back to playing with OK.

Next, stand at different distances, pick up the line and say her name, DAISY, then COME as you run away from her (yes, away from her). Your enthusiasm will excite her and COME will have a big draw. When she gets to you, draw her focus up to your eyes and reward her big time.

A Real Lifesaver

It's true! The Emergency DOWN really does save lives. Even I have a story to tell. I was leaving my training classes with my Husky, Kyia, when a tennis ball slipped loose from my pocket and started rolling toward the busy road. Kyia, sweet thing, wanted to help and ran innocently to collect it. In a panic I shouted DOWN and she dropped like she'd been shot. What a good girl! She got a few extra biscuits during the car ride home.

USING THE FLEXI-LEASH

This is a good teaching tool. Dogs love the extra freedom, and their increasing distance gives you the opportunity to practice your lessons. Use it informally during walks to reinforce the commands that follow. But don't rely on it when you're on a busy street. It is not strong enough to totally restrain most dogs, and the line can get tangled around legs.

Name

Call out your dog's name enthusiastically, DAISY! If she looks to you, praise her. That's all that's required. Just a glance. If she ignores you, quicktug the line — and praise her once you've got her attention.

Wait

Say WAIT to instruct a sudden halt. If your dog continues forward, quicktug the line and say NOPE, WAIT.

Sit-Stay

Practice some distance control by asking your dog to SIT, then STAY. Increase your distance from her incrementally. As you leave your dog, the Flexi-leash adds resistance to the collar, so condition your dog with the Tug Test (see page 110) before you try this.

Heel

Use HEEL to call your dog back to your side. Call her name, then say HEEL as you slap your leg and walk toward her. Mark the moment your dog circles back to your side and reward her enthusiastically. Walk on with her at HEEL, and vary the distance.

Nope

Use sparingly and only when your dog has alerted to something inappropriate. Your dog's ears will show you where her attention is, so watch carefully! If her ears are pitched forward, notice what's riveting her attention and, if appropriate, quicktug the Flexi-leash and say NOPE! Immediately refocus her attention with a command or a toy.

Emergency Down

This exercise can be a real lifesaver! It harkens back to dog pack behavior, when the leader signals the group to quickly seek cover, and should be used as no less of an emergency in our world.

1. Stand next to your unsuspecting dog.
2. Suddenly command DOWN in a very life-or-death tone (the tone you'd use if a loved one were about to walk off a cliff).
3. Kneel down quickly as you bring your dog into position.
4. Wait a moment, then release with OK.
5. If you're using a clicker and food, you can lure and mark quick DOWNs. Phase out treating and rewards within five days.

Soon your dog will catch on and will begin to comply on her own. Once she does, begin extending your distance from her. This is a serious life-or-death

The Emergency DOWN says, "Hit the dirt!"

direction, and is rarely given at close range. This exercise could save your dog's life if you two are ever separated by an oncoming vehicle.

This exercise is very stressful! Limit your practice to two sessions of three Emergency DOWN sequences each week.

USING THE TREE STATION

You may tie your long line or a 15-foot leash to the base of a tree or post, making sure all knots are secure. Leave the line on the ground and follow this sequence:

1. Warm up with five minutes of regular on-leash practice. Stop your dog next to the tree station and attach the line discreetly to your dog's buckle collar.

2. Remove her regular lead and place it on the ground in front of her. Keep your hands free.

3. Say SIT and STAY and walk out 10 feet. Extend your distance as she gains control.

4. Run your fingers through your hair and swing your arms gently back and forth to emphasize that your dog is off lead.

5. If she falls for this and darts for a quick getaway, wait until she's about to hit the end of the line and shout NOPE! Return her to her position, keeping calm, cool and collected, and repeat the exercise at closer range.

Secure your dog to a station and you can really work on the long-distance STAY.

🐾 Motivation Matters

When your dog disobeys, try to figure out from her body language if she's motivated by anxiety, confusion or defiance. If she's confused or anxious, let it go. Calmly return to her side and reposition her gently. Repeat the same exercise at close range. If your dog breaks defiantly, however, say NOPE as she hits the end of the line. Reposition her and repeat the exercise at close range.

6. As your dog improves, practice an out-of-sight SIT-STAY.

7. Practice DOWN from a SIT-STAY and a DOWN-STAY.

Encourage her good reactions with a sound marker and a reward.

USING THE INDOOR DRAG LEAD

Place the 10-foot lead on your dog when she is indoors and you can watch her. Every couple of minutes, stand by the line and give a command (SIT, DOWN, WAIT, COME). When she responds, mark the moment with YES or a click and reward her. If she looks confused, step on the line and calmly say NOPE. Recommand enthusiastically and help her into position.

For example, if you command DOWN and she gives you a blank stare, say NOPE and recommand as you guide her into position. Always praise your dog when she is in the right position, regardless of her initial cooperation. Your understanding will help her overcome any off-lead confusion.

USING THE SHORT LEAD

Once your dog is responding to the drag lead, progress to a short lead. Attach it to your dog's buckle collar and use it to reinforce the stationary commands SIT, STAY, DOWN and WAIT, and the proper position for HEEL and COME.

Three times a week, bring your dog into a quiet room and practice a command routine. At first hold the short lead, but then drop it once you've warmed up. Slap your leg, lure her with

A short-lead application for HEEL.

food if she seems confused and use hand signals and peppy body language to encourage your dog's focus. If your dog drifts or lags, calmly pick up the line and

guide her. Jerking motions to grasp the leash will cause her to shy away, so just be smooth!

OFF-LEAD WRAP-UP

As you work through these exercises with your dog, keep in mind that she's trying to read and anticipate your behavior just as you are trying to anticipate hers. Think for a minute. If I were to ask your dog to describe you, what would she say? "Fun to be around, happy, confident and in control." Or would she say, "Impatient, scary to get close to when I'm off-lead, easily fooled or unsure"?

Your dog has an opinion of you and responds to you accordingly. Make a good impression. Stand tall, direct her confidently and don't be afraid to have a little fun. That's what having an off-lead dog is all about!

 Risky Business

Allowing even the best dog off lead in an unconfined area is a risk. It's better to let your dog free in enclosed areas and keep her safe from traffic and unnecessary accidents by using a leash everywhere else.

When will I know that I can trust my dog off lead?

You should feel it. It's like learning to ride a bike or play a new sport. It's usually not a smooth road in the beginning; some days you'll get a quick and happy response, other days will feel more like your first day of lessons. Stay cool, though. Frustration is a sign of weakness and will diminish your control. Keep your dog in an enclosed area as you practice so that if she starts to act cocky, you can retreat immediately. And don't hesitate to go back to long-line or on-leash exercises for a quick review.

It's so frustrating when my dog ignores me. I feel like I'm going to explode! I want to hit him.

Feeling like hitting something is fine. Hitting your dog is not. It would erode your relationship and diminish his off-lead trust. If you're really angry, walk away calmly. Remember: Retreat is not failure.

My dog breaks every time I leave him in a SIT-STAY on his Flexi-leash.

Did you practice the Tug Test? Pivot in front of your dog and tug forward gently as you remind STAY. Once you've done that, increase your distance slowly. For example, if your dog breaks every time you walk out 15 feet, then practice at 10 feet for a week. Gradually move up to 11 feet, 12 feet and so on. In addition, don't face your dog as you walk out. Walking backward invites a COME response. Instead, walk out confidently, with your back to your dog, and pivot at your final destination. Remind STAY.

Don't the lines get caught around trees and doors?

Yes, they do. Clip all lines to the buckle collar or Gentle Leader and never leave your dog unsupervised with a line or leash on.

When I shout NOPE on the tree station, my dog crouches down and barks at me. I find it hard not to laugh.

Don't laugh! You'll be undermining your efforts and teaching your dog that when you're separated, the games begin. Instead, close shop (cross your arms and look away). Completely ignore her and wait until she's through with her silly display. When she calms down, take her back to her original position and repeat an easier version of the same exercise. If she just won't quit, place her on the leash and do some beginner exercises before calling it a day.

When I go to correct my dog, she stays just out of reach.

Watch that body language and negative eye contact. Being off the leash is as nerve-wracking for her as it is for you. Look at the ground as you return to your dog. If she's still out of reach, kneel down and wait. When she approaches, take her collar gently, reposition calmly and work at close range.

> ### 🐾 Grounded!
>
> If your dog gives you some defiant canine back-talk (a bark or a dodge), step on the lead, tug it firmly as you say NOPE, and station and ignore her for 15 minutes. She's been grounded with no TV.

My dog picks the long line up in her mouth and prances around me like a show horse.

Clever girl! She's found a way to get your attention. First, ignore her. Play with a stick or one of her favorite toys, refusing to share it until she drops the line and sits. Keep her focused on objects other than you and on listening for directions. If all else fails, pick up the line as far from her body as possible and reel her in. Try soaking the end of the line in Grannick's Bitter Apple or Tabasco sauce overnight, so having it in her mouth is a lot less fun. If she's still acting cocky, quietly go inside and watch her discreetly from the window.

When I place my dog on the short lead, I can't get near her.

You'll need to work on your drag lead for another week or so. When you try the short lead again, attach the drag line to the handle of the short lead and urge her cooperation by focusing on good behavior and controlling her by stepping on the drag lead if she darts away.

Chapter 8

The Encyclopedia of Canine Etiquette

If only I had a dog biscuit for every time I hear the phrase, "My dog knows he's been bad!" Solving behavior problems requires the highest level of creativity and understanding. You need to see the issues from your dog's point of view. Most dogs don't consider their behavior to be bad, especially when it gets them more attention, relieves anxiety or causes a change in the environment (bark at the scary letter carrier and he disappears). Your dog's misbehavior results from the stress of not understanding who is in charge and what's expected of him. A confusing dilemma. Poor doggie! Let's help yours out by pretending you're my client.

The first thing I always have my clients do is make a list of what they love about their dog. (So take out paper and pen and make your list now.) Although the list may be short, it's never blank. Next, I have them list their frustrations. (You keep writing too!) "I can't housetrain my dog." "He digs up the backyard and barks at passersby." "He chases the cat and knocks the kids down." "He chews everything he can get his mouth on."

From here we work to create a program that is as much about restructuring the dog's surroundings and day-to-day interactions as it is about a specific issue. I teach them, as I will teach you, that a frustration, whether it's housebreaking, chewing or jumping never develops in a vacuum. All problems are a mix of the interactions between a dog and his environment. And I think you'll conclude, as my clients do (always with a smile on their face), that solving problems is a learning process for people as well as dogs. In fact, I believe this so strongly that I've put it under my name on my business card:

Simply Sarah
Simply Sarah Inc.
PO Box 420
Bedford, N Y 10506

Sarah Hodgson
Teaching Dogs, Training People

As we address your specific issues, make a four-column chart and share it with friends and family. In the first column detail your frustration. In the next column list your goals. Then decide on the words you'll use in training, and finally the routines and lessons you'll follow. For example, for housebreaking:

Frustration	Goal	Words	Routine
I just wish my dog would stop peeing on the carpet and let us know when he needs to go out.	Peeing outside	OUTSIDE	Supervise him in the house, keeping him on a leash or in a small room or crate.
	Signal he needs to go out	GET BUSY	Restrict attention until after he has peed outside in the designated area.
		YES!	Stick to a specific routine: Go to one door saying OUTSIDE; ring a bell hanging on the door; open the door and go to a predetermined area close to the door; say GET BUSY while he goes; say YES or click and reward with attention or food.

Remind everyone that consistency is a must. Communicating what you consider to be good behavior boils down to helping your dog reorganize his priorities according to your plan. For your dog to start changing, he has to respect and understand you and everyone else involved in his care.

Many of the following solutions use techniques from Chapters 3 through 7. Please read them as needed.

AGGRESSION

Aggression is an interesting phenomenon. For the dog, it's adaptive. Aggression grows out of a need for order. And order in the dog's world is based not on democracy, but on a hierarchy where every team member has a specific rank. This concept of hierarchy is central to canine psychology. Your dog views you and your family as dogs, and the whole of you as a group. If you think of your group as a team, every team needs a captain. If your efforts don't convey that you're in charge, your dog will have no other option than to assume this position himself.

The position of leader is not taken over lightly. The leader takes on multiple responsibilities, from patrolling the territory to being responsible for the safety and whereabouts of each member of the group. Imagine the mental concern of a dog who perceives himself in charge and yet is left alone eight hours a day! Or a passive dog who nervously tries to keep everything organized and suddenly finds a strange, hyper child in his face. The role of group leader can be nerve-wracking, especially when, in reality, your dog has so little control of your world.

Although many people are embarrassed to admit to it, most dogs show aggression in some situations, whether with their owners, strangers, other dogs or furry little tidbits running around the backyard. If you're dealing with an aggression problem, you're not alone. Aggression is a normal form of canine communication, similar to human frustration or anger.

There are breeds more prone to aggression, and bossy puppies have a greater likelihood of asserting themselves as adults, but aggression is seen in dogs of every personality type, from strong to fearful, and in every breed. There are no hard and fast rules here. If a dominant puppy is not given the proper instruction from his owners, or a passive puppy is coddled too much, both will develop an

 Don't Add to the Problem

If you've got an aggressive dog, please spay or neuter the dog. It will help reduce the dog's aggression, and it's the responsible thing to do. Aggression toward humans is a genetic trait, and you wouldn't wish your situation on anyone else.

In addition, 10 million pets are put down each year because there are not enough homes for them. Ten million! That's 165 times the number of people who fill the stadium for the Super Bowl each year. Unless you're a responsible breeder, do the right thing and make sure your dog doesn't add any offspring to this statistic.

over-inflated sense of themselves. Both will grow up with the idea that their humans are subservient and in need of a leader to provide direction and control. When those same owners try to direct their dog or discipline him, the dog sees his owners as stepping out of line and thinks they must be reprimanded like a delinquent child. Since dogs can't send naughty owners to their room, they may snap, growl or bite. Same concept, different communication.

This, however, is not the only type of aggression. Aggression comes in many forms. The next section describes in depth eight categories of aggression and how you can begin to understand, resolve and, if possible, prevent it.

Eight Types of Aggression

This section deals with the many forms of aggression. It is a serious and sober topic. If you're having a problem, get professional help! Seek a well-known and respected canine behaviorist or trainer in your area. Your veterinarian may be able to recommend someone.

My recommendations are just that — recommendations. Do not follow them if you are unsure whether they apply to your situation. Stop in your tracks if your dog is making you scared or growling at another member of your family. *Aggression, if approached incorrectly or with caution or fear, can result in a serious bite.*

- **Dominant aggression:** In the hierarchy of the home, this dog is boss. He goes where he wants, when he wants. Although he may respect a strong member of the household, he'll assert himself over anyone small or soft. Step out of line and try to direct a dominant dog and watch out — you may get bitten!

- **Territorial aggression:** This dog is protective of his property, home, yard and/or car, and considers it his responsibility to determine who comes near and who goes away.

- **Protective aggression:** Some people consider it honorable that their dog defends them, but when it's against the letter carrier or a friendly neighbor, the situation must be re-assessed.

- **Predatory aggression:** Many dogs can't resist a good chase. If this behavior is not controlled, it may spill over to other pets, children and the wheels of cars and bicycles — and eventually, to anything that moves.

- **Spatial aggression:** This dog views himself as boss and would prefer no interruptions when eating food, resting or chewing on a toy or bone.

- **Fear-induced aggression:** A passive dog who (by default) views himself as in charge will tend to react aggressively when stressed. What he really wants is a leader to interpret the situation and protect him.

- **Dog-to-dog aggression:** Dogs aren't hippie-like in their attitudes. They have strong likes and dislikes. Dog-to-dog aggression results when dogs don't see eye to eye. It is also influenced by human interaction, both in multi-dog households and day-to-day meetings with other dogs on the street. In addition, if your dog thinks he's your leader, the body language and interest of another dog may spark a protective reaction.

- **Psychotic aggression:** This dog shows erratic or fearful responses in very atypical situations, and will be unpredictable. Most, though not all dogs in this category, are the result of poor breeding or early stress.

A Closer Look at Dominant Aggression

The potential for developing this type of aggression can usually be seen in puppyhood. An active pup who steals clothing for fun, barks for attention, leans against his owners when in new environments or around strangers or successfully solicits attention whenever the mood strikes him, is dominant. Although the aggression may never surface, all too often it does. And when it does, the problem lies not with the dog, who thinks his leadership qualities are appreciated, but with the owners, who must now assert themselves to solve the problem.

ADVICE ON DOMINANT AGGRESSION

In essence, you must stop being the servant and become the leader.

- Use EXCUSE ME if your dog leans against you, presses a toy to your body or blocks your path. Thank him for getting out of the way.

- Consider using a Gentle Leader head collar. The pressure it puts over the muzzle and behind the ears is at acupressure points that communicate your dominance passively. Don't miss the opportunity.

- Create stations in every room you share with your dog. No getting on the furniture until the hierarchy is rearranged, and then only with permission. Station your dog to the side of a room and reward him for settling down. No sharing your bed for now; create a station there, too.

- Teach your dog to WAIT at every door or threshold or staircase, because leaders always lead. Feed him just twice a day and use WAIT (on leash, if necessary) to enforce self-control.

- Practice a 5- to 10-minute lesson from Chapter 5, using your enthusiasm and rewards to motivate your dog's happy cooperation. HEEL and DOWN are especially important.

In addition, you must:

- Ignore your dog's attempts to get your attention. Close shop (crossing your arms and looking to the sky) if he paws, jumps, whines or stares at you when you're busy. If he's too physically annoying to ignore, review other options in the Jumping section of this chapter. Review the Leading and Stationing exercises in Chapter 3 and begin them immediately.

- Train your dog to keep off the furniture until he's more respectful. I can hear some of you whining, but this is not an option. Leave a short leash on your dog to move him off the sofa or bed (physical maneuvering may spark an aggressive response). Create stations and use them.

- Diminish the constant petting and staring rituals by 80 percent. Constant attention from you communicates subservience and a need for direction. Use all the self-control you can muster!

- Do not look at your dog unless he has responded to you. If you want to pet him when he comes over, instruct SIT or DOWN. No free body rubs on demand. (Imagine a loved one interrupting your meal for a quick back massage. I don't think so!) You're a servant no more!

If your dog growls during any of these efforts, such as when you move him out of your way, don't push it. *Stop everything until you get professional help. Your problem is serious.*

 ### Shelter Dogs, Small Dogs

There are lots of things that influence aggression. Is your dog from a shelter? Shelter dogs all suffer from shelter shock — the experience of being locked in a cage in someplace unfamiliar. No matter how proactive a shelter is, it's not the same as a loving home.

Some former shelter dogs may be possessive around food and/or territorial about your home. I know this from personal experience, having adopted four of my last five dogs from shelters. I'm not discouraging adoption, but do be mindful of a dog's experiences, be sympathetic and get ready to do your homework.

Small dogs suffer, too. To them many things are overwhelming, from bending over them to picking them up when they're anxious or afraid. Every dog has a unique personality and history that affects the way he behaves. Consider life from your dog's paws.

A Closer Look at Territorial Aggression

Dogs who act threatening when strangers approach their home turf are territorial. This problem is encouraged by:

- Passive or placating owners. Lovely people, but too soft for many protective dogs, who consider their territorial behavior as necessary for the group's survival.

- When delivery people approach and leave the home territory, the dog thinks he drove them away and his aggression is reinforced.

- When the owners are home and react to a territorial response by yelling or physical handling. A dog can't understand this in human terms and concludes that the situation must be very suspicious for his owners to react this way.

- When a dog reacts aggressively at home, in a car, along a fence line or on a tie-out, he is warning all intruders to stay away. Since most people and other animals passing by go away anyway, he considers himself victorious and his territorial aggression is reinforced.

- When dogs are isolated during greetings or visits, they may develop frustrated territorial aggression. Not good. In a normal group of dogs, the leader permits or denies entry to a visitor, who is then sniffed out by the rest of the pack. Isolation frustrates this normal process and will encourage a more assertive response the next time the doorbell rings.

ADVICE ON TERRITORIAL AGGRESSION

Territorial dogs feel their efforts are warranted and appreciated within the group. To reclaim order and command their respect, you must be assertive. Not mean, but assertive. For many of my clients, this sense of authority does not come naturally, but resolving this issue is not optional.

To assert yourself:

- Practice Chapter 5 lessons daily, preferably twice a day, to communicate your willingness to take charge.

- Keep your dog with you, secured on a leash or at least dragging one. Leaving him outside alone for hours tells him he must play the role of protector.

- Review Stationing and Leading in Chapter 3. Either lead him or secure him at a station set up to the side of each room. No getting on the furniture for now.

- Consider using a Gentle Leader. This collar reduces the negative restraint around the neck and places your dog's body in a submissive posture.

- Use EXCUSE ME to clarify your position as leader. If your dog leans, steps on, blocks or asserts himself in front of you, say EXCUSE ME and move him to the side or bring him behind you.

- Leave a leash on your dog. Practice the basic words in Chapter 4 and use the leash to control barking and assertive behavior. Interfere after two barks with a quicktug and a positive recall back to your side. Praise and treat your dog for compliance.

- Leash your dog when people arrive. Use BACK if he crowds the door or visitors. If need be, station your dog until he calms down. When people approach, keep your dog behind you and do not give him any attention until his tension is reduced. Use the treat cup or jingle jar to help associate company with positive rewards.

- No more yelling or physical corrections. Both make matters seem more threatening than they are. To calm your dog, set the serene example.

A Closer Look at Protective Aggression

This dog thinks his job is to protect his owner from other people and dogs. Even away from his territory, he will react aggressively if anyone approaches. It is not uncommon for dogs to develop this sort of relationship with a young child or a passive, inexperienced owner. The owner — man, woman or child — is perceived as weak and in need of protection.

ADVICE ON PROTECTIVE AGGRESSION

Both you and your dog need training. You must learn how to take charge, especially when other people and dogs are around. It's time to assert your authority and prove to your dog that you're not only capable of protecting yourself, you're capable of protecting him too!

- Gentle Leaders really help. Requiring little strength, they lead your dog in a naturally submissive posture. Pressure on the lead also closes their mouth should a stranger surprise you.

- Practice Chapter 5 lessons daily, preferably twice a day. Teach your dog that you'll give direction from now on. Once you've mastered the lessons at home, practice them in the far end of a parking lot (away from people) and slowly progress into town. Emphasize STAY, DOWN and HEEL.

- Watch your dog's ears! The ears are his antennae and their position is a sign of dominance or insecurity. When the ears are upright and tight, your dog is in an assertive mode. If they're pinned flat, he's unsure and frightened.

Not So Tough

I remember a client who brought her Australian Shepard mix, Shadow, to my office. He was so aggressive I couldn't get near either of them. On a hunch, I asked her to toss me the end of the leash and, on the count of three, to run behind the back of the building. Thankfully, I was right. He didn't fall in love with me, but he went from threatening a bite to shaking in fear. Once the owner was out of sight, the dog's aggression turned into concern for her whereabouts and outright worry about my presence. No sign of aggression. Fortunately, this owner-dog team worked on a Gentle Leader and followed through with my instructions. They continued training for five weeks. The problem was eventually solved, but not without effort and dedication.

Your goal is two relaxed ears around a new situation. Use your command words to direct your dog (familiar sounds are comforting) and praise him for cooperating.

- See if a group training class is offered with an instructor who is knowledgeable about your specific issues.

- When walking around the neighborhood, keep your dog at your side. Letting him walk you conveys the wrong message. Allow quick bathroom breaks, then back to HEEL. Protective dogs are focused on body position: Whoever is in front is responsible.

- If he asserts himself or leans against you around company, tell him NOPE, THAT'S NOT YOUR JOB! Bring him back to you your side. You're the boss. You're his protector now!

A Closer Look at Predatory Aggression

Most dogs still possess a chasing instinct. Predatory aggression, however, is more intense. It borders on obsessive-compulsive behavior. If you have encouraged your dog's chasing behavior by egging him on, stop. It's not funny.

Teach your dog the meaning of NOPE, and use it whenever you notice his desire kindling. If you have a Nordic breed or terrier, the only way to totally curb their predatory instinct is to contain them, either on lead or in a fenced enclosure. After one of these dogs kills a small animal, their chasing instinct becomes stronger. This instinct, however, rarely transfers to children. For other solutions, please contact a professional.

Kill the Sprinkler

Some dogs develop predatory aggression toward strong sounds (a doorbell or weed whacker) or inanimate objects like a broom or lawn sprinkler. It sounds entertaining, but for the dog it's no laughing matter.

I have a group of three accomplished Collies I work with: Beamer, Thomas and Oz. They are all certified therapy dogs. Beamer is as steady and sweet a Collie as you could ever meet. However, to watch him transform when the sprinklers are turned on is nothing short of fascinating. He attacks those units with the gusto of a Jack Russell Terrier, pouncing and grabbing until the sprinkler system is turned off.

To resolve this issue, we had to start our lessons outside his Red Zone — the distance from which the sprinklers did not bother him. Using his clicker and treats, we slowly got closer and closer until we were actually getting wet. Each time he went into predatory mode, he heard NOPE and received a quicktug, until we were right up next to sprinkler working on SIT-STAY and DOWN. And although Beamer can control his impulse with his mom or teacher present, he still has to be brought inside at watering time.

ADVICE ON PREDATORY AGGRESSION

To discourage your dog's predatory response:

- Work through the basics in Chapters 4 and 5. Once your dog has mastered them, take him to new places where you'll seem more worldly and in charge.

- Determine your dog's Red Zone: the distance at which the distraction does not affect your dog. Work outside it initially. Gradually reduce the distance as your dog's focus improves.

- Use a training collar that issues a sharp cause-and-effect correction. The chain collar or self-correcting collar can work well if used appropriately. The instant your dog alerts to an animal or object (watch for his ears to pitch forward), quicktug the leash and say NOPE! Refocus with a familiar STAY or HEEL.

- Play the swing toy game to re-channel your dog's impulses. Take a plastic gallon milk jug and remove the lid. Slather peanut butter or cream cheese on the inside and outside of the opening and tie the handle to a 10- to 15-foot rope. Go into a field (either fenced or with your dog on a long line) and swing the toy around. Toss it into grass or bushes, keeping it moving until your dog is spent. If he likes to tug, tie toys to trees or stair banisters to encourage him to tug on something that won't come loose.

A Closer Look at Spatial Aggression

A dog who shows aggression while eating, chewing, sleeping or being groomed or cared for by a family member, stranger or other dog professional (veterinarian or groomer) is showing spatial aggression. It is usually tied in with dominant, territorial or psychotic aggression (follow the suggestions in these sections, as well).

If you adopt a dog from the shelter, you may see this behavior. It's nothing personal; just the result of living in such closed quarters where rations are prized and competition seems high.

Based on a dog's reaction when approached or handled, different levels of aggression are observed. The following description is based on a dog chewing a bone.

Level 1: Does not release the bone, tail wagging broadly. Usually seen with puppies, this dog is conflicted about sharing his prize.

Level 2: Hovers over the bone, body stiffens, tail still or short purposeful wags. "I really love you, but this is my bone and I don't want you to touch it."

Level 3: Throaty growl, tight, stiff body, may show teeth. May snap if pushed. This reaction is common in maturing dogs who may have been disciplined in the past but simply won't back down anymore. If this sounds familiar, get professional help!

Level 4: Belly growl showing teeth. This dog will quick-bite if pushed. After the bite, these dogs hover over their bone, their tail moving in short, deliberate, stress wags. Serious warning: You need professional help!

Level 5: Either a ferocious growl or lack of any vocalization, followed by a dramatic bite sequence. Continued growling and/or hovering posture over the bone until the person has left. This is a very sad situation. This dog doesn't trust anyone.

Where does your dog fit in? If it's Level 3 or above, call for help. The rest of you, read on.

 Displaced Aggression

This form of aggression is seen when a dog gets worked up and is prevented from attacking the source of his frustration (another dog, a noise or visual stimulation or a small prey animal). He settles for the closest thing, which can be your arm or another unsuspecting pet. If your dog is prone to this reaction, it's easy to see but hard to eliminate (but not impossible). Teach him to follow your direction, use a Gentle Leader (or a muzzle) when the trigger cannot be contained or avoided, and know the stress signs to prevent injury.

ADVICE ON SPATIAL AGGRESSION

Remember, this is advice is for Levels 1 and 2 only. Level 3 and up, call for professional help!

Proceed with caution. Don't freak out, beat your dog or scream. These reactions will only reinforce his notion that you're confrontational. In his mind, your dog thinks you've got prize envy. To help your dog accept you as less threatening, follow these steps. I'll use the food dish as an example:

1. Do not make a power struggle out of the feeding ritual. For example, some owners make their dog sit and wait before every meal. This is excessive and encourages food frustration. Ask your dog to SIT, but release him right away as you put the bowl down.

2. Find your dog's Red Zone. Is he OK when you're five feet from his dish but no closer? Use the suggestion below, initially working at five feet until your dog feels more comfortable.

3. Use your treat cup or jingle jar to alert your dog of your arrival. If your Red Zone is too far, stop and toss him the treats. Continue doing this until you can stand over him and drop treats into his bowl.

4. If you're using a clicker, click and treat the moment your dog lifts his head from the bowl to greet you.

5. Slowly phase out shaking the cup until you can approach his bowl calmly. When you get to his side, toss the treat into the bowl and leave.

6. Next, try kneeling down as you shake the cup and toss a treat into his bowl.

7. When this passes without tension, try placing the treat into his bowl with your hand. (Any signs of aggression? Stop. Get help.)

8. After you've offered your dog a handful of treats, try stirring the kibble with your hand.

9. If you're successful, continue this procedure once every other day for a week. Next, after offering a handful of treats, try lifting the bowl. Give it back immediately and leave. Repeat once a week only.

If at any point you are frightened or unsure, call a professional. Human fear is suspicious to dogs, and they often act aggressively. I cannot guarantee you will not get bitten in the process. Be your own judge, proceed as long as you and your dog are comfortable and call help if necessary.

PUPPY PREVENTION

To make sure your puppy gets used to occasional interruptions around her bowl, follow the procedure above as a precautionary measure. If your puppy thinks your approach means he's getting something good, he'll never be concerned!

Approach the bowl, treat cup in hand.

A Closer Look at Fear-Induced Aggression

In every litter there will be shy puppies. Mama's boys (or girls) who depend on her wisdom for safety. In human homes, these dogs continue their dependency and are often overly coddled by well-meaning people. The dog often interprets this as human insecurity. So the dog assumes leadership of the group, not because he wanted it or it was in his nature, but because no one else volunteered for the position.

Although these dogs are insecure and wary of new situations, they think their people are more scared! Their timidity, which surfaces in new situations, may turn into overwhelming fear if they're not given proper direction and support from their owners. These dogs may react aggressively due to the stress of not knowing how to handle the situation.

Although shyness is a temperamental trait, there is also a learned element to the behavior. When an owner attempts to soothe a frightened dog, the attention reinforces the fear. Additionally, when strangers or caring professionals back away from a threatening dog, the take-home message is that aggression works!

Petra

Petra is a 13-month-old Greater Swiss Mountain Dog. She's a happy dog with two loving owners. Her temperament is delightful, except for one big problem: She growls when she's approached while eating.

After questioning her owners, I discovered that Dave, her father, handled the situation by shouting and removing her food dish. But instead of solving the problem, this made it worse. I also learned that Dave had never disciplined Petra for anything else.

Poor Petra! Her growling had to do with a natural instinct to protect food. Instead of reassuring her, Dave's reaction created more fear and aggression. Poor Dave, too. He felt horrible as I explained this to him. But after two weeks of following my detailed instructions, he and his wife were able to pass close by Petra's food dish. Now, instead of growling, she wags her tail and looks for a treat.

ADVICE ON FEAR-INDUCED AGGRESSION

This problem demands a lot of understanding and patience. You cannot correct a fearful dog (you will only increase his fear) or soothe him. Your attention will reinforce the behavior.

- Teach your dog you're not weak. Practice lessons twice a day, focusing on words and exercises from Chapters 4 and 5.

- Consider using the Gentle Leader. When a dog is scared, the steady pressure across his head is more reassuring than a neck jerk or a harness hold.

- Lead your dog around your home and neighborhood to show him you know how to run the show. Reinforce WAIT at all thresholds and use EXCUSE ME if he crowds you.

- Create comfy play stations with mats and toys and a pre-secured leash. Practice 30-minute quiet times during the day. When your dog is stressed, keep him by your side. Familiar words, like HEEL, STAY and WAIT, are reassuring.

- Set the example by staying relaxed: The calmer you are, the cooler you are as a leader.

- A large part of the problem is that the fearful dog feels no one has control of the situation. Keep your dog on his leash, and act confident and secure in new situations. Encourage everyone to ignore him until he comes forward. Use your treat cup to encourage a more positive association to unfamiliar situations.

The Dog's Choice

The fascinating thing when studying aggression is that dogs really do control the level of damage they inflict. With a possible thousand pounds of pressure per square inch of their jaw, a dog makes a conscious choice if, how hard and where (body, arm or face) he wants to bite. To put it in human terms, when angered a person chooses how to confront the issue: from words to physical posturing to a push or a punch.

- If you have company visiting and your dog is afraid, keep him with you. As your dog relaxes, lay a trail of treats to your visitor's feet and end the trail in the palm of his or her hand. Another plus with visitors is to let your dog smell the visitor's hand together with yours.

A Closer Look at Dog-to-Dog Aggression

Aggression between dogs occurs when they perceive their territories as overlapping (this can happen anywhere, because some dogs think their territory is very extensive), or when there is a hierarchical struggle in a multi-dog household. It is often exaggerated by well-meaning owners who scream or pull their dog back when he is showing aggression. This only adds to the tension.

ADVICE ON DOG-TO-DOG AGGRESSION

First of all, relax! Human tension makes aggression worse! And remember, a little aggression is totally normal. Dogs don't always get along.

Now let's divide this section into two categories: in-home disputes and on-the-road bickering.

In-home disputes arise when the hierarchy of the group is undetermined or undermined. Whenever there are more than two dogs in a home, the dogs must establish a hierarchy. The leader is usually obvious, even to first-time dog owners. He or she pushes the other dog out of the way for attention, dominates toys and food and is the first to pass through doors.

This natural hierarchy is often undermined by well-intentioned humans who coddle the underdog. When this happens, the dominant dog becomes frustrated and is more prone

What About Sex?

Sex often has little to do with dogs getting along. That said, two snappy females under the same roof is the hardest situation to remedy. In every situation, the dogs must know that people are in charge of the hierarchy above all else!

A Boxer Who Doesn't Want to Be King

Rocky is a one-year-old Boxer. His people are a newly married couple. I met with Rocky and his mom, Cathy. When I arrived, Rocky came over to me in the driveway, which surprised Cathy because his usual habit was to bark, growl and then hide behind her legs. Even though there was vocalization, I could tell Rocky was unsure. As he approached, he made no effort to check on Cathy's reaction to my arrival. Friendly and chipper, Cathy reassured Rocky as she welcomed me. The first clue.

Inside, we sat around the dining room table with Rocky between us, firmly leaning on Cathy's leg. The second clue. Cathy detailed the history from picking Rocky up at the breeder at six weeks old to a wary adolescence to what she saw as a defining moment: His stay at the veterinarian when he was neutered at seven months old. After that, she noticed an approach-avoid pattern with company and a growing concern with new situations.

When I asked her how she handled his caution, she illustrated by leaning in and telling Rocky everything would be OK. The third clue.

An incident at a local playground two days before my visit had her very worried. Rocky snapped at a child. Cathy was bent over holding Rocky in her arms, her face pressed into his, when a child approached quickly from the side. Though no contact was made, the child startled Rocky and he snapped the air. The fourth and final clue. I outlined the issues.

Rocky is an innately sensitive dog who has assumed the role of leader and protector by default. Early separation from his primary family left him feeling overwhelmed and unsure. (Many canine behaviorists now say 12 weeks is a better time to separate a puppy from this mother and littermates.) Cathy and her husband John's innocent and smothering "first-child" love for Rocky was translated as submissive puppy play. As Rocky matured, he viewed their constant affection as subordinate, and although he had no innate drive to dominate, he had no other choice. One of them *had to* be the leader.

From this resulted the aggression. Passive dogs exalted to the position of leader show similar patterns: the approach-avoid routine, constant leaning, the trapped look when stressed or cornered, often paired with growling.

Cathy was the one who needed the most training. Fortunately, she took on this responsibility. Outside Rocky is told to HEEL and SIT-STAY. Cathy must lead the walks and stand tall and confident when Rocky is stressed. Inside, Rocky has a quiet-time station next to (not on) the couch and a greeting station when company arrives. In addition, Cathy and Rocky are taking classes to improve his interactions with people, dogs and children. Fascinating stuff!

to fight, basically to show the humans how tough he really is. The underdog, naturally inclined to back down, now fights back to confirm the humans' expectations of him. What a mess!

To calm things down:

- Structure the house, creating stations for both dogs. Give the Top Dog the choice spots near you in each room.
- Pay more attention to the Top Dog.
- Feed, greet and play with the Top Dog first and most. Spend more time training him. The other dog will follow.
- If they fight, praise the Top Dog and ignore the other. I know this method sounds cruel, and it *is* hard (I had to do it), but trust me — it works. If you're having difficulty, bring in a professional.

On-the-road bickering often results from a lack of early socialization or inappropriate handling at the onset of maturity. Although tightening up on a leash is an instinctive human response, a tight hold heightens a dog's anxiety and turns what would normally be a curious reaction into a threatened response. And if one dog's body language is threatening, another dog will follow suit.

If you've got this problem, assess how serious it is. A training class might be the perfect solution, teaching you how to assert yourself and act as the leader when you meet another dog. For now:

- Use a Gentle Leader. It will control your dog's body naturally, tucking his head into a submissive posture. Since it requires little physical strength, even tense moments are manageable.
- Train your dog to understand that you're in charge. Work on the lessons from Chapters 4 and 5. Familiar words give your dog a sense of calm direction, especially when he is stressed.
- Keep your dog next to you when you're walking. Leaders lead and make all executive decisions for the group.
- Don't be afraid to say no when someone asks for a doggie play date or even a quick meet and greet. Not all dogs are dog friendly. My terrier mix can't stand other dogs when she's on a leash. Although that disappoints me, she came from a shelter and I'm sure she has a good reason. When she's on leash, I tell people she's not dog friendly and that's that. She needs me to speak for her, and I do. She's a super people dog and we love her just the way she is!

PUPPY PREVENTION

The next time you bring home a new puppy, enroll in a puppy class immediately. In my puppy kindergarten classes, I allow 10 minutes of off-lead play. It's a great time for the puppies to socialize with each other and with people.

A Closer Look at Psychotic Aggression

It's very rare that I come across a psychotic dog or puppy, but they do exist, and for me not to address the issue would be irresponsible. This problem is identified by erratic or fearful aggression responses in very atypical situations, which can often be traced back to early puppyhood. There are two categories:

1. **Erratic viciousness:** At unpredictable intervals, this dog or puppy will growl fiercely from his belly. It may happen when his owner passes his food bowl, approaches when he's chewing a toy or even walks by him. At other times, the dog is perfectly sweet. A Jekyll-and-Hyde personality.

2. **Fear biters:** These dogs show dramatic fear or a startled bite response to nonthreatening situations, such as their owner turning a page of the newspaper or moving an arm suddenly. They can act extremely confused or threatened when strangers approach. (Many well-educated dog people use the term "fear biter" incorrectly. There is a big difference between a dog or a puppy who bites out of fear and a fear biter. Don't automatically assume the worst if someone labels your dog with this term.)

Please don't panic if your dog occasionally growls at you or barks at the letter carrier. A lot of dogs and puppies growl when protecting a food dish or toy, and the guarding instinct is strong in many breeds. These behavioral problems can be cured or controlled with proper training. Many biters can be rehabilitated.

The situations I'm speaking of involve severe aggression: bared teeth, hard eyes, a growl that begins in the belly and a bite response you'd expect from a trained police dog. These personality disturbances are seen very early, usually by four months of age.

It's both frightening and tragic, because nothing can be done to alter this behavior. If you suspect that your puppy might have either of these abnormalities, speak to your dog's breeder and veterinarian immediately, and call a specialist to analyze the situation. These dogs must be put down. In my career, I've seen only a few cases, and all were purchased from unknown or suspect breeders.

The Last Word on Aggression

I specialize in rehabilitating aggression. Nothing gives me more pleasure than to see a situation resolved. If you have an aggressive dog, the first thing you must do is consult a professional in your area. Immediately! The dog world does not need another bite on the record books. Next, keep the little things in mind. If your dog is allowed free access to your furniture and bed, you're communicating that you're equals. Aggressive dogs don't dig equality; they need to know who is boss. If you don't assume the role, your dog will.

A Tale of Three English Cockers

The players here are three English Cocker Spaniels: GB (male, two years old), Parker (male, one year and 10 months) and the newly rescued Jennie (female, one year). The people are Mark and Dan.

What tension when I first walked into this household! Parker was belly growling and not letting Jennie walk across the floor. GB and Parker were getting into impulsive arguments over space and attention. Mark and Dan were first trying to correct, then soothe. Mark was miserable and wanted to move out. Dan (a dog hobbyist) was trying every technique he'd ever read — simultaneously!

"Stop right there," I said with a somewhat worried smile on my face. Honestly, during that first two-hour session, I had no idea if their relationships would mend (both the dogs' and the people's). The hierarchy had run amok. Everyone was bickering. And Jennie, who was recently adopted, was showing all the signs of fear aggression (probably learned in her previous home).

All the dogs received Gentle Leaders. Stations were established and routines organized. GB was obviously the Top Dog and was not to be disciplined or isolated. Parker was actually far more passive than he appeared; he was just being exalted by the humans, leaving him in a constant state of tension and as a target of GB's frustration. I told Mark and Dan to follow my daily plan to the letter and that I'd see them in a week.

Well, you couldn't wipe the smile off my face when I revisited them. The tension had evaporated. Gone! The dogs were leashed and getting along. The daily fights had subsided, save one argument when the dogs were handled by a stranger. GB was delighted to be king again, Jennie was playful and gaining confidence, and Parker, though confused, was calm and serene. At the time of this writing we're still in the process, but I know with Mark and Dan's hard work that peace is possible.

Remember that aggression is no small problem. And there are no guarantees. If your dog has bitten, you cannot be sure he won't do it again. Your effort to remedy the problem will only help, however. And in any case, this is your only option. Passing an aggressive dog on to another home or into a shelter would be irresponsible. You'd be responsible if the dog bit someone else. Get help if you need it!

BARKING

Dogs bark for lots of different reasons. They bark for attention, when they feel threatened or in defense. Sometimes dogs bark to communicate a desire to play or frustration. Vocal dogs bark at every sound they hear and every motion they see.

 **Out of Control**

A little barking goes a long way, but when it's out of control it's a clue that your hierarchy needs reshuffling. Whether your dog is barking to protect you or your home, or simply to protest or demand attention, he's assuming the leadership role. Follow the exercises in Chapters 4 and 5 to convey your authority and teach your dog how to behave, before correcting him.

But to every problem behavior, there is a human element. Understanding the role you play is the first step in solving your problem.

Prerequisite: Teach your dog the meaning of NOPE from Chapter 4, using a food level distraction in your first lesson. NOPE, when taught properly, catches the impulse and arrests the behavior. Follow the lesson to the letter. Both of you need an understanding of NOPE before you can deal with the barking. Next, teach your dog the basic words found in Chapter 5, from HEEL to COME. These words will give your dog a new leash on life (no pun intended!). He'll catch on — because a barking dog is a bright dog — and will learn to be more focused on what you have to teach him than on what's going on around him.

Attention Barking

This type of barking generally begins at about five months of age, when smart puppies are in their bratty stage. If you paid attention to it then, you're probably paying for it now.

The best remedy for this problem is the old cold shoulder. I hate to sound like a broken record, but ignoring an attention-getting behavior is the best line of attack. If your landlord is threatening eviction and you simply can't close your ears, try these other cause-and-effect reactions:

- Walk out of the room. Go into the bathroom and shut the door. Cause-and-effect: Barking brings isolation.

- Use a deterrent like a water spray gun or a can filled with 10 pennies. When he barks, discreetly startle him. "Discretely" is the operative word. Be very secretive about the correction, so it seems to come from the environment, not you. Otherwise, he'll learn he can get away with barking when you're not around.

Meanwhile, exercise your dog and stimulate his brain. Go for a walk and teach him to HEEL. Enroll in a training class or practice the exercises from Chapters 4 and 5. Bratty dogs are just bored. Tapping your dog's intelligence will stimulate his cooperative side! Anybody, a dog included, would rather hear how clever they are than how annoying.

Startle Barking

If your dog is suddenly startled or frightened by an unexpected object or person, he may bark. Don't caress him. Attention reinforces anxiousness. Simply act confident and approach the object or person happily. If you set the example, your dog will follow. Meanwhile, work on HEEL and STAY lessons to teach your dog to stay close and mimic you when he's unsure.

Defensive Barking

You probably want your dog to bark at strangers, but you certainly don't want him to threaten your houseguests. When your dog responds to a knock at the door, don't shout at him or egg him on. Keep him on leash when you're expecting company. When he starts to bark, calmly approach him, quicktug the leash as you say NOPE-SHHH in

 **No Yelling!**

Never yell at a barking dog. When you yell, it sounds like you're barking too! You're having a bark-along, and, in your dog's mind, he started the fun.

a "shame-on-you" voice (remember shouting equals barking). Next, say BACK as you direct him to your side with HEEL or to a pre-designated station with SETTLE DOWN. When he calms down, mark the moment with a YES or click and treat.

You have the option to hold the leash, secure your dog to a station until he calms down or let him drag the leash if he's better mannered that way. You're letting your dog know that alarm barking is OK, but the Top Dog (that's you!) ultimately controls the situation.

 **The Set-Up**

Ask a friend or family member to stage a doorbell set-up. Have them unexpectedly ring the bell while you're practicing lessons on leash. If your dog alert barks (once or twice) and then stops, praise and treat him. If he overreacts, quicktug and refocus him with BACK and HEEL. If possible, have them ring the bell at one-minute intervals so that you can condition a proper response in your dog.

Play Barking

Play barking is cute. A dog gets so excited as he's playing with you that he starts to bark. Often if a dog is not calmed down at this point he may get snappy. If this sounds familiar, rather than scolding your dog and encouraging more hyperactivity, calm him with soft rubs or refocus his energies on a toy. If you're unsuccessful after 10 seconds, end the play session. Next time you play, attach a short lead to enforce a calmer attitude.

Frustration Barking

Dogs are not a solitary species. They thrive on interaction and are frustrated when they're confined away from their group. To communicate this, they often resort to barking. And barking often results in attention. Once again, the response rewards the behavior.

The first remedy for this problem is exercise and training. Your dog must learn to respond to *your* barks — especially WAIT and STAY. Try to keep him with you when you're home, leading or stationing him. Stage practice departures where you come and go every minute. If you come back to a hyper, barking, jumping dog, ignore him. Wait until he's calmed down, and then greet him with calm pats. Stage 15 to 25 departures a day, doubling the departure time as your dog feels more assured of your return. Above all else, avoid rescuing a barking dog. Wait until he's settled down. Buy wax earplugs if you need them. When your dog quiets down, have some quality bonding time (he'll likely be exhausted).

If you have a marathon barker or one you just can't ignore, you may try a cause-and-effect sequence to discourage him. Secretively spray his crate with a strong stream of water or toss a can filled with pennies. Your dog must not think this is coming from you — the environment is corrective, you're reassuring. (Another option is the citronella collar discussed on page 196.)

Sound and Motion Barking

This passionate creature is attuned to everything! Things you could never hear or see become monumental events for this dog. Here are a few options to consider.

- Lessons are a must, as they teach your dog to put you above outside distractions. When everything is distracting, getting your dog's focus is a real plus. If you can pinpoint a time or distraction that really sets your dog in motion, work your dog outside of his Red Zone (the distance from the distraction at which he can stay focused on you). Slowly inch closer to the distraction. If food is a strong drive, use it to encourage your dog's attention.

- Can you block off your dog's access to areas that are most stimulating? I know a Wheaten Terrier named Duffy who is totally bonkers when the school bus arrives in the afternoon. Lessons helped and so did blocking the

The Opposite of SPEAK

One fun way around the barking issue is to teach your dog SPEAK. And then from SPEAK, teach SHHH. Broadway, watch out!

- To teach SPEAK, whenever your dog starts barking, use this command and a snappy hand signal (you can make one up) to egg him on. If he doesn't make the connection, try to secure him out of reach as you bait him with a toy. Most dogs bark in frustration — seize the moment! Say SPEAK and praise, praise, praise, but no food.
- Now on to SHHH. After four or five barks, stand tall and in a low, flat voice say SHHH as you stamp the floor with your foot. The second your dog stops, instantly click and treat. Yeah! Now redirect with a familiar command, like SIT or PAW.
- Practice two or three sequences, then quit for the day.

access to the front room from 2:30 to 3:30 until he had a better handle on his impulses. Sometimes the most obvious solutions are the most effective.

- When you're home with your dog keep him on leash. Correct any alert barking with a quicktug and NOPE, and quickly refocus him on an appropriate distraction toy. In my house we say KILL THE DUCK (politically incorrect, I know) and my terrier races over and shakes her duck around. Clever girl!
- Play the swing toss game from Chapter 4 to give your dog an outlet for his energy. Investigate other toys that slowly dispense food as your dog plays with them, such as the Buster Cube and Jolly Balls. They're great for dogs with high prey drive.

My Golden Retriever barks during play, but I want him to bark when new people come into the house. What can I do?

Not much. Golden Retrievers are more concerned with making friends than scaring people off. Teach him SPEAK on cue, and have him bark when he hears someone at the door. Good luck!

I ignore my dog when he barks, but it doesn't work. Whether he's outside or in, he just keeps it up. What about an electric barking collar?

A diehard. Your dog obviously knows that eventually you'll give in. If you react once in 10 times, your dog will bark another 10 times. Believe me, I know. I had a barking machine once named Calvin. The first two words he learned were SPEAK and SHHH. I also used a head halter to handle him. This calmed him tremendously. Next, I bought wax earplugs. And until he learned better manners,

No-Bark Collars

There are no-bark collars on the market. Shock collars that zap a dog with a bolt of electricity — I'm not a big fan of that. Though it may solve the barking problem, it generally creates a whole host of other issues such as household destruction and self-destructive habits. Have you ever seen a dog who chewed a hole into his own fur or licked himself to the bone? It's not a pretty sight.

I recommend using the citronella barking collar. It is sound activated and releases a blast of citronella under a dog's chin when he barks. It works most of the time, but it needs to be monitored to make sure the citronella box is replenished and the collar is secure. And, like any negative deterrent, a dog needs an alternative activity to stave off frustration. A good bone or a toy will do.

I didn't leave him outside alone. Your dog must learn that you control situations. Otherwise, he'll think he does and be frustrated when he's separated from you, which leads to barking. As for the no-bark collars, I don't endorse the electric ones. They create more problems than they solve. Check into a citronella barking collar. I've found this to be helpful in situations like yours. Above all, a steady teaching path, patience and perseverance are the strongest remedies.

My puppy whines a lot. What can I do?

Ignore him. Whining is a common reaction to wanting to have or do something and not being able to do it. Sometimes I wish I could whine. Your puppy is probably entering puberty or adolescence. It's a stressful time and he's just letting his stress out. It will pass. If you pay attention to the whine, however, you'll create a lifelong whiner.

CHASING

Like barking, chasing is another instinctive behavior that dates back to ancestral times when dogs had to chase prey to survive. Even though we provide their meals and dogs rarely bring down what they chase, it's still a fun pastime and many dogs do it. If you've got a chronic chaser, read closely. You've got some work to do.

Car Chasing

This is a big no-no. Although very fulfilling ("Look! I chased off that gigantic Tin-o-sourous and saved the day!"), it's a deadly game for your dog as well as for the drivers. There are several approaches to dealing with this problem, but the first precaution is to keep your dog leashed when he's not confined. If you're considering a fence for your property, keep it back from the roadway to discourage border chasing, which only aggravates an ingrained ritual. If your fence came down or your dog escaped, it could be tragic.

Buckaroo

Buckaroo, a usually docile five-year-old Labrador Retriever-Springer Spaniel mix, has the best ears in Westchester County. Big, black, oversized and as smooth as velvet, a quick touch melts all stresses away. His transformation when a car passes his home is unimaginable. Hair up, body rigid, he flies from one corner of his electrically fenced property to the other — a distance of a quarter mile — barking with intent to kill. When the car passes, he returns to tail up, lips parted panting in a happy grin, as loving and calm as the moment before.

I correctly concluded as I sat with his friendly, laid-back family that the only time they yelled at and scolded Buckaroo was when he chased cars. Since the yelling came from behind and basically followed Buckaroo as he ran the perimeter of his property, he perceived their vocalizations as supportive. The scolding he received after the fact was not linked to the car, but to the overall situation (his family only got cross when cars were around), making him more wary when cars approached.

When I asked them to walk him on the street, Buckaroo pulled forward and crouched to chase the car. Oh my!

Buckaroo got a quick lesson in HEEL, STAY, NOPE and WAIT. He was fitted for a chain training collar and a long line for yard work. Each time a car was heard in the distance, we watched Buckaroo's ears (a dog's antennae). As soon as they pitched forward, we ran back toward the house saying NOPE as the leash tugged him, and HEEL to call him back to our side. In addition, he learned to walk at HEEL on the street and each time he alerted to a car he was corrected with NOPE and directed TO THE SIDE, where he was praised with food and attention.

Like many dogs I work with, Buckaroo has a thing for cars. He was re-inforced for all his assertive behaviors.

The key to remedying this problem is to think a few steps ahead of your dog. When you hear a car coming, make a big fuss about running to the side of the road. Say TO THE SIDE as you run like you're about to be bombed. When you get to the side, instruct your dog to WAIT behind you. If he so much as looks at the car, say NOPE and quicktug the leash. You must interrupt the thought process to solve the problem. Mark the moment he's centered on you with YES or click and treat.

Another entertaining and sometimes completely effective method is to ambush your dog. Stage a drive-by with two friends in the car: one at the wheel driving slowly, the other secretively perched by the backseat window or sunroof. Keep your dog on a long line to supervise how close he gets to the car. As the car drives by, have the passenger lob cans filled with coins or water balloons or sound off a fog horn to startle your dog.

If it works, you'll know right away. Your dog will run fast and far and never want to chase a car again. It's worth a try, although don't be disappointed if your friends lack coordination and the whole set-up is a wash. For some dogs, the chasing instinct is too strong to be dissuaded by corrections mid-chase.

I have two dogs who love to chase cars. How can I get them both to stop during walks?

Buy a coupler — which enables you to attach both dogs to the same lead. Familiarize yourself and your dogs with it. Next, ask someone to drive by while you handle both dogs on the coupler. As the person drives by, watch your dogs. As they lower their heads for the chase, say NOPE and run to the curb saying TO THE SIDE. Pet them reassuringly when you've made it to the sidewalk. Repeat, repeat, repeat until your dogs start running to the curb every time they hear a car. Good dogs!

My dog no longer chases cars on the street, but when people come into the driveway he runs at the wheels and jumps at the car window.

You're probably paying attention to your dog when he does this. Even negative attention will reinforce this routine. To stop this little game, do the following:

1. Repeat the set-up I just described, asking a friend to come over and honk the horn when they arrive. Put your dog on a leash and encourage him to retreat at the horn sound as well as the car.

2. Have a friend hold your dog on a leash and encourage your dog's retreat as you arrive, honking your horn.

3. Do not yell at your dog from the car as you drive up. This is interpreted as barking and will spur him on.

4. Have a water mister adjusted to jet stream. When your dog jumps on the car, do not look at him. If you get out when he's jumping, you're reinforcing the jumping. Instead, spritz his body (below the shoulder) and stay in the car until he sits or retreats.

People Chasing

Use the same technique you used for car chasing with bikers and joggers. Ask a friend to help you as you work your dog on a leash or long line and training collar; preferably a Gentle Leader. Correct your dog the second he thinks about chasing anyone. Once he's in motion, it's too late.

If you're honestly concerned your dog may bite a passerby, call a professional. You've got a serious problem on your hands.

Cat Chasing

Squirrels, deer and other four-legged animals fall under this heading, too. You'll need a four-legged volunteer, or you can use what the environment provides. Once again, catching the thought process is paramount. The second your dog's ears go up (a sign of anticipation), say NOPE as you quick-tug the leash and redirect your dog back to your side. Next, place a light 20-foot line on his buckle collar. When he starts stalking, run in the opposite direction and say NOPE as your dog hits the end of the line.

 **Sometimes It Never Works**

Use your judgment. If your dog is flipped out and clearly wants to kill your cat, don't attempt to bring them together. Cats can recognize the intent to kill; it's horrifying. There are cases when a dog and a cat cannot live together. If you're unsure, ask a professional.

If you've got a cat under your roof, the key is to limit your dog's freedom for a week or two, keeping him attached to you to make sure he's supervised or stationed, so your cat learns that puss reigns again. Each day:

1. Lead your dog into the room your cat occupies. Have a SIT, STAY and HEEL lesson, correcting any interest he shows in the cat's whereabouts.

2. As they get more comfortable in the same room together, station your dog into a far corner of the room. Stay calm; correcting any overtures your dog makes with a quicktug and NOPE, THAT'S UNACCEPTABLE. Your cat will love it! You may notice a sudden reappearance and paw cleaning just out of reach. Cats are quite comical.

3. Now for the big test: Take your dog (on leash) and cat into a small room, such as a kitchen or small bathroom. Correct any canine alert with a quicktug and NOPE. Give your dog familiar directions like SIT, STAY and DOWN. Mark his cooperation with YES or click and treat.

Slowly a relationship will develop between your cat and dog. Let your dog drag his leash for awhile so you can intercede if things get out of hand. Fall back to stations and supervised meetings, if necessary.

Child Chasing

Kids and dogs: The perfect match. Well, sometimes. Until the dog is racing after the children, knocking them over and grabbing the backpacks off their backs. Then it's not so perfect.

In the dog's defense, however, children can seem like interactive puppies. They squeal, run and jump around. They push back really hard, which brings the rest of the family running. Like it or not, dear doggie, this chasing game has to stop.

This set-up requires a few volunteers. Little volunteers, that is. If you haven't got kids, you'll need to borrow some. Here's what you'll do:

1. Place your dog on his leash and training collar. Bring him to your side.

2. Ask the children to run in front of you, but watch your dog.

3. As he lowers his head for a lunge, say NOPE sternly as you quicktug the leash. (Correct the thought process!)

4. Tell your dog to HEEL and ask the kids to keep running back and forth until your dog gets conditioned to their movements.

When you've mastered this procedure, try some distance control by placing your dog on a long line. Extend your distance from him as your little volunteers race around in front of you. Every time your dog thinks about a chase, correct him by snapping back on the lead, saying NOPE and calling him into a HEEL position.

CHEWING

Dogs chew for many reasons. Like children, dogs are enormously curious about the world around them and they love to explore, especially as puppies. Kids use their hands; dogs use their mouths. Both are capable of going to great lengths to satisfy that curiosity. At around 14 weeks, puppies begin to teethe. Teething children may keep you up at night, but they will not chew your furniture to alleviate their discomfort. Your puppy will.

As they get older, chewing alleviates the boredom and anxiety of being left alone, undirected or over-disciplined. And for dogs who don't fall into any of those categories, destructive chewing is just plain fun. Imagine, from your dog's perspective, tearing all that stuffing out of a pillow or shredding a whole stack of papers. Some breeds are obsessively oral — the Sporting and Nordic breeds quickly pop to mind.

If a puppy gets attention, even negative, for inappropriate chewing, his habit will continue. Uh-oh! Are you

 **Quick Fix**

Though indirect, exercise and lessons help calm chewing habits tremendously. A tired, well-educated dog has less nervous energy. This dog feels more important, smart and physically exhausted.

thinking this might have happened to you? Well, don't worry. We can handle this problem.

Most dogs get more attention for chewing what they're not supposed to! The first step in teaching your dog better chewing habits is to get him turned on to chewing his own things. Here are some ideas:

- **Encourage before you discourage.** Teach your dog the words BONE and TOY. Each time you play with him, emphasize these words and make a big fuss when your dog seeks out his own chew toys. Dogs love attention, and if they get it for chewing their own things, that's great!

- **Keep things organized.** Organize an area for your dog in each room. Aside from it being just plain nice (don't you like knowing where to sit when you go into a room?), the consistency of it really helps. Put a mat down and return all chewies to your dog's mat if they become scattered. If you have young kids or other pets, tie the dog's bone to the station to keep it from disappearing. Each time you enter the room, tell your dog SETTLE DOWN, GET YOUR BONE and praise him tremendously.

- **Provide limited chewing objects.** Given too many toys to choose from, your dog may confuse his objects with yours. Ask your veterinarian's advice about the best chew toys. I like (for my dogs, not me) knuckle bones, sterilized hollow bones (good for stuffing), pressed rawhide and vegetable bones. I pick my dog's top two favorites and buy multiples to spread around the house. If your dog is a fan of rope or stuffed toys, which are so similar to household objects, buy only one and leave it in the crate or take it out for play time. Offer a bone to your dog if you're talking on the phone, chatting with company or reading the paper.

- **Keep your dog attached.** If you're dealing with a puppy or a delinquent chewer, lead or station him to control his rambunctiousness around the house. This enables you to control his actions and keep him out of trouble when he's with you.

- **Teach your dog to find his bone.** In the beginning just say BONE whenever you offer it. Later, play a game where you encourage your dog to find it. Wave it in front of him saying BONE! Then put your dog in a STAY or have another family member hold him. Start out hiding in easy spots, then slowly progress to real detective work. Say WHERE'S YOUR BONE? as you encourage your dog's enthusiasm. If he looks confused, get down on the floor and show him how to use his nose to find his treasure. When he does, cheer and reward him with food and attention.

Once your dog gets hold of something or has already destroyed it, forget about it. If you correct a dog with something in his mouth, he'll think you envy his prize ("It must be valuable if this person wants it"). And if you discipline a dog after the fact, you're ensuring a repeat performance. If it's destroyed, stay calm or go punch a pillow, but leave your dog out of it. If your dog got something you rather he didn't, you have a couple of options:

- If you suspect it's attention-getting behavior, it probably is. Walk out of the house or into another room. Most dogs drop the object immediately and wait by the door.

- Leave your dog on a drag leash or curtail household freedom altogether until you work on your lessons and the correction method explained below.

- Place treat cups around the house. Each time your dog or puppy puts anything in his mouth that he's not supposed to, shake the cup and say WHAT DID YOU FIND? If he drops the object or brings it to you, say THANK YOU FOR SHARING and go on like it was nothing. Better to have a dog who's intent on the grab-and-show than the grab-and-go!

Remember, once it's in your dog's mouth, it's considered a prize. Corrections just don't work after the fact!

The problem with disciplining dogs is that they often get the wrong message. Your attention puts more value on a particular object. They learn to covet the object, hiding it somewhere or simply grabbing it when you're out of the house or not looking. This makes people more frustrated, which leads to a heightened sense of anxiety for the dear doggy, which leads to . . . you guessed it, more destructive chewing. It's like a person who bites their nails: The behavior gets more intense when they're stressed.

 **A Swift Kick**

If you cannot lift the object, kick it. I know, you'll look ridiculous kicking your dishwasher. But hey, if the method works, use it!

Instead, set up situations that convey that the object is bad, not the dog! In the meantime, work through your lessons so that your dog will have a greater appreciation for your opinions. Read carefully!

1. Place a tempting object on the floor. A crumpled paper towel can be quite irresistible.

2. Bring your dog to it on his leash.

3. The instant he approaches the object, quicktug and say NOPE.

4. Pick up the object, shake it forcefully and correct it harshly. SHAME ON YOU! BAD PAPER TOWEL! Look at the object, not the dog. The object's bad, your dog's an angel.

5. Toss the object on the ground. Vent your frustrations. Correct it again. It's a very naughty object. Then calmly look to your dog and command, LET'S GO.

Correct the object, not the dog!

My dog baits me. He picks up something he knows is important and stands just out of reach. What can I do?

Your dog is smart. He has learned what gets your goat. He doesn't really know the object is important. He just knows it will spur you into action. First of all, put all treasured objects in a safe place. Next, leave a not-so-important object about and when your dog takes it and baits you with it, leave. Yes, leave. Walk out of the house, shut the door and come back in a couple of minutes. Refocus your bewildered dog with a toy, and casually pick up the object. Do not correct your dog for this. Chasing him around communicates only one thing: prize envy. Eventually this game will lose its magic and cease.

My dog is no problem until the laundry basket comes out. Then he goes crazy!

You've got some setting up to do. Here's an idea: Soak a bunch of old socks in Grannick's Bitter Apple or Tabasco sauce, fill the laundry basket and lay a newspaper over the clothes. Place the sauced socks on top of the paper and act like it's any other load. Your dog will get quite a shock this time around. Have a bowl of water awaiting him, but do not soothe his reaction. Next, spray some Tabasco sauce along the edge of the basket, and correct your dog any time he thinks about investigating it. (Also set up the above sequence and correct the laundry: BAD LAUNDRY! BAD SOCK!)

> ### 🐾 Nasty Noshing
>
> If your dog's a furniture fanatic and he's adverse to Grannick's Bitter Apple, here's what you do. Spray his favorite piece each day. Yes, every day, until his tastes refocus on more appropriate toys. If you catch him noshing on, say, the leg of your chair, discretely spray it while he's chewing. Say nothing. It's a cause-and-effect reaction. When he pulls away, suggest BONE.

DIGGING

Digging is another favorite canine pastime. Dogs do it for a whole host of good reasons: to get cool, to alleviate boredom, to mimic their human parents' gardening techniques, for fun, or, like my dog Hope, to chase rodents deep down under, where they hide! Short of keeping your dog confined to hard surfaces and structured leash walks for the rest of his life, you'll have to make some concessions in this department.

Do

- Exercise your dog. Tired dogs have less restless energy.
- Teach lessons to stimulate your dog's mental activity.
- Select a dig spot. Pick one area in which your dog can dig to his heart's content.
- Go to the area ahead of time and hide some favorite biscuits and toys.
- Go to the area with your dog each day, instructing GO DIG! Have a dig-fest and cheer him on.
- If your dog's a die hard, place his own stool or some red pepper flakes in the hole and cover it up.
- If you catch your dog digging somewhere he shouldn't, correct him with NOPE and then tell him (escorting him to his dig spot, if necessary) GO DIG!

Don't

- Garden in front of your dog. The old "monkey see, monkey do" rule applies here.
- Discipline your dog after the fact. It simply makes no sense.
- Spray your dog with a hose or set mouse traps. That's cruel!
- Put the dirt back into the hole. That's confusing; now you're digging in the same spot, too.

GARBAGE GRABBING

Garbage grabbing gets a lot of attention and it is most rewarding! To rehabilitate your little garbologist, stop giving him all those after-dinner goodies. I know, I know: they'll go to waste. But if your dog can have your leftovers in his bowl, he'll want them from the trash.

Next, place your garbage someplace your dog can't get it — in a bin with a tight-fitting lid, then inside a cabinet, for example. Prevention is the most sensible cure. If your dog is still rummaging around, try one of the following:

- Walk your dog by the garbage on leash. Toss something irresistible into the trash. The second he starts to show interest, quicktug the leash and say NOPE. Rush up to the can, and kick and scream at it. Do not yell or look at your dog. Tell your dog LET'S GO and move on to the next activity. If he passes this test, place him on a 10-foot drag lead and correct him from behind. Walk him by the can again and note his reaction. If your dog ignores the temptation, give him a hug. If not, you need to be more forceful with the can — yes, the can. Do not look at your dog. Look at and correct the BAD GARBAGE!

- If your dog is sound-sensitive, construct a pyramid of penny cans on top of or next to the garbage can. Place 10 pennies each in six cans, and arrange them with three on the bottom, two in the middle and one on top. Tie a string to the middle can on the bottom row and hold the other end. When your dog shows interest, pull the string and shout NOPE.

- The last thing to try is the balloon stay-away. Blow up a few balloons and pop them one at a time with a pin with your dog present. As each one pops, act afraid yourself. Don't pay any attention to your dog. Just act it out and trust me, he'll be watching. Next, tape the balloons to the edge of the garbage can and leave them there a couple of weeks.

My dog is an angel when we're in the room.
It's when we leave that he gets into trash trouble.

A wise guy! Mr. Clever. There are several approaches you can try:

- Set up a bitter-tasting lure by soaking a paper towel in Grannick's Bitter Apple or Tabasco sauce and leaving it on top of the trash. Repeat this until he loses interest in the trash.

- Set up the penny-can pyramid and booby-trap him when you've left the room.

- Set up a mirror so that you can keep your eye on the garbage can even when you're not physically present. When you see your dog approaching, step in and correct his thought process.

HOUSEBREAKING

There are so many variables in a good housebreaking schedule — your dog's age, temperament and even his size. Did he come from a pet store, shelter, breeder or is his background unknown? And then there's you — your lifestyle weighs into the process big time. Those who are home all day can devote more structure and attention to the process. Even your patience level can be a factor: Frustration (yours) unsettles a dog's nervous system and this leads to more elimination.

Four Steps to Get You Started

Step 1: Organize a structured plan for you and your dog. Decide where you want your dog to go. On paper or outside? Some working parents have to mix methods, and although it's confusing a dog will learn in time. Once you decide, organize the bathroom area. If it's paper, put several sheets down neatly in a private corner. I repeat, neatly. If you're taking your dog outside, designate one door of the house to use for bathroom breaks until your dog is fully housebroken, and select a bathroom spot close by the house. Walking your dog all over neighborhood is not good practice. Would you toilet train a child by sending them to the neighbors? Keep your dog in your yard and close by the door. Tell everyone in the house the plan. Consistency is the key to learning.

Step 2: Assign words to the act of taking your dog to the door or the paper. OUTSIDE or PAPERS works for me. Each time you escort your dog to the area, repeat the word in a clear, directional, important-sounding tone. If your dog is clever and outgoing, hang a bell next to the door leading outside. Before opening the door, flick the bell with your fingers as you repeat OUTSIDE.

Step 3: Once you reach the papers or outside area, ignore your dog. Wait until he eliminates and say GET BUSY as he does. In time, you'll be able to open the door and say this phrase, and your dog will know just what to do.

Step 4: Seize the moment! If you're using a clicker, now's the perfect time. Click the moment your dog finishes eliminating and reward him with a yummy snack. If the clicker is not a part of your plan, say YES! to give your dog a sense of accomplishment.

Preventing Accidents

To prevent housebreaking accidents you need to be extremely organized and positive. If you live a chaotic life, downshift for your dog's sake. Follow these guidelines and the program in Chapter 4. In principle, dogs are clean creatures who prefer absorbent surfaces and don't like to hang out where they eliminate. Their clean nature makes the housebreaking process easier.

Creating a Routine

A good routine is the foundation of any housebreaking plan. Get your dog focused on a routine, and encourage everyone to help out and follow the rules. Here are the elements involved in your routine:

Pick "The Door": Pick one door through which to take your dog outside for bathroom breaks. Each time you go to the door, say OUTSIDE. Repeat it every three seconds until you are at "The Spot."

Pick "The Spot": Designate a five-foot-by-five-foot area in your yard or house as "The Spot." If you're outside training, locate the area near "The Door." If you're paper training, cover a large area, slowly decreasing its size until it's appropriate for your puppy's needs.

Pick "The Word": Use a short, snappy command like GET BUSY or DO IT when your dog squats to eliminate. Say it once or twice, and praise him calmly when he finishes. You'll appreciate this when he wants to go out in the pouring rain at four in the morning.

CONTAINMENT

The fastest way to housetrain your dog is to keep an eye on him. Use the leash to station or anchor your dog, or crate or isolate him when you can't supervise him (a less desirable alternative). You may allow short periods of supervised freedom after he's emptied his bladder.

YOUNG PUPS

Puppies under 12 weeks of age have little bladder control and cannot separate the need to go to the bathroom from the action of doing so. Don't correct a young dog. They'll catch on as they grow up. Young dogs need to go out after a meal, a nap, play or isolation. Watch them closely during these times. Although their signals may be subtle, most puppies get very hyper and nippy before they eliminate and tend to move away from the group. When you think your puppy needs to eliminate, take him to his designated spot *immediately*. And *always* praise him when he does the right thing in the right place!

FOOD

Ask your veterinarian to help you select a good dog food and a feeding schedule. When feeding time arrives, place the food and water bowls down for 15 minutes, and then remove them. If your dog can't stay still for the allotted time, crate or station him with his bowls. If he doesn't eat, don't worry! He may need to skip a

meal or two before he gets in the habit of eating at mealtimes. It is easier to housebreak a dog on a consistent feeding schedule. His last feeding of the day should be somewhere between 4 P.M. and 6 P.M., as it takes about six hours for his bowels to cycle.

WATER

Make water available during feedings. Additionally, have water available before you take your dog to the bathroom. Don't give him free access to water yet, or he may turn into a fountain. Remove all water after 7:30 P.M. If you think he's thirsty, give him some ice cubes to lick, as they absorb faster into the bloodstream.

NO FREE RIDES

Avoid carrying your dog to his bathroom area. He must learn how to navigate the route on his own. If you've got a young puppy who can't navigate stairs, give him a quick lift and then put him down.

FIRST THINGS FIRST

When you wake up in the morning or come home at night, don't greet your dog until after he has eliminated. Put his leash on and walk to "The Spot," saying OUTSIDE or PAPERS! As he goes, command GET BUSY, then greet and reward him happily.

THE OUTSIDE ROUTINE

Your dog will need to go out after feeding, exercising, napping and isolation. Use the following chart as a guide:

Age	Daily Trips to "The Spot"
6 to 14 weeks	8 to 10
14 to 20 weeks	6 to 8
20 to 30 weeks	4 to 6
30 weeks to adulthood	3 to 4

CORRECTIONS

Do not hit or yell at your dog if he makes a mistake. A lot of people want to know how to correct a dog after the fact. "Does the old discipline of rubbing their noses in it still work?" No, it doesn't. In fact, it *never* worked. I can think of nothing more disgusting. If you didn't catch him in time, you're the one who must take responsibility. Remove him from the room and clean the area with a 50-50 mixture of white vinegar and water. Do not clean the area in front of him (that's the sort of thing a subordinate pack member would do, not a leader). The only time you can correct your dog is if you catch him in the thought process or just as he's starting to go. Then startle him by making an unfamiliar, guttural EH, EH, EH! sound, and command OUTSIDE! You want your dog to think the ceiling is falling when he eliminates indoors but that everyone is so happy when he goes to his place. Be patient. He'll get there.

TEACHING HIM A SIGNAL

Before you take this step, make sure your dog understands the routine. One morning, take him to the door on leash without commanding OUTSIDE. Don't say anything — no pats or eye contact — just walk him to the door. Stand still and

Incorporate a signal bell into your routine.

pay attention. He's accustomed to marching right out, so he may start whining, jumping or pulling. If you've incorporated a bell into your routine, he may ring it. When he does, praise YES! OUTSIDE! Take him to "The Spot." When he catches on that he must give you a signal before you go outside, start using this system in rooms farther away from the door.

A Housebreaking Schedule

In the following chart you'll find a typical housebreaking schedule. I know it may seem like overkill, but I root for success, not mistakes. You can cut out walks as your dog develops bladder control and he learns to give you a signal. Remember to keep the bathroom area close to the house and reward elimination with attention, treats and/or walks.

A TYPICAL HOUSEBREAKING SCHEDULE
(A dog needs to be taken outside or
to his indoor papers at each of these times)

At-Home Canine Parent	Working Canine Parent
Early morning wake-up	Early morning wake-up
Right after breakfast	Right after breakfast
Midmorning	Lunch break/dog walker/papers
Right after the afternoon meal (if applicable)	Midafternoon, outside or papers (for puppies) Arrival home
Right after dinner (4 to 6 P.M.)	Right after dinner (4 to 6 P.M.)
Before bed (9 to 11 P.M.)	Before bed (9 to 11 P.M.)
Middle of the night (young pups and sick dogs)	Middle of the night (young pups and sick dogs)

If you're regularly gone six to eight hours a day, you'll need to leave papers down for your dog for emergencies. Leave your puppy in an indoor pen or room, sectioning off an area with papers or incontinence pads. Fold the pen up when you arrive home and dispose of the soiled pads.

What about installing a doggie door?

If you have a securely fenced yard, it's something to consider. You'll need to follow the same guidelines in your approach to housetraining, but instead of escorting your dog out the door, you'll go through the people door and lure him out through his doggie door. In other words, you still have to teach him what to do.

There are two major drawbacks to these doors: The first is that your dog may be stolen when left alone. Such things really do happen! The second is people are tempted to forego lessons. This is a problem because a dog assumes a self-reliant and inflated view of himself, which can lead to a whole host of problems from aggression, to running off, to destruction and, dare I say, housebreaking!

My dog doesn't give any signal. He just sits and watches me until I take him out.

You'll have to watch for subtle signs and then praise him wildly before going out. This will encourage a more revved-up reaction. If he shows absolutely no sign, jump around a little (encouraging a bark or a jump) before you say OUTSIDE. Soon he'll pick up the routine.

Where should I put the crate?

Ideally, in your bedroom. If you're concerned about messes, lay paper underneath. Being around you makes your dog calmer and more likely to sleep through the night.

My dog eliminates in the crate. What should I do?

First, check with your veterinarian to make sure your dog doesn't have a urinary tract infection or worms. Perhaps your crate is too big. If so, make it smaller. You can buy crate dividers or you can rig one yourself. Additionally, remove all absorbent material from the crate. Some dogs love to pee on absorbent things. If you're still having problems, find a professional behaviorist or trainer; your dog may be suffering from separation anxiety.

My 10-week-old Cairn Terrier wakes up at 3 A.M. and whines. Should I take him out?

Yes, but don't make a big thing of it. Take him to his spot, bring him back in and go back to bed. Period. Right now his bladder is too small to make it through the night, but if you play games at 3 A.M., he'll keep getting up at 3 A.M.

Will I have to crate my dog forever?

Not unless you want to. Eventually, when your dog can hold his urine, try stationing (see Chapter 3). Once sleeping at his station has become a habit, crating him will not be necessary.

My dog just wants to play outside. He thinks the carpet is for peeing.

Do not walk around or play with your dog when you take him out. Calmly walk to the selected area, stand still and ignore your dog until he has gone to the bathroom. If he doesn't do anything for five minutes, take him back inside, ignore him and crate or leash him for 15 to 30 minutes. Then take him outside again. Once your dog eliminates outside, praise him and play a favorite game. Soon he'll learn that eliminating outside is what begins playtime!

INEDIBLE INGESTION *(PICA)*

Dogs who ingest nondigestibles such as plastics, clothing, foil and rocks have to be watched carefully. Although an occasional crayon or pen cap can pass through the system, other objects can't and your dog will need immediate medical attention. If you have a dog who does this watch his stools, first to ensure that he is having them regularly (once or twice a day) and second to examine them for any abnormality. Ah, what we do for love!

The impulse to eat the inedible cannot always be remedied, and can have fatal effects. It is easiest to resolve with young puppies or dogs who are just starting to show signs of the behavior. As puppies, dogs with this propensity are very oral.

 **Keep Cool**

Do not get tense or angry at your dog if he beats you to something and swallows it. Call your veterinarian. Ask if you should induce vomiting or just watch his digestion carefully. Do not pick up anything he values in front of him, because if you "eat it," he'll want to do the same.

To resolve this problem, you must work hard at controlling your behavior. Yes, your behavior. If you scream or chase a dog every time he reaches for something inappropriate, you're actually encouraging him to continue. It's that prize envy concept again: By devoting time and energy to getting it away from your dog, you're giving the object a lot of power. The only two alternatives for your dog are to run fast or swallow the evidence.

Remember, get help if you need it, but first try these measures:

- Consider a Gentle Leader. When your dog starts to scrounge, a gentle pull will close his mouth, enabling you to redirect him.

- Keep your dog leashed inside and outside until the problem subsides. Carry a treat cup or jingle jar with you to condition a willingness to show you mouthed objects — the grab-and-show, not the grab-and-go!

- Provide good chew toys. I'm a huge fan of hard, knuckle-type bones, sterile bones that you can stuff with peanut butter and vegetable-based bones that your dog can chew, destroy and digest.

- Read and practice teaching NOPE as outlined in Chapter 4 and in the Chewing section of this chapter.

- Teach your dog WAIT, HEEL and STAY — the first step in self control.

- Once your dog is turned on to listening, teach him the fetching games outlined at the end of Chapter 5. Exercise, exercise, exercise. Tired dogs are less fidgety.

- Once your dog has learned HEEL, use it as you walk and discourage all sniffing.

- Bring along a distraction toy and play with it when you walk.
- Each time your dog sniffs at garbage, spritz the object with Grannick's Bitter Apple or another disgusting liquid and say NOPE calmly but firmly. Continue walking in an upbeat manner.

JUMPING

Everybody knows a jumper. Little jumpers and big jumpers. Wild, knock-over-the-furniture jumpers and muddy-paw-prints-on-your-pants jumpers. The most popular excuse for this behavior is, "He's just saying hello!" Not true! He's saying, "Thank you for teaching me this excellent way of getting attention! I'll do this again and again and again!"

Let's take a closer look. All dogs start out as attention-seeking puppies. And it's true, all puppies are irresistible. When they jump, they get lots of love, plenty of attention and a few kisses to boot!

Puppy Lesson #1: Jumping is an interactive behavior, definitely worth repeating!

But as puppies gets bigger, their charm wears off. They get pushed and shouted at for a behavior that was once encouraged.

Puppy Lesson #2*:* Jumping is still interactive and still worth repeating!

Puppies can't resist the interaction! They continue to jump; you continue to push. Jump, push. Jump, push. Help!

To rehabilitate your jumper, encourage before you discourage. Use SIT for everything your dog loves: your attention, walks, toys, food and treats. My favorite is the Silent SIT.

The Silent SIT: Go into a quiet room with a clicker, treat cup or favorite toy. Stand in front of your dog and entice him to jump by waving the object in front of his face. If he does jump, close shop, pull the object up as you cross your arms over your chest and look up. When he stops jumping, try it again. Say nothing. When he sits, YES or click and give him the goodie. Now, spread some treat cups or toys around the house and repeat this sequence throughout the day. Ask for household cooperation. The more he gets it right, the faster he'll understand that sitting gets rewarded!

Ignore your dog: If jumping gets the smallest morsel of attention, it's reinforced. And it doesn't matter if it's negative or positive attention. Most dogs perceive negative attention as confrontational play. Enforce the Four Paw Rule (four paws on the floor) in your home today. Share the plan with friends and family members! Although ignoring sounds tough, there are several ways to go about it.

- Close shop. Cross your arms over your chest and look up. The ultimate snub.
- Do a spray away. Do not spray your dog in the face or look at him when you're spraying! Simply spray a vapor boundary between your body and his. This also works great with company. Binaca breath spray, a plant

My girl Whoopsie Daisy at her greeting station.

mister or Grannick's Bitter Apple all work well. Decide what's most effective and buy multiples.

- Do the reverse yo-yo. Place your dog on a drag lead when you're expecting company, tying a knot in the lead where it touches the floor. When company arrives step on the knot and let your dog jump up and get brought down until he figures out it's better to just sit. Magic — that's what gets the attention!

- Leash your dog or secure a short leash to his collar. When he jumps look away, grasp the leash and swipe him off to the side. Keep doing it over and over if necessary. No attention until he's calm.

- Create a station to the side of the greeting room. Secure him during arrivals. Wait until your dog is contained to let him meet and greet.

What Kind of Jumper Are You?

The reaction you choose is determined, in part, by what category your dog's jumping fits into.

ATTENTION JUMPERS

If your dog jumps on you for attention, close shop. Shop re-opens for polite dogs only! It can be as simple as that. If he's unbearable, leave him on a short leash and swipe him off as you continue to ignore him. When he gets down, pause for at least five seconds, instruct SIT and pet him. Soon he'll catch on that sitting is all the rage.

GREETING JUMPERS

Mom's right again: Good manners start at home. When you greet your dog after an absence, stay calm! If you go nuts, you're teaching your dog to go hog-wild when the door opens. Instead, give him a special bone and ignore him until he settles down. If he's banging around in his crate, don't open it until he's quiet. Instruct SIT when he calms down, and pet him gently. Reinforce calmness and you'll be doing both of you — not to mention your guests — a favor!

COMPANY JUMPERS

When company arrives, get control of your dog before you open the door. Either leash or station him. Tell him WAIT as you open the door and give him a special "greeting" bone or toy, one he gets only when company comes (I use a tennis ball for my Border Collie and a stuffed duck for my terrier). You'll need to train your company, too. Insist that they ignore your dog until he's calm. I agree — company is often harder to train, but do your best! If your dog is bouncing, swipe him off with the leash and say NOPE as you present his "greeting" toy. Consider the "reverse yo-yo" detailed previously. When he settles down, reward him with attention and treats. Brace your dog while your company pets him. If your company is staying for a visit, anchor your dog at your side and give him a special toy.

FURNITURE FANATICS

You must decide right now if you want a furniture dog. Do you want your full-grown dog jumping on the couch, sitting in your favorite chair, hogging the bed? If that sounds like your plan, read no further. But if you'd rather have your dog on the floor or getting up only with permission (my personal plan), read on. Create a station right up near your furniture. Encourage your dog to SETTLE DOWN by setting out a comfortable bed and a favorite chew. Praise your dog when he lies quietly or chews. If your dog continues to jump on the furniture, secure a leash to an immovable object to prevent or control this.

If you want permission control, wait two weeks before you allow your dog onto any furniture. Your dog must bond to his place before your teach him the whole permission deal. Then, bring your dog on a short leash to your

A Tip for Puppy Owners

Control yourselves! Puppies are so irresistible. I know it's hard to keep them on the floor, but you must start now if you don't want them on the furniture later. You can still cuddle to your heart's content; just get down on the floor to do it!

chosen spot on the couch, tap the cushion and say UP, UP! He'll look at you like you've lost your mind — "what?" — but continue to encourage him. He won't need too much coaxing. After a cozy sit, take the short leash and instruct OFF as you get up together. Resist the temptation to invite him up every day. Old habits will resurface.

COUNTER CULPRITS

Not all dogs choose human targets. Some find the defrosting turkey on your kitchen counter to be far more interesting and will perform mind-boggling gymnastic feats to get it. If you have a counter culprit, set up a tempting situation. Put your dog on his leash and get some tasty human food out from the fridge. If he even pauses to consider what's on the counter, tell him NOPE and quicktug.

Scold the food, not your dog! BAD TURKEY! BAD! BAD! If you catch the thought process, your dog will be impressed. If he still steals when you leave the room, you can try soaking bread in Tabasco sauce and letting him self correct. Occasionally a pyramid of cans filled with pennies and tied to a chicken leg can be pretty daunting. Some clients claim a booby trap mousetrap tamed curiosity. What works for one dog may not work for another. All you can do is try, try, try!

Can't I ever let my dog jump on me?

Believe it or not, yes. But not now. First you must teach him not to jump. Once he understands that, you can instruct UP and let him jump on you with your permission. If he tries it without permission, close shop or swipe him away.

Close shop!

What do I do when my dog jumps at me when he's on leash?

Are you holding the collar too tightly? That can be frightening for dogs who feel like they're being strangled. If that's not the problem, your dog is confronting your control and needs a good HEEL lesson. For now, don't buy the confrontation. Try ignoring him completely. Seriously — wear an old coat if his nails are too sharp. If your dog still persists, carry a spray of Binaca or Grannick's Bitter Apple, discretely spraying a boundary between you two until your dog learns to back off. Still out of luck? Try using the Gentle Leader to convey your authority calmly and without force or confrontation. Don't face your dog; this posture reinforces his confrontational efforts.

Some corrections make my dog wilder. What am I doing wrong?

It sounds like your dog isn't taking you too seriously. You'll need to do some foundation training to get him focused on you. Are you bending over to correct him, yelling or using your hands to push him away? All these corrections are interactive and encourage rougher play. Perhaps your dog just has a lot of energy or needs to go to the bathroom more often. Check it out.

My dog ignores the counter when we're around, but as soon as we turn our backs he jumps right up. It seems like a game.

An opportunist! Try stationing your dog for awhile, telling him to WAIT as you leave the room. Then try the same set-up without stationing. Also, correct the surfaces your dog shows interest in.

I have a Toy Poodle and I don't mind him jumping.

You may not mind, but your houseguests might. Teach your dog to ask permission to come up. When he jumps, ignore him temporarily and when he gets down, instruct SIT. Next, instruct UP and lift him into your lap. Soon he'll come and sit for permission instead of jumping. Remember, a well-mannered dog can be selectively spoiled!

MOUNTING

Don't be too embarrassed. Mounting is more a sign of dominance than of sexual preference. This, however, does not make it acceptable. Mounting dogs are bossy dogs who get over-stimulated in exciting situations. To rehabilitate yours, teach him that he's not king of the castle. Practice HEEL, WAIT, EXCUSE ME and STAY, for starters. Include the kids, using a Gentle Leader so that they can control him. In addition:

- Leave a short lead on your dog.
- Do not face off with a mounting dog. No eye contact or pushing.
- When the mounting starts, calmly grasp the short lead and snap down firmly.
- Once your dog is grounded, stand very tall, glare at your dog and say SHAME ON YOU in your most indignant tone. Station your dog for 15 minutes with no attention.
- If your dog is mounting other dogs or the kids, keep your approach calm and repeat the preceding procedure. Do not storm into the situation; this will heighten your dog's excitement.

Note: If your dog acts aggressively, terminate the corrections and seek help.

Why does my 11-month-old male Husky mount my eight-year-old male Labrador-mix? What's going on?

It's a dominance thing. Nothing more. Let them work it out. And once they've established dominance, support it. (See "Multi-dog Households" in the Appendix.)

NIPPING/MOUTHING

Puppy nipping is natural, until about four months. After this time, nipping blurs the lines of authority. It's pushy and can lead to adult aggression. Better to nip it in the bud, so to speak. To eliminate nipping:

- Encourage before you discourage. Teach your dog to give KISSES by rubbing butter on your hands. This is a great activity for kids too! Even a dab on a baby's foot can go a long way toward associating positive feelings. (If you've got an aggressive dog, do not let him interact with children or babies of any age. Get help before you proceed.)

- Ask yourself: Does my dog need something? Some dogs, especially as puppies, nip when they have a need they can't fulfill. Nipping is hardest when they have to poop or can't put themselves to sleep.

- Any time your dog licks you, say KISSES. If he just won't stop, that's pushy too. Nudge him off with your leg, say THAT'S ENOUGH and ignore him.

- Dogs who nip love to interact. In fact, they can't leave you alone. Refocus this negative energy into positive play and teaching games.

- Eliminate all tug-of-war and wrestling games. Period. They encourage nipping and aggressive play.

How you handle the nipping itself depends in large part on the age of your dog.

Young Puppies

Puppies under 14 weeks are naturally oral. They nipped their mother softly when they were weaned. She tolerated soft mouthing, but if they nipped too hard she gave them a clear message to back off. When puppy siblings played, they nipped each other, too. Rough play and hard nipping elevated a puppy's position in the group hierarchy.

Face Off

At this age, puppies like to interact around your face. Yes, it is a sign of affection, but they also bite faces in play. Don't let your puppy near your face when he's excited. Puppy play bites can hurt!

When you bring your puppy home, he wants to know whether you're the mother figure or a littermate. To communicate leadership, ignore all soft mouthing. Yes, ignore it. If you screech or pull your hand away, you're reinforcing it with attention and submissive puppy play. If your puppy keeps nipping, ask yourself if he might need a bathroom run or if he's tired or hungry. Nipping can be equivalent to a young baby's cry.

If all else checks out and your puppy bites down hard, say NOPE and either step toward his body or quickly pull your puppy's head away from your hand. I repeat: Pull your puppy's head away from your hand. Do this with a leash or a quick flicking of his collar. Don't pull away from him. Too gamey. Say KISSES, whether you're encouraging your puppy to lick or he chooses to on his own.

Use treats to reinforce every good impulse, from chewing on a bone to not nipping you when you're together. Format the memory of positive interactions, praising your puppy every chance you get. If your puppy is getting wild, refocus his energy with a chew bone or toy. See the "Puppies" section of the Appendix for other suggestions.

Mature Puppies

As your puppy matures (older than four months), teach him not to place his mouth on human skin. Encourage before you discourage: Make sure all his needs are met and he knows an appropriate alternative, like KISSES. Use your clicker and food rewards! Consider changing to the Gentle Leader head collar; the pressure on the muzzle conveys dominance. It truly has a calming effect and is a good conditioning tool, especially with young children.

You can also try two corrections:

1. Place your puppy on a short lead and correct any and all mouthing by pulling his head away from you as you glare at him indignantly and say NOPE. Refocus on a more positive behavior like KISSES, TOY or BONE. Remember, don't pull your hand out of his mouth because it will encourage rougher play.

2. Buy Binaca breath spray or Grannick's Bitter Apple or simply fill mister pumps with water. Keep plenty around the house and some in your pocket. Whenever your dog mouths, say NOPE indignantly as you discreetly spray the part of your body your dog is nipping on. Get your dog to withdraw from your space and don't move your hand from his mouth. Encourage KISSES or BONE and then praise your dog. If he ignores you, ignore him.

I've tried various corrections, like holding my
five-month-old puppy's mouth shut or smacking his snout.
They seem to make the situation worse.

Your puppy perceives these corrections as confrontational play. I don't encourage these methods. I find that acting indignant and disappointed works better. Pull your puppy's mouth away from your hand. If he just won't quit, walk away.

> ### 🐾 Three Strikes and You're Out
>
> If your dog just won't stop nipping, correct him twice and try to refocus his energy. If he nips again, calmly take him to his station or crate for some quiet time. Don't get angry or make a fuss. You both need a little cooling off!

I have three kids and one dog. They love to wrestle, but they don't like it when Buddy (my seven-month-old Keeshond) plays too rough. Help!

They're small. They're energetic. They love to race around and play games. And I'm not talking about your dog! It's easy for dogs raised with children to mistake these little creatures for other puppies, and that can lead to some pretty wild behavior — on both their parts. You're faced with a double whammy: training your dog and controlling the kids.

- Any time your kids can't slow down, you should station, crate or lead your dog away from them.

- Avoid getting angry or frustrated at any of them. Your energy will only excite or frighten your dog. Help your kids see that too much enthusiasm ends play time.

- Put your dog on leash and stage a set-up. Encourage the kids to run in front of you. If your dog starts to charge, quicktug the leash and say NOPE! Repeat this until your dog chills out. When he does, click and treat and practice some familiar lessons like SIT, STAY and DOWN.

- Small children may pull on your dog's coat or explore around his face. Condition your dog to accept this handling by treating and praising him as you gently pull his coat and handle his face. He'll be more accepting of the children if you accustom him to such treatment first. Meanwhile, condition your kids not to do things that might hurt the dog. How you do that is up to you!

- Encourage your kids to play with your dog when he's calm or chewing a bone. Teach them how to use the treat cup and introduce them to luring exercises. Kids have more fun when they're successful. Make this a special time with you and your kids. Reward both for being calm!

RUNAWAY DOG

If your dog is running away, the first question to ask yourself is, why? In fact, is he truly running away or is he simply roaming to satisfy some other need? Few dogs run away — most are driven by an instinctual drive they just can't ignore.

- Unneutered male dogs can smell a female dog in heat up to a mile away. Please have your dog neutered for his own safety and to do your part to reduce the 10 million unwanted pets who are put to death each year. Ten million! Don't add to the numbers.

- When walking your dog off your property, keep him at your side. Allowing him to wander and pee on every bush and post may seem nice, but your dog is marking his territory. Off leash, he will patrol this area.

- If your dog's a social butterfly, he won't be able to resist the sounds of other dogs and people around your neighborhood.

- Is your dog a budding garbologist, taking every opportunity to raid the neighbor's trash? It's a very self-reinforcing behavior.

There is one solution to each of these problems: containment! Either keep your dog on a leash or install a fence. It's a scary world out there, full of automobiles, poisons and dognappers. Although your dog may feel like he can control his world, he can't.

If your dog has truly run off, follow this checklist:

- Notify the police and the highway department (if applicable).

- Call friends for help.

- Walk the neighborhood with a recent photo and a pad of paper. Leave your phone number at each house.

- If a night or a day should pass, call and speak to the local animal control officer and all surrounding animal shelters.

- Make posters about your lost dog with a recent photo and put them up everywhere.

- Contact all local animal hospitals.

- Call all animal professionals, from veterinarians to pet stores to training centers.

Above all, stay as calm as you can. Getting upset loses valuable time. You've got a job to do now. And a prayer wouldn't hurt.

Another key in solving this problem is — you guessed it — teaching your dog lessons that communicate your

Welcome Home!

Whatever you do, *never* discipline your dog when he returns home. Who'd want to come back for that?

leadership. Lessons make your dog feel like a full-fledged member of your team. And when that happens, he'll stay closer to home. Your dog won't want to go wandering off alone anymore; your love and structure has tamed him.

SEPARATION ANXIETY

Separation anxiety is the canine equivalent of a panic attack. This poor dog is in such a sorry state that he can't track or control his reactions. He's lost his grip on reality. The symptoms include intense pacing and blocking your departures, excessive salivation and vomiting (especially when left in a crate), destructive chewing (shared furniture and doorways), house soiling, whining and excessive barking. In short, this dog acts as though he's trapped in a world that's falling apart. If this sounds like your dog, ask your veterinarian's opinion and consider professional help. It's often curable.

There are lesser forms of anxiety that I'll cover here. These dogs may exhibit similar, though less intense, reactions. For example, when alone, your dog longs for your companionship, and because chewing fingernails or watching the soaps isn't an option, he may settle for your couch.

Dogs with this problem fall into one of two categories: passive or dominant.

The Passive Dog: This dog clings to his owners when they are home, soliciting attention often and getting it. This leads to overidentification, not unlike a child who clings to his mother's leg. This dog is confused about himself and depends on his owners' presence to reassure him. When they're gone, the anxiety sets in.

The Dominant Dog: This fellow thinks he is king of his castle. Ruler of the roost. When his owners, whom he considers his subordinates, leave, his anxiety is in their best interest: "How will they survive without their great leader to protect them?"

With either type of dog, resolving the problem means training the dog. For the passive dog, training will help him feel he has a secure leader and a personality all his own. For the dominant dog, training will place him in a subordinate, carefree pack position. If you need help training your dog, get it. In the meantime, follow these ground rules:

- If you come home and find your dog has damaged the house, never correct him after the fact. **Never.** Your dog will associate corrections not with the destruction, but with your arrival, and he'll be more anxious or frustrated the next time you leave.

- Avoid theatrical hellos and goodbyes. Lavishing your dog with kisses, biscuits and drawn-out declarations of devotion do not reassure him. They stress him out.

- Leave a radio playing classical music to cover unfamiliar sounds.

- Place your dog in a dimly lit area to encourage sleep.

- Leave a favorite chew toy with him. Rub it between your palms so it has your scent.

- If you're leaving for more than six hours, try to find someone to walk your dog. Otherwise, proof the house against his destruction by setting up an

> ### 🐾 Strong Bonds
>
> Dogs with this problem are very strongly bonded and emotionally connected to their group. In fact, the problem is they're a little too bonded! They've slipped into the can't-live-a-second-without-you category. Imagine a spouse or a child with that problem. It would be sad and disruptive. Help your dog get over his emotional dependency so you can both enjoy life a little more.

indoor pen. It folds nicely so that you can store it away when you're home, and it can be expanded before you leave to give your dog space when you are gone for extended periods. Dogs get cramped when left in crates for over six hours and develop hyper-isolation anxiety.

- When home, temporarily decrease your physical attention by 50 percent. Do not give in to solicitations. Although giving in relieves your guilty feelings, it is too sharp a contrast from being left alone all day.

- If possible, get a kitten for your dog. Kittens are super companions, and they are great company for dogs if they're raised together. Getting another dog is also an option, although it's better to wait until you've resolved this problem.

The next step in remedying your dog's anxiety is a series of practice departures. Station your dog in a familiar spot. Instruct WAIT. Leave the room for 15 seconds. Return. Ignore him until he's settled down, then praise him lovingly. Repeat this procedure 10 times or until he stays calm. Continue these short separations until he shows no anxiety. Then, double the separation time and repeat the procedure. Continue doubling the departure time until you're able to leave the room for 30 minutes.

Once your dog is comfortable for 30 minutes, go back to short separations. But this time leave the house. Gradually work your way up to spending 30 minutes out of the house. Then start over; this time, get into and start your car. With patience, you'll be able to build your dog's confidence and leave him for longer and longer periods of time.

If you seek help, make sure you avoid trainers who encourage discipline.

Why is training so important for dogs with separation anxiety?

Think of your dog as a kid. Kids need parents. If they don't have them, they lose their sense of themselves and behave in a frightened or manic fashion. Dogs need a leader, just like kids need a parent. Training communicates that you're applying for the position. Successful training takes a lot of pressure off your dog. Someone else is on the lookout. Someone else is in control. Your dog thinks, "I can just relax. I can just be a dog. I don't have to be the leader."

STIMULATED SPRINKLING

Whatever you do, don't correct this behavior. It's involuntary and often out of pure respect, and if corrected it gets much worse. Yell at a submissive urinator and he'll empty his bladder!

Stimulated sprinkling comes in two forms: excited and submissive. Both, initiated during greetings or discipline, indicate that the puppy or dog cannot contain either his excitement or his anxiousness about the situation. He's overflowing, so to speak.

To resolve this issue, understand it first, than establish a calm, take-charge attitude so your dog puts faith in your interpretations of new situations. First of all, decide which category your dog falls into: Is he sprinkling from excessive submission or excitement? If it's submission and you're heavy-handed with the discipline, back off. Get help or read the appropriate sections of this book. You're scaring your dog, not teaching him.

Respect for Mom

If you've got a young puppy who is doing this, don't worry. It's normal; puppies often pee out of respect for their Mom and the behavior is simply transferred. They do grow out of it.

The first step is to teach your dog/puppy to watch you. Use confidence-building techniques (clicker training, targeting) to teach your dog that he can win approval by staying focused and calm. SIT, DOWN, STAY and HEEL are helpful.

If your dog sprinkles when people come to the door, put treat cups and jingle jars nearby. Condition your dog that the sound of the doorbell or knock means a reward. Practice this when no one else is around and your dog is hungry. Link the bell, a direction (SIT-STAY) and food. When visitors arrive, try these ideas:

- Keep your dog on a leash, or station or crate him behind the door.
- Have everyone ignore him for five to 20 minutes until he calms down.
- Rather than a face-to-face greeting, take out a treat cup or jungle jar and have the visitor run through a quick word sequence: SIT-DOWN-STAY.
- Kneel and pet his neck to avoid him feeling submissive.

If it's you that your dog empties his bladder for:

- When you come in, ignore your dog until he's completely calm.
- Use your treat cup to get his attention focused out and command SIT before petting.
- Kneel down to pet him, rather than leaning over.

If your dog is timid with certain people, have everyone (including you) ignore him. If you soothe him, you reinforce his fear. If your dog approaches the person, have them shake the treat cup or click and offer him treats. If he is calm, have the person kneel and pet his chest.

If your dog piddles during greetings or play sessions, ignore him or stop the play until he has better bladder control.

> **Be Prepared**
>
> Keep paper towels and an odor neutralizer handy. Clean up quickly and calmly. Do not correct this behavior, because your frustration will put more emphasis an already anxious situation.

I have a four-month-old puppy who is very shy, and three young kids. The kids are rough and frighten the pup. When he's frightened, he pees. And it's getting worse. Is it possible that the puppy is unsuited for our chaotic household?

Yes, it is. I can't tell based on your question alone, but you may want to get an unbiased and professional opinion. If so, the fairest alternative for both you and the pup is to find him a home in a quieter household. Perhaps with an older couple. If you decide to get another puppy, do more research into temperament and breed type. Test your new candidate before you bring him home. Pick one with a strong sense of self. Good luck!

STOOL SWALLOWING (COPROPHAGIA)

Dogs swallow two kinds of stools: other creatures' and their own. Both behaviors are pretty disgusting. But, believe it or not, both are natural. Completely natural. Kind of makes you glad you're not a dog.

Other Creatures' Stools

These are actually quite a delicacy — for dogs. They find them tasty. Corrections, unfortunately, make it worse. Your dog will think you want them, too. So he gulps faster.

Most dogs outgrow this behavior if you feed them a balanced meal twice a day and ignore their stool fetish. Try to distract your dog if you catch him in the act, and refocus him on a favorite activity. If you're suffering from litter box blues (dogs seem to love what cats leave behind in their litter box), put the litter box in an inaccessible area or correct the box as outlined in the Chewing section of this chapter.

The Dog's Own Stools

Although this is probably the grossest thing you could ever think of, in dogland it's just a handy way to keep the den clean. When your dog was a puppy he watched his mother do it (in fact, the problem is more common in female dogs with strong maternal instincts), and when he sees you cleaning up after him, he thinks . . . well, you get the picture. To halt this habit, clean up after your dog (when he's not watching) and try the following:

- Don't correct your dog when he shows interest in his stool. If you fuss, he'll gulp.

- If your dog is showing interest, refocus him on a favorite game: GET YOUR BALL!

- Ask your veterinarian to give you a food additive that will make the dog's feces distasteful to him. I know, what's more distasteful than dog poop? But such things do exist.

- After your dog is finished eliminating, spray the pile with something distasteful such as Grannick's Bitter Apple, Tabasco sauce or vinegar.

TIMIDITY

Timid dogs look so sad. You just want to soothe them, like you'd soothe a frightened kid. But dogs are not kids and they'll think your soothing is a sign of your fear. Compromised body postures and high-pitched tones translate into canine distress signals. Now you're both afraid! That's a big problem.

To help your dog, you must mirror the attitude you want him to adopt. Act confident when he is afraid of noises and unfamiliar objects. Act happy when you're greeting visitors. Although it may take time (only your dog can tell you how long), be patient and consistent. Work through your lessons to convey to your dog that you're the full-time leader no matter what happens during the day. His accomplishments will build confidence; he'll adopt a "can-do" attitude. Consider using a Gentle Leader — it's the difference between holding a frighten child's hand or grabbing their shirtsleeve. Stand up straight. Relax your shoulders. Smile. Whether it's a bag blowing in the wind, a sharp noise (like thunder) or an uncommon face, act calm, face the feared object and ignore your dog until he starts to act more like you. Here are some everyday situations.

Objects

Whether you're helping your dog overcome his fear of the vacuum cleaner or a startling novelty on the scene (a leaf bag or new furniture), stay calm. If possible, leave the object out and investigate it yourself as if you were a dog. Remember, dogs sniff objects, they don't stare at them. Place delicious treats nearby and on

Cody and I Make Friends

I have a Standard Poodle friend named Cody who wanted nothing to do with me when we first met. Although timidity is a trait, Cody also has a comical side. We worked on target and clicker training. Cody loved to perform, so we also worked on tricks. We went to town and his mother bravely protected Cody's space, telling everyone to steer clear for now. This helped Cody gain confidence slowly. Although Cody will never embrace the world with Lassie's flair, he's not skittish anymore. He'll even give you his paw and wave goodbye. And I even get a kiss!

the object. If it's a new object, go up and investigate it solo. If your dog is on a leash, don't drag him over — that's freaky! Just let him watch you, his brave leader, and reward his interest.

If it's a machine, work with a family member to determine your dog's Red Zone (the distance at which he can tolerate the noise) and have him/her run the machine at this distance while you work through your lessons with food rewards and attention. Gradually decrease the distance. Also, make a tape of the noise and play it at slowly increasing volume while playing with your dog or feeding him.

People

Teach your dog HEEL and direct him through every new meeting. Ask the person you're meeting to avoid all eye contact, kneel to the side of your dog and, should they get close enough, pet from under your dog's chin. If your dog wants nothing to do with a visitor, fine. Don't let it affect your positive attitude. No attention to your dog when he's withdrawn; that would reinforce his impression, not yours.

If your dog is a food hound, try to ease his concerns with a treat cup or jingle jar. Blaze a trail of goodies to your friend's side and leave a jackpot of yummies in their hand. It may take weeks for your dog to warm up to anyone.

Play Dates or Puppy School

If your dog is fearful or has not been socialized with other dogs, you may get a big theatrical reaction on your first social outing! He may scream before other dogs even touch him. He may hide under the chair or try to climb in your lap. Don't cave in. Soothing will not help him. Socializing is one of life's realities. The best thing for you to do? Play with the other dogs or puppies. Show your dog how to get along. Set the example.

Thunder

Some dogs have a purely physical reaction to thunder. Biometrics, the earth's alignment — I couldn't say for sure, but their body goes into panic mode. These dogs need to be safely confined during thunderstorms; some need medication. There are other dogs who are fearful (thunder scared me as a kid), but instead of learning how to cope, they somehow got the message that thunder really means the sky is falling. Maybe they were in transit during their first storm, away from mom but not yet in a loving home. Perhaps their new family coddled them, giving a more fearful impression, or they were left out in a pen. Whatever the root cause of the fear, there are measures you can take to ease their concern.

Let me start with the don'ts. Don't coddle your dog. Don't permit him to hide under the sheets or climb into the closet. Don't isolate him. This will make the fear worse. Depending on how bad your situation is, try one or all of these approaches:

- Turn on some classical music and play it loudly.
- Lead your dog on his leash while you act completely calm. Set the example. Read a book, play music or watch TV. Show him how to cope with the situation. If your dog is jerking on a neck collar, use a Gentle Leader or harness. Let your dog have his fears, just don't respond to them. When he calms down, pet him lovingly.
- Find (or make) a thunderstorm tape recording. Play it on low volume while you play your dog's favorite game with him. Slowly increase the volume.
- Ask your veterinarian for tranquilizers to soothe him before a storm.

My dog is terrified of anyone new who comes to the house. He slinks down and will run into the back of the apartment if he can. If I keep him in the front room, his mouth tightens and he Velcros himself to the back of my legs.

Your boy is feeling out of control, and at this point he's not looking to you to guide his interpretations. Start basic lessons pronto, 5 to 10 minutes a day. Emphasize the DOWN and STAY. Next, practice leading him in the house. To resolve timidity I often use the Gentle Leader; this collar puts supportive pressure on the dog's head, rather than constant pressure around his neck. (When a dog is overcome with dread, the neck collars often add an element of asphyxiation, which can accentuate the fear. Gentle Leaders, on the other hand, leave a dog feeling guided, not trapped.)

These exercises communicate your willingness to give direction and be responsible for your dog throughout the day. Once you've mastered them, invite a friend over at a specific time. Ten minutes before your friend arrives, strap on your snack pack with an abundance of treats and a clicker, if you're using one. Put your dog on leash and warm up leading her around.

🐾 Fearful Aggression

If your dog is so afraid that he's showing aggression, tail tucked, body pulled back, ears flat, call for help. His fear has overwhelmed his coping skills. Do not knowingly put your dog in stressful situations.

When the doorbell rings, act nonchalant (any excitement may trigger her insecurity). If possible have your friend ring the bell five times at 20-second intervals before you go to the door to answer it. When you answer to door, instruct HEEL and bring your dog behind you. Greet your friend warmly, inviting her in — all the while keeping your dog behind you. Sit with your friend and speak about anything but your dog. As your dog's body relaxes, click, treat and pet him calmly.

If he's still a bit nervous, instruct SETTLE DOWN at your side as you offer him a bone to chew away his tension. If he's showing confidence, lay a path of treats down in your friend's direction. Praise any courage. If he's getting close to your friend have a jackpot of treats waiting. If your friend is there on a long visit, lead your dog in the house. If your dog is comfortable and your friend is confident, hand over the leash and let your friend instruct your dog using familiar words. Mutual communication soothes anxiety.

My dog is deathly afraid of the vacuum cleaner and the weed whacker. How should I handle this? He'd run into traffic if I wasn't holding on (tightly!) to the leash.

Poor guy! He's a sound-sensitive softy. For starters, leave the machine out so he gets accustomed to seeing it without the loud sound. Place a bunch of tempting treats nearby and on the body of the machine itself and praise your dog when you see him investigating it. Since your dog will mimic the one he loves, get down on all fours and pretend you're sniffing the object and eating the treats yourself!

Next you'll have to determine his Red Zone (the distance he can be from the running machines without reacting to them): 10 feet, 20, 50? Whatever it is, work your lessons there, slowly reducing the distance as your dog gets more comfortable and familiar with the sound.

🐾 A Lifelong Journey!

The magic of your relationship with your dog is that it never ends. Dogs aren't like the latest gadget, a novelty that collects dust in the corner or ends up on some back shelf in the basement. They are next to you through life's ups and down, challenging you to stay in the moment, wagging their tail when you're happy and comforting you when the day is heavy. The efforts you've made to create a mutual language, to teach manners and sharing, are a part of both of you now. It's the efforts that can't be seen that are the most measurable. Enjoy!

Jodi Buren

Appendix

PUPPIES

Whoever started the rumor that puppies are so cute that they make perfect gifts and spur-of-the-moment purchases — please sit down. Puppies are a lot of work and are a tremendous responsibility. But they can be a lot of fun, too! Here are some hints to help you along.

Puppies and Babies

Babies are a great point of reference in raising pups — and vice versa. Both are a lot alike. They go through developmental stages, they need to be potty trained and they have to be taught good manners. When they are young, they are focused more on themselves and their own needs than on you. They learn best using positive reinforcement and structure rather than harsh discipline. The main difference between them and us is that puppies use their mouths instead of their hands to explore their world. Remember this as your puppy is mouthing everything in sight. It's natural. Completely natural.

Puppies Under 12 Weeks

A puppy under 12 weeks old is like a child under six months old. Corrections don't make sense for one this young. Would you yell at a five-month-old baby for grabbing your earring or swiping the crystal off the dining room table? I hope not! Your efforts would be just as fruitless with a young pup. They're going to nip and chew just like a baby pulls and grabs. All you can do for now is patiently remove whatever you don't want them to touch and redirect their attention.

It's a Puppy

I know. Puppies can be really frustrating. They chew, jump, nip and pee where they're not supposed to. But after all, they're just puppies and that's what puppies do. They're not acting out of spite or to make you angry, so try to calm down. Harsh corrections or yelling will only frighten your puppy or, worse, egg him on. Instead . . .

Have Fun

Encourage good behavior before you address the naughty stuff! Puppies learn really quickly and they love hearing positive affirmations: You're so clever. You're so beautiful. You've got the best paws! Clicker training, treat cups and jingle jars turn pups on to a lifetime of learning and listening. Your puppy pees outside — you click and treat. You shake the treat cup and he sits for attention. You shake the jingle jar and he comes racing. What a great puppy! What cool puppy parents!!!

Socialization

If your puppy is too young to go out, invite the world in. Inoculated dogs and other puppies can come for a visit. You can dress up in silly costumes, have a hat party with family and friends, and invite the postman in for a cup of coffee. If your puppy is given the green light from his veterinarian, take him out on a safe collar and leash. Keep him at your side and approach all people and dogs respectfully. Enroll in a puppy class, too!

Snowflakes

Like snowflakes, no two puppies are alike. Every puppy is unique. Your puppy will have his own special personality, which will determine how you communicate with him. Does he have a passive or an active temperament?

Passive puppies like direction and shrink from making independent decisions. They feel most secure and calm near their group. If you've got a passive puppy,

---

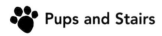 **Pups and Stairs**

One of the cutest miracles I get to perform is teaching puppies to handle stairs. I'll tell you my secret. Once your puppy is large enough to make it downstairs, avoid carrying him. He'll develop learned helplessness. Instead, brace his rib cage securely in your hands and help him manipulate his body to do the action. If you've got extra people to help, have them shake a treat cup and cheer him on. "You're a can-do puppy!" Give him a heap of praise and a jackpot of treats when he reaches the top or bottom! (If yours is really frightened by the whole flight, carry him to the bottom or top few stairs and coach him on the rest of the way.)

train him with a gentle hand and avoid giving him corrections. Ignore all anxious, shy or fearful responses, because your attention will reinforce them. Passive puppies can develop into sweet, gentle, adoring pets if they're handled properly. If given too much attention for shy or insecure behavior, however, they may develop separation anxiety or chronic timidity.

Active puppies have a strong sense of themselves. They are outgoing, unafraid and funny. Training and moderate corrections may be needed to focus their attention. Always a part of things, they can make a dynamic addition to any household. Left untrained or isolated, however, they can be very disruptive, annoying and destructive.

Needs

Puppies under nine months old are motivated by five primary needs: hunger, thirst, sleep, play and elimination. If at any point they have a need that is not being met, you'll know about it. They will act out. Some dogs will bark or whine; others will nip or jump. If your dog is acting up and just won't quit, ask yourself, "Could he be trying to tell me something?" Remember, naughty behavior is often a puppy plea for help.

Getting everyone involved is key. Consistency rules! Same routine, same words. When pups are hungry, they must be fed. A consistent eating schedule is a must. When puppies are tired, they sleep. You cannot drag them around when they're zonked. When young puppies have to go, they get very rambunctious and nippy. And when pups have energy, they need to release it! Wild and crazy energy spurts are normal, and puppies can have as many as four a day. The best thing for you to do at these times? Let your pup have freedom in an enclosed yard or kitchen while you climb a tree or stand on the counter tossing toys out randomly for your puppy to chase. No, I'm not kidding. Wild pups get nippy, and corrections only make them wilder — now they think you're playing, too. It's better to wait until their engines cool before you attempt to reason with them.

A Puppy Needs Chart

Make a Needs Chart for your puppy. Use the template below to assign a word(s) and a routine to each need. Over-emphasize your words and encourage everyone to do the same. In the Routine column, assign a specific location and routine to each task. It will help your puppy identify where to go and how to communicate to you when a need is coming. Show your chart to everyone. Consistency and repetition create understanding.

Here is a sample Puppy Needs Chart. Of course, you can change the times and other particulars of the routines, and even change the words you associate with them.

Need	Word	Routine
Eat	HUNGRY	Feed at 7 A.M., noon, and 4 P.M. Fill the food bowl, encourage him to SIT and place the bowl down next to the sink. Puppies over five months can eliminate noon feeding.
Drink	WATER	Lift the water bowl up from floor, fill and place next to the sink.
Bathroom	OUTSIDE or PAPERS and GET BUSY	Take the dog out the side door, to same spot in the yard, beside the garage. Puppy must go before he gets any attention or playtime in the yard.
Sleep	SETTLE DOWN or TIME FOR BED	Lead the puppy to his mat or confined area, and secure him if necessary.
Play	BONE, BALL or TOY	The basement, hallway and den are designated indoor play areas. Make sure all four paws are on the floor before you toss any toy.

Maturity

Like babies and tadpoles, your puppy will grow up. Before you know it, he'll stop chasing every blowing leaf and will grow accustomed to the long wagging thing at the end of his body. If you handled his youth correctly, his maturity will bring a consistency to your world that will not change with the seasons or time. He will truly be your best friend.

KIDS AND DOGS

I once gave a lecture called "Kids and Dogs: Constant Companions or Sibling Rivals?" in which I stressed that raising children and dogs together may not be as effortless as those reruns of *Lassie* might lead one to believe. Both creatures are in need of constant attention and care, and it is crucial that a child be encouraged to help with the family pet. Encouraging children to help care for the family dog helps reinforce a constant companion relationship.

Don't get me wrong: I think dogs can make wonderful companions for children, but there are hidden responsibilities and considerations to keep in mind.

Help!

Know when to ask for it. If your dog is becoming less tolerant of your child, showing signs of aggression or creating such havoc that your normal daily routine and your parental responsibilities are overloaded, call a professional trainer or behaviorist immediately. They can really help. Ask your veterinarian for a referral.

Expecting a Baby?

Congratulations! Here are some tips to get your four-footed family member ready for the new arrival.

Carry a doll around the house. If you can find one that cries or eats, go for the big effect! Use the SIT-STAY as you pretend to change the diaper and a SETTLE DOWN when you feed the "baby."

Keep your dog with you as you prepare the baby's room. Create a station area for him in the corner or right outside the door, so you won't have to exclude him when the baby comes. Exclusion can cause new-infant-resentment syndrome, and you wouldn't want that!

Use treat cups and clicker training to reward your dog's cooperation. Leave them around the house so when the baby arrives, you'll already be set up.

You've given birth! A miracle to behold. Before you come home, ask a spouse, friend or family member to show your dog a used bed cloth or diaper. Familiarizing him with the scent will help him feel more comfortable when the baby arrives. Also use the baby's name to create a warm, group feeling and help your dog accept the new addition: "Let's go feed Ryan!"

Your homecoming! The big day. To help your dog ease into the transition, ask someone to handle him on his leash as you come through the door. If you feel up to it, let someone hold the child and greet the dog as usual. After he's calmed down, allow him to sniff nearby as you praise and treat him lovingly. The start of a beautiful relationship!

Cool Sayings and Catchy Phrases

Kids, like adults, really turn off when they constantly hear "don't." In fact, it's human nature to do whatever we're told not to. But you can be clever and use positive (and cool) terms like:

- The Four Paw Rule: Four paws on the floor!
- Close shop: Fold your arms and look up from the dog.
- Peacock position: Stand up straight when addressing the dog.
- Treat cup name game: Teach the dog the kid's names.
- Swing toss: A fun chasing game that teaches to dog to run *with*, instead of after, the kids.

Attention, Attention!

Kids love it as much as dogs do and, like dogs, they're not concerned about whether it's negative or positive. A lot of times children will tease their dog just to get their parents' attention. Keeping this in mind, praise all positive interactions. Take time to notice your child when he pets the dog calmly or helps out with the feeding. If you see any rough play or teasing, calmly remove your dog from the situation and isolate him in a crate or private room. Don't discipline the dog; just remove him peacefully. Ignore your child for 15 minutes to let him know that rough play ends interaction time.

Teasing

Children, especially those under eight years of age, tease dogs. It's a fact of life. Although teasing can be minimized, it can't be eliminated entirely. To help your dog get accustomed to the way children handle animals, mimic it yourself. Pry your dog's mouth open, handle his feet, tug his coat, and, as you do, praise him and give him treats. The next time you catch your child handling him properly, praise them both and let your child be the one to give him a treat!

Dog Stress?

Is your young child or baby stressing out your dog? Does he jump when your child crawls across the floor? Does he dodge oncoming toddlers? If so, he needs help overcoming his anxieties. Try shaking a treat cup or using the clicker and a treat every time the child is near. Acting happy will give your dog a good feeling and dislodge all those old tensions. A negative response communicates anxiety and puts a real strain on their relationship. Act happy and he'll be happy!

Caring for the Family Dog

Although children under five cannot be expected to perform any care duties without help, older children and other household members can and should assume some of the responsibilities of taking care of the dog. To encourage everyone's participation, make a fun project out of all the necessary duties (brushing, feeding, walking, exercise and training) and design a special roster to hang on your refrigerator. Be creative in your encouragement, and avoid getting angry for lack of cooperation. Anger, after all, is just another form of attention. We're not so unlike our dogs after all!

While it's important to involve your children in your dog's care, the adults in the family must ultimately take responsibility for the dog. If your child forgets to wash the dishes, you can leave them to pile up in the sink to teach him a lesson. But you cannot let the dog be neglected while you to teach your children about responsibility.

 You Set the Example

You are your children's best example. You can teach your children not to tease through the power of your example and positive reinforcement of calm interactions. If you're calm and structured with your dog or puppy, your child will copy you. If you're frantically confused or you encourage rough play, your child will copy that behavior, too. The choice is up to you.

 **Who's Your Top Dog?**

To determine who is Top Dog in your pack of pooches, observe your group's behavior. The Top Dog is the one who insists on being the first through the door, pushes the others out of the way for attention and ends up with all the toys between her paws. There are no size restrictions or sexism in dogland. You may be surprised to find that your five-pound female Maltese is running the show!

MULTI-DOG HOUSEHOLDS

Having two dogs can be twice the fun! Or it can be double the trouble. The outcome is in your hands. Here are some hints for making it easier.

A Dog Is a Dog, But . . .

While dogs have certain similarities, each has a unique personality and temperament that will affect the way they relate to their world. In a multi-dog household, everyone must be sensitive to the needs of each individual dog.

Hierarchy

Personality affects the way dogs relate to one another. In a group of two or more dogs, a hierarchy will develop, with the most outgoing, assertive dog becoming Top Dog.

Privileges

Once your dogs develop a hierarchy, you must recognize it by giving all the household privileges to your Top Dog. She should be fed, greeted, petted and allowed out first. If you pay more attention to the subordinate dog(s), you can cause discontent among the ranks — which may lead to fighting.

Almost Twins

Raising two dogs of the same age can be quite a challenge. Resolving housebreaking, chewing, nipping or jumping habits can double your workload. You'll have to pay close attention and be very consistent.

On the other hand, raising two dogs can be twice the fun if you're considerate of their individual needs and train them to be more focused on you than on one another. Often, when raised together, puppies will develop opposite personalities. The more outgoing one becomes Top Dog, while the other dog is more passive. Although it's tempting to console the introvert, remember the laws of nature, which instruct you to defer all privileges to the Top Dog; and the attention factor, which reminds you that if you pay attention to an introverted dog, you'll get an introverted dog. Here are some other hints to prevent problems:

1. If they're together 24 hours a day, your puppies will form a strong bond to one another and be less attached to you. To prevent this, separate them at least twice a day for individual lessons and play periods. If possible, have them sleep in separate bedrooms.

2. Use individual crates for housebreaking, chewing and any sleeping difficulties.

3. Feed the puppies separately. If you feed them together, the Top Dog may grab all the food.

4. Support their hierarchy. Feed, pet and greet the Top Dog first.

Different Ages

"Monkey see, monkey do" could not apply more to this situation. Puppies raised with older dogs pick up a lot of their habits — both good and bad. To discourage a younger dog from learning bad behaviors, resolve your older dog's problems first. In addition, follow the same suggestions I made for dogs of the same age.

If you've welcomed a mature dog into your pack, you'll need to observe the new hierarchy and respect it. When I brought my Labrador Retriever into my family, he quickly dominated my eight-year-old Husky. Although this arrangement broke my heart at first, once I supported their system, everybody was happy.

Discipline

If you don't know who did it, you can't correct either dog. That's the rule. If you find a mess after the fact, forget it. Disciplining your dogs will only weaken your connection to them and strengthen their connection to one another. For suggestions on resolving specific problems, see Chapter 8.

Is Wrestling OK?

Yes, to a degree. Teach TAKE IT OUTSIDE and say this whenever your dogs get out of hand. If that's not an option, leave them on short leads and calm them by saying SSHHH! as you pull them apart. Instruct SETTLE DOWN on a mat and refocus their energy on chew toys.

The Name Game

Teach your dogs two names: their personal name and a universal one that you can use when they're together. Try DOGS, GIRLS, BOYS, BABIES — whatever works for you. This system simplifies things when you have to call them. DOGS, COME! is a little easier than BUDDY, FIFI, DAISY, MARLO, COME!

Feeding

Feed your dogs separately. Place your Top Dog's bowl down first. If you're having difficulty keeping them separated, station them apart on their leashes for meals.

Toy Wars

I know, you want them each to have a toy, but one dog keeps insisting on having both. You give the toy back to the other dog and the Top Dog takes it away. Give-take-give-take. Remember your Top Dog rule: If the Top Dog wants both, he gets both. Period.

Dog Fights

Whatever you do, don't yell! Yelling is perceived as threat barking and will actually make the problem worse. If a dog fight breaks out, the best thing to do is walk out of the house and slam the door. No words or discipline, just an abrupt departure. It's usually your presence that prompts an argument. You can also try breaking up the fight by dumping a bucket of water on their heads or turning a hose on them.

Once things have calmed down, review your actions. Were you supporting the underdog? That's not good. After the fight has been settled, you should isolate the subordinate and praise the Top Dog. I know it sounds cruel, but if number one feels supported, he won't threaten the other dogs. Additionally, if you catch a fight before it begins, shame the underdog and reward your Top Dog with attention. I know it feels unnatural, but remember that your dogs aren't human and they don't think you are, either. If the dogs are fighting frequently, call in a professional.

References

NAMES TO KNOW IN THE DOG WORLD

Steve Appelbaum
A well-organized man, teaching dogs and people
(800) 795-3294
www.animalbehaviorcollege.com

Sarah Hodgson
That's me!
Simply Sarah Inc.
P.O. Box 420
Bedford, NY 10506
www.dogperfect.com

Karen Pryor
Clicker queen
Sunshine Books, Inc.
49 River St. Suite 3
Waltham MA 02453
www.clickertraining.com

Sue Sternberg
Shelter advocate extraordinaire and behavior specialist
Rondout Kennels
4628 Route 209
Accord, NY 12404
www.suesternberg.com

Jack and Wendy Volhard
Precision training for home and competition
Top Dog Training School
30 Besaw Rd.
Phoenix, NY 13135
www.volhard.com